conran's

# CREATIVE HOME
# DESIGN

# conran's

# CREATIVE HOME DESIGN

NONIE NIESEWAND

and David Stevens

LITTLE, BROWN AND COMPANY
BOSTON · TORONTO

First U.S. edition.

Library of Congress Catalogue Card No. 86-82581

First published in 1986 in the United Kingdom by Conran Octopus Limited.

Conceived, designed and produced by
Conran Octopus Limited
37 Shelton Street
London WC2H 9HN


Printed in Singapore


Reprinted 1987

# CONTENTS

HALLS      6

LIVING ROOMS      24

KITCHENS      80

DINING ROOMS      146

BEDROOMS      154

BATHROOMS      204

GARDEN DESIGN      228

PLANTING      272

PRACTICALITIES      296

INDEX      302

ACKNOWLEDGMENTS      304

# HALLS

First impressions linger, but many times visitors step inside to find a neglected hall, rather than a welcoming introduction to the occupants' style and taste. Unlike other rooms, halls are not usually given over to any particular function – aside from postal deliveries and meter reading – and it is easy to forget about them. When you first move in, the hall may be the logical place to stash boxes and cartons – whether still packed with possessions waiting to be put away or already emptied of their cargo. Later, any item relating to the outdoors may also find its home in the hall, from winter coats to gardening implements to summer sports equipment.

To make a grand entrance, you must first think of the hall as a room in its own right, and then start by making sure that everything in it is intentional or has a place. Tidy away the coats and hats on decorative stands, add an umbrella stand and build cupboards around unsightly meters and fuse boxes. Such cupboards can be designed to store cleaning equipment as well. If you have a favourite outdoor hobby, the entry hall is the place to store the gear in a practical and pleasing still life display. For example, an angler's rods, hamper and umbrella can be mounted beneath an arrangement of fishing prints; the paraphernalia of a sporting life – trophies, flags, pennants, crossed skis, cricket bats, golf clubs – can be teamed with pictures which reflect the enthusiasm in an arrangement which is easily dismantled when the gear is needed.

Halls can also be adapted to other functions, and are especially good as storage areas. There are many imaginative ways to use the dead space under the stairs. Open shelving can transform a hallway into a library; racks of wine create a vintner's cellar; picture rails and hooks establish a personal picture gallery. Halls lend themselves easily to closed cabinets or open shelving systems.

A mirror is always a useful hall accessory, since it is the place to keep up appearances before making an entrance or exit. Good lighting changes a dull cloakroom into a brightly welcoming area. A skylight admits natural light, under which houseplants thrive.

When all the rooms of a house radiate from the hall, the way the space is decorated sets the tone for the whole house scheme: you can make a bold statement or start out with a restrained approach.

## PLANNING CHECKLIST

- ■ Have you measured the hall areas and left enough space for doors opening outwards?
- ■ What items and equipment require storage space?
  - sports equipment
  - linens
  - overflow from other rooms
  - cleaning supplies
  - books
  - coats
  - boots
  - hats
  - umbrellas
- ■ Do you want storage systems you can take with you when you move, such as hatstands or adjustable shelving, instead of built-ins?
- ■ What features do you want or need in the hall?
  - notice/message board
  - storage shelves, or cupboards
  - telephone
  - mirror
  - seating
  - houseplants
  - pictures
  - boot rack
- ■ How many other rooms are visible from the hall that will influence its decoration?
- ■ Will any special activity areas be needed, such as a small desk, ironing board or sewing table?
- ■ Are electricity or gas meters or fuses sited in the hall?
- ■ Is the hall well lit and welcoming?

*The elegant lone white wire chair in this hall — a collectors' piece originally designed by Harry Bertoia in the fifties and still reproduced today — makes a firm sculptural introduction to a home that has other collectors' pieces, not many, but all reflecting the eclectic taste of the owner.*

The front door opens to reveal the first glimpse of your home. A folksy and countrified hallway follows naturally after an old, stripped pine door and can be created (even in the inner city) with flagstone-effect vinyl flooring and pastel rag-rolled walls accompanied by furnishings such as a stripped pine table and a bentwood or bamboo hatstand. A faceless, blank white door leads easily into an empty, minimalist-style hall, perhaps lined with storage cupboards disguised as plain walls. A heavy, panelled wood door would belong at the entrance to a formal hall.

1  In a room of such formal simplicity as this hallway, striking keynotes set a stylish tone. The black and white chequerboard floor – made up of linoleum tiles rather than traditional marble and laid on the diagonal to make a diamond pattern – emulates grand entrances of the eighteenth century. The white walls have been carefully marbled with hand-painted veining and even fine lines to enhance the illusion of marble slab panelling. A simple white bench with grille-like upright slats to screen the modern flat-panel wall-mounted radiator provides a hallway seat for removing muddy boots or waiting for the grand double doors to open, their stripped wood façade an invitation to step inside.

1

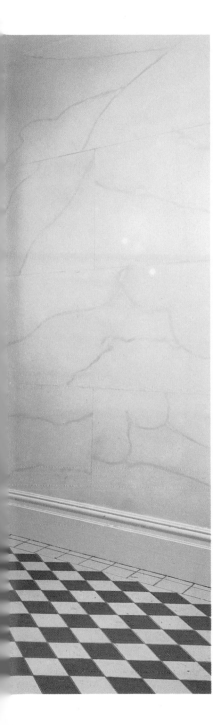

2

3

2   *To complement the grand scale of the arch leading to the kitchen, there is a matching semicircular fanlight above the double front door leading into this cheerful entry hall. Red and blue emphasize the dramatic, soaring structures of the architectural joinery and ironmongery. The bright spots of unpainted wood – in the front door panels, the enormous kitchen door and the kitchen cabinet doors – supply a yellow tone which rounds out the primary colour scheme. Immaculate white paint unifies natural surfaces, from the brick kitchen base units to the walls Such textural contrasts are enhanced by the soft fawn carpet underfoot.*

3   *In this more traditional style of hallway, the same fawn carpet is used under very different circumstances. Here, lemon yellow dado rail and skirting board visually lengthen the corridor without making it seem too narrow. It is in fact wide enough to display a generously proportioned, two-drawer telephone table. The table decorations – a green houseplant and baskets – are echoed further down the corridor by the natural basket, and by the large houseplants visible in the living room. The door is painted a gleaming, glossy white – the perfect foil for its Art Nouveau-style stained-glass window panel.*

1    *When halls double as storage areas for invasive household clutter, the limitations they impose can lead to original schemes which become features in their own right. Here, a very tall, conventional storage cupboard acts as a visual anchor for an unusually graceful staircase. The cupboard transforms a stair-well into practical storage space, but because the staircase is open-treaded and backed by a large window, the effect is not at all dark or gloomy. Venetian blinds echo the horizontal slats of the louvred doors. A terracotta pot and a chrome-edged perspex stand are the only furnishings.*

2    *In this late nineteenth-century Italian farmhouse, a box-like entryway with three doors opening into it and limited natural light has been transformed into a bright linen room with a combination of traditional and modern furnishings. A well-planned, careful facelift replaced the door at the end with an arch, and added ultra-modern linen chests with pencil-case roller shutters whose undulating curves echo those of the arch, and which are tall enough to house an ironing board. A wall-mounted lamp provides task lighting for ironing. The traditional style of the house is maintained by the Vienna cane and wood sofa positioned beneath four etchings.*

1

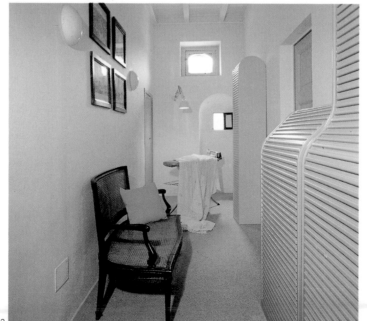

2

3

3 *This ingenious storage system was designed to complement the spacious period style of a late nineteenth-century London apartment. Based on the look of classical exterior stonework, this imposing hall of cupboards is fronted with modular panel doors. Here, the detailing is superb, from the highly polished wooden floorboards to the glossy, monochrome, custom-built cupboard units. No surface lacks enlivening embellishment, from the segmented wall panels to the curved alcoves.*

4 *Although this storage system seems almost an integral part of the original building, it was clearly designed to take careful account of the needs of the modern owners. Here, one cupboard from the restrained line-up is opened to reveal shelves to accommodate the usual array of household paraphernalia.*

4

1  *In this tiny hallway, little wider than the door, both walls are lined with open bookshelves for browsing when the door is closed. A downlighter recessed into the ceiling is not only a space saver in this incredibly small room, but also a necessity — anything else would have blocked the door.*

2  *Space around and above doors which would otherwise be wasted can often be used for storage shelving. Here, a stripped pine door has been made into an impressive feature by display shelves filled with a collection of decorative baskets and bears.*
*This hall's countrified look is strengthened by the stripped pine staircase and the pretty green and white wallpaper, with its tiny floral pattern.*
*It accommodates a great deal without seeming cluttered.*

3  *Here the angular, uncompromising lines of a joist are echoed and enhanced by the triangular top half of the stylish bookshelves, a shape doubtless imposed on the designer by the space available beneath a flight of stairs. The elegant flooring has been laid so that the pattern of narrow tiles runs from wall to wall, thus visually widening this long, narrow hall.*

4

5

6

7

4 When hall space is at a premium, even the smallest areas can be brought into use. The tallest area under the top tread of this modest staircase has been made into a broom cupboard, with a washing machine tucked neatly into the remaining space.

5 Halls must often house working mechanics which most people prefer not to look at, but which need to be easily accessible to servicemen and suppliers, such as electric fuse boxes, timers or gas and electric meters. In this hall, these essential but unsightly boxes are hidden behind a stripped wooden door.

6 Fashion footwear for every occasion is neatly hidden behind the carefully shaped doors of this custom-built, below-stairs cupboard which was designed to meet the highly individual requirements of the owner. Space between the shelves is evenly proportioned to hold shoes from the flattest moccasins to the highest stilettos, with boot rails provided in larger compartments.

7 Instead of boxing in the space below stairs to make a cupboard, a low table has been built in beneath this open-tread staircase to provide display storage space akin to a sideboard. Scarlet woodwork links the whole area.

1   *Conventional staircases, such
as those you find fitted into
townhouses and
condominiums, can seem
identical, apparently offering
little scope for individual
treatment. Even so, the
creation of pattern underfoot
through a combination of
wood, tiling, carpeting and vinyl
flooring can add interest to
otherwise dull treads and
risers, and visually link the
stairs to the hall.
Here, the staircase is very
much an extension of the long,
narrow, corridor-like hall. The
dramatic, formal tone of the
entryway is established, not so
much by the white floor tiles,
with their black insets and
border, as by the furnishings: a
dark sideboard flanked by two
plaster busts and potted palms.
The Victorian theme is
reinforced by the Grecian key
pattern of the carpet running
up the stairs and the polished
wood bannister.*

2   *This gently rising staircase
features natural wood treads
raised on plastered white
concrete blocks. The series of
broad wooden landings seems
like a terraced entry hall. The
crisp Mediterranean style is
reinforced by the curved
archway that frames the stairs
and an arrangement at the top
which combines blue and
white Mediterranean pottery,
green houseplants and a white
porcelain figurine.*

## DECORATING A STAIRWELL

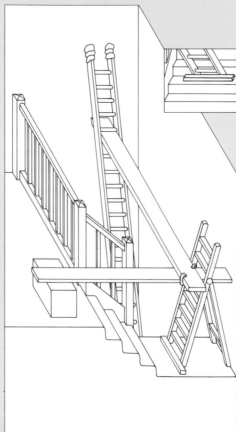

To wallpaper, paint or otherwise decorate a stairwell, first
construct a safe working platform. Take up any stair
carpets and make a scaffold system using ladders and
planks, checking that the ladders are perfectly secure. **1**
Wrap cloth around ladder tops to prevent damage to wall.
**2** Secure steps and ladders by chocking against wood
strip screwed to landing or stair. **3** Use two boards if
unsupported length is over 1.5m (5ft). **4** Clamp the top
board to the bottom one to prevent slipping.

1

2

3

3  *A conventional, boxed-in staircase with solid treads and risers would have transformed this open hall into a dark, narrow corridor. Instead, the staircase occupies very little floor space indeed. Its simple wooden treads are supported by fine, closely set balusters suspended from the upper floor, permitting a clear and unimpeded view of the handsome terracotta flagstones of the floor below. The clean, modern lines of the staircase do not detract from the traditional air of the carefully selected, handsome furnishings. The wonderful, ornately carved old chest, the centrepiece of the entryway, is complemented by the fine wooden bed visible in the bedroom. The blue and white Delft jug, brimming with colourful tulips, evokes the mood of a Dutch old master painting, perfectly in keeping with the portrait hanging on the wall above. Even the smallest details – the brass curtain rod and the antique maps visible as you climb the stairs – contribute to the atmosphere of simple and tasteful comfort.*

1   Every detail conspires to link this generously proportioned landing, itself something of an indoor garden, to the room created by the roof-top garden outdoors. The large windows admit enough light, even when the slatted blinds are drawn, to maintain the lush greenery of the houseplants which twine around the balusters, spilling into the stairwell.
The draughtsman's work table tucked into this unlikely corner is well positioned, both for contemplating the charming view outdoors and for taking advantage of the natural light, which can be supplemented by the clamp-on task light when necessary. The natural coir flooring and slatted blinds tone well with the tiled paving and brick wall outdoors, and the red accent of the drawing table legs and chair is picked up by the scarlet geraniums.

2   Instead of the usual balustrade and handrail, this Art Deco landing features a sculptural curved barrier at the head of the stairwell, like the entrance to a maze. The landing is very simple, with a beige wall-to-wall carpet and a flat, black disc-shaped wall lamp which softly illuminates the area. The only furniture is an Art Deco-style desk whose clean lines contrast with the highly figured wood from which it is made. A few well-chosen Art Deco-style objects complete the decoration.

1

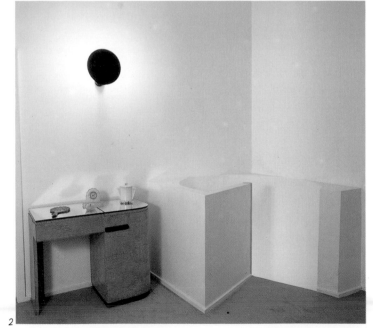

2

3

3  *In this unusual upper-storey design, skylights and an open well combine to create a much more light and spacious atmosphere than you would expect from a corridor at the top of the house. Custom-built wooden bookcases squeeze maximum storage into this tiny area, including a unit which houses stereo equipment. Light switches have been built into a convenient spot on one bookcase, rather than into the less accessible wall. Houseplants come into their own in an area such as this, which has no particular function. Some are planted in decorative ceramic pots, some hang from the ceiling; one occupies a coopered wooden tub and one climbs up a special support to cross the ceiling. The varieties grown here — from fern to spider plant — all have fairly low light requirements. With the ample natural light admitted through the skylights, the houseplants can be placed wherever they look best, rather than clustered near the windows.*

1   *Handsome pine floorboards, stripped of all finish to reveal the mellow gold colour characteristic of older wood, feature in this simple entrance hall. The shapely bannisters of the staircase have been painted a clean white, while the walls are covered with a busy, fresh blue and white pattern. Matching blue skirting boards and architraves complete the picture. A bamboo hatstand also houses a large, dramatic fern and is flanked by matching bamboo-framed mirrors and uplights with pearly shades modelled on old gas lights.*

2   *The beauty of the herringbone-patterned parquet stands on its own in this handsome hall, complemented by the stripped pine door and frame at the end. Hand-marbled walls contribute an elegant touch.*

3   *An expensively elegant woven carpet in blue and pink extends the eye from a small hallway up the stairs, giving the illusion of more space than there really is. The small pink pattern of the carpet has suggested the colour for the skirting boards and architraves.*

4   *This hall welcomes the visitor with a warm, patterned rug on a natural jute carpet, while the wooden stair treads echo both the honey colour of the rug and the wooden furniture which decorates the hall.*

5 The gently rising treads of this townhouse staircase are carpeted to match the hall and living room in a heavy-duty jute twill. Decorative detail and visual interest are added by the wooden battens which anchor the carpet firmly to each tread. An appropriate grade of carpet is important for a staircase, since stair carpets get a lot of rough treatment.
The fine white balustrade contrasts nicely with the dark hardwood of the handrails. A baby's cot is tucked neatly away under the stairs, making use of otherwise dead space.

6 The large-scale linoleum tiles of this elegant hall were copied from designs employed in the Cathedral of San Marco in Venice, although the geometric trompe-l'oeil could just as easily have been inspired by a modern artist such as Escher.

7 The linoleum tiles of this hall were also inspired by patterns found in old European churches. Here, a giant black and white chequerboard floor found at Alton Abbey in England is reproduced in a small domestic entry hall. It shows how large-scale pattern can be used in a small space with dramatic effect.

8 Here a diagonally laid chequerboard pattern is created on a smaller scale with tiny black and white tiles.

1   *This narrow, enclosed hall could be dark and uninteresting, but has been transformed into an unusual and elegant picture gallery. The yellow walls have a moulded black picture rail from which pictures hang on special clip-on cords. The choice of pictures — all old black and white architectural photographs — contribute to the effect of Georgian formality. The black and yellow theme has been maintained throughout. The architectural features of the hall — the door panels, the architrave and the winged figure above the door — have not been given a distracting treatment. Only the modern flat-panel radiator and door handles have been picked out in black.*
*Since the corridor is dark, even, diffused light is supplied along its full length from behind opaque panels.*

1

2 *A muted blue dado rail emphasizes the sweep of this staircase and contributes to a theme of blue woodwork — balustrade, skirting boards, architraves, mouldings and dado rail — which ties the disparate elements of this staircase and landing together. By painting the area below the dado rail in a darker tone than the walls above, an effect similar to that of dado panelling has been achieved.*
*The sort of special paint effect employed here can be used to texture and colour walls to make them unique. Broken colour finishes (often called 'distressed' finishes) can be achieved in two ways. Either paint is added over a background colour — with a sponge, by spattering or by using a brush to emulate marble or wood — or a top coat of paint in a second colour is partly removed by rags, combs or special brushes.*

3 *This monochrome blue landing in a Scandinavian-style house could seem cold — blue is normally considered a cool colour. The light streaming in through the window and the pretty blue and white drapes add warm touches. Only a white chair and white floorboards deviate from the colour scheme. The floorboards have been painted such a high-gloss white that they act as a mirror, reflecting light into all corners of the room.*

1 *A theatrical strip of unshaded giant light bulbs mounted on a beam of unpainted wood at the apex of an arched ceiling illuminates this narrow corridor. The impression that this wooden beam is in fact a structural joist is reinforced by the natural wood cross-beams on which it rests. This system casts a strong light upon the pictures hanging on the walls and the terracotta floor tiles, into which black contrast tiles have been laid to form an attractive pattern.*

2 *This tiny hall leads to all the rooms of the house – bathroom, bedroom and living room. It illustrates how easily various factors can affect the quality of light available. In the yellow hall itself, an uplighter washes the wall with atmospheric yellowish light. The same type of uplighter in the white bathroom next door casts a much brighter light, but even this has a much more yellow cast than natural light. Whatever the light source in the other two rooms, the effects are completely different, and the room opposite the bathroom emits a contrasting bluish-grey light.*

1

2

3

## HALLWAY LIGHTS

Round and oval bulkhead lights

Wall-mounted uplighters

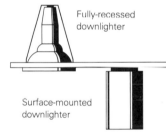

Fully-recessed downlighter

Surface-mounted downlighter

## LIGHTING STAIRWAYS

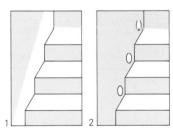

1    2

Good lighting is essential for staircase safety. **1** Install a light source, probably a downlighter, at the head of the stairs so that each step casts a sharp shadow or **2** use recessed lights at the side of each step to illuminate each step clearly and create a stylish feature.

3  *The appearance of any room can be altered or improved with the right lighting, the effect of which will depend largely on the surfaces being illuminated. In this bright landing, a frosted-glass door takes on a burnished metallic gleam, like the light fitting itself, under the low-voltage lamp suspended from the ceiling. Ordinarily, mirrors and glass are used to reflect light, but here even the highly polished dark floorboards shine. White walls also reflect light, contributing to the overall gleaming effect. By contrast, the matt black finish of the other metal feature in this landing — the modern cast-iron staircase — absorbs light, creating a clean black line. When choosing lighting for landings and staircases, remember that bright general illumination is not the only consideration. Lights must be sited so that each step is delineated from the other by shadow. The downlighter in the landing at the head of the stairs enhances the contrast between the black open-tread stairs and the white walls.*

# LIVING ROOMS

The total effect you want to achieve should be in your mind as you gaze at the space designated to your living room. That way, you establish priorities. The minimalist who dislikes clutter will clearly concentrate on storage that conceals everything behind immaculately finished façades, paring down and refining all that is there. The traditionalist sets up skirted tables for displaying collections, hangs pictures, plans curtain drapes with swags and flounces, picks complementary patterned papers. Country enthusiasts in urban areas will be scouring antique shops for dressers and wicker with pine, whitening floorboards, picking paint finishes and assembling a pastel palette of patterned prints.

It helps in planning a house to recall its functions, room by room. The living room is primarily an area for relaxing, either with friends, in which case you need several seating options, or watching television or listening to music, in which case you need wall storage systems for both. Bear in mind acoustics as well as sockets, since placing the television and sound systems for best picture and sound is a very exacting exercise. Then decide what you can retain of existing possessions. You may have moved house with furniture that is too big for the new room, or too bulky to fit against a wall or too shabby for new surfaces. Consider ways of revamping it if the shape is right but the finish is tired. Can you afford to be ruthless and abandon it, or will you settle for paint transformations? Sometimes the simple addition of a single beautiful plant, or a floor uplighter behind a collection of objects on shelves, can transform a dull corner.

Work out the background colour scheme once you have assembled the pieces that you know will have to be placed in the room. To help you pick a colour scheme, you can choose a coloured, patterned fabric you like and then distribute those colours in varying amounts throughout the room. Professional decorators pay great attention to detailing: skirting boards, cornices, radiators and door lintels can be brought into focus with accent colour.

Colour choice should be determined by whether your room faces north or not, since a greyer light will not complement a blue room, whereas a sun-splashed room can take a much cooler palette of greys and charcoals with silvery blues.

## PLANNING CHECKLIST

- Have you measured the living area and made a scale drawing (see page 27)?
- Have you decided which of your furniture to keep or refurbish?
- How many people will use the room on a day-to-day basis? *This will determine seating requirements.*
- Have you provided storage and seating for all likely activities?
  - entertaining
  - music
  - game playing
  - reading
  - TV watching
  - sewing
  - conversation
  - writing
- What is the focal point of the room?
- Will children or pets use the room?
- Do you anticipate living in the house for a long time so that it is worth installing built-in storage systems or platform seating?
- Do you want furniture you can take with you when you move?
- What electrical wiring, outlets and special fittings will be required?
  - lighting
  - television
  - microcomputer
  - aerial outlets
  - stereo
  - broadcasting
  - video
  - cable outlets

*Expensive decorating schemes and furnishings are not necessary to create a stylish interior. This room shows how the simplest elements – modular cube storage, an adjustable-height table, two simple sofas, pillows, houseplants – can work to create an individual room.*

*Few people have the opportunity or the budget to completely redecorate a living room from scratch. Whatever your circumstances, making a plan will ensure that your time and effort result in a living area to suit both your pocket and your life style.*

*These room plans present two possible treatments for the ground floor of a typical small terrace house. In the first, the area is divided between living room and dining room, each of which has its own doorway to/ from the main hall. Elsewhere on this floor, a large kitchen is devoted entirely to cooking. This would suit a household where entertaining revolves around small dinner parties, but whose ordinary evenings do not require seating for large numbers. The fireplace has been made the focal point of the living room, with a sofa and chair grouped for viewing television or conversation. The second plan illustrates an open-plan treatment of the same area with the partition wall removed. Dining facilities are incorporated into the large kitchen (not shown), and the living area embraces both rooms. The smaller area is furnished for study and viewing television, while the larger area, with two sofas grouped around a low coffee- table, will comfortably accommodate a large conversational group.*

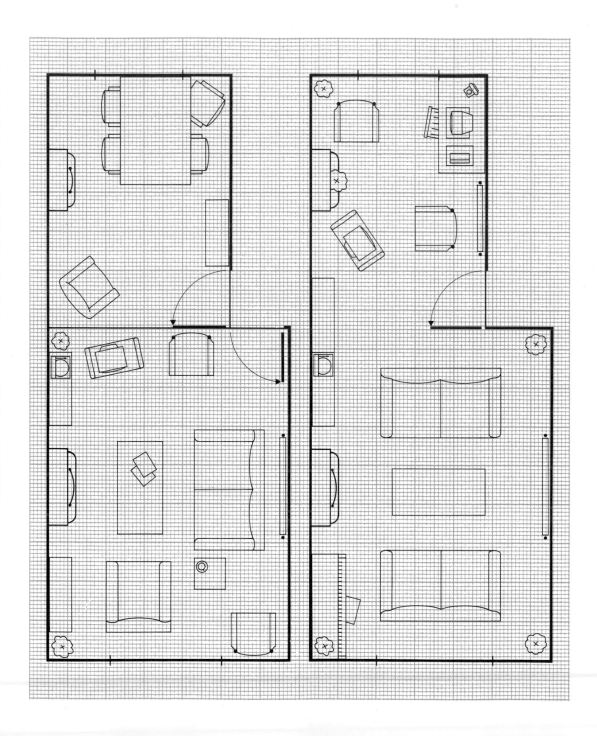

## MAKING A PLAN

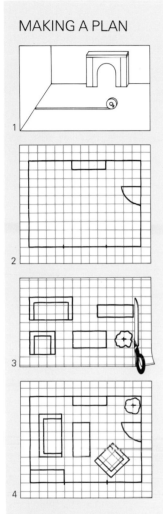

**1** Measure your living room.
**2** Make a scale drawing which includes all permanent features, such as doors, windows, cupboards and fireplaces. **3** Also make a scale drawing of each piece of furniture. Cut out the pieces.
**4** Use the cut-outs to plan your lay-out in miniature on the scale drawing of the room.

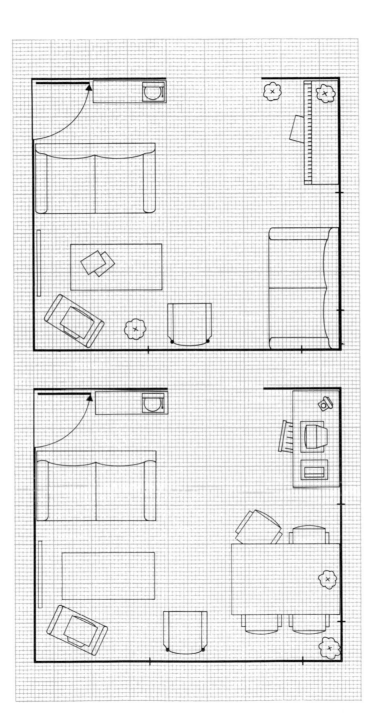

Whether large or small, the problem with living rooms is the amount of furniture they are expected to accommodate. This problem becomes acute when you are confronted with a very small flat or apartment where the living room must serve dual purposes.

These two room plans present possible treatments for a living room in a small flat. As is often the case in tiny apartments, use of space in this room is complicated by the existence of two doorways. Not only must you leave enough room for the door to open fully, but you must also allow for the flow channel – the route from the door to major pieces of furniture or appliances.

The first plan illustrates a lay-out appropriate when there is enough space to eat in the kitchen or in a separate dining room. An open, L-shaped flow area permits easy entry from either door. An upright piano occupies one corner, and a sofa and chair grouped around a coffee-table provide the main conversation/television viewing area in another.

The second plan is very similar, but would be more suitable in a smaller flat which lacks dining space in the kitchen or a needed study area. Instead of the piano, there is a small desk with typewriter and telephone. A modest dining table and chairs occupy the space in front of one window.

*These two photographs show how the same space in a modern townhouse can assume completely different dimensions and traffic patterns by simply rearranging the furniture. The positioning of furniture is critical to the success of a room. The trick is to find a focal point in the room around which to centre your plan, from lay-out to details.*

1  *A small cotton dhurry rug the same width as the two-seater sofa is placed in front of the sofa so as to define an area for seating and conversation. The trestle table opposite the sofa can either be used for work, as here, or for dining. It has been sited slightly off-centre with respect to the rug to make for easy access to and from the kitchen. This arrangement also allows for movement between the stairs and the kitchen via the path created behind the sofa and in front of the simple bookshelf which houses the telephone in a conveniently central location.*
*The arrangement of furniture in this small apartment has been well planned to flexibly accommodate the owner's life style and requirements. Although divided into defined areas by the placement of the furniture, the whole space is unified by the use of colour, especially the small accessories and items which pick up the rich blue of the carpet underfoot.*

1

2

2  Here, the same space is given a completely different treatment. There are many alternatives to the traditional three-piece suite of living room furniture. If, as here, you choose a pair of two-seater sofas instead, it is possible to add different chairs at a later time, perhaps when you have more space or a larger budget. The sofas face one another for easy conversation, with two matching Parsons tables placed symmetrically at both ends of each sofa. Two vase-like opal glass table lamps provide a soft upward glow. The space nearest to the kitchen becomes a dining area. The table, made from stained oak veneer with chrome legs, has a detachable extension leaf which is folded down when not in use, but provides more seating for extra guests at larger dinner parties. There is enough space to turn the table vertically if so desired, rather than horizontally as shown here, and for the handsome Bauhaus-style side chairs, made from chrome and grey-lipped woven cane.
This arrangement combines yellow striped wallpaper and neutral grey carpet, softer lighting, pictures on the wall, yellow cushions and a loosely draped, subtly patterned white cloth on one sofa.

1 *A living room that doubles as a work space requires graceful furniture and sensible, but not too workmanlike, storage. When the microscope and task light are removed from this desk, it is transformed into an island dining table. The swivel chair on rollers can be wheeled away when entertaining. A long continuous bookshelf which lines the junction between walls and ceiling in place of the more usual cornice is decorative and functional.*

2 *A simple, screen-like partition separates this small work space from the living room. An L-shaped opening in the partition prevents the tiny area from being too cramped, dark and poky for comfort. The work space is entered by walking around and behind an angular table built up as an extension to the partition itself (see page 35 to view this room from the other side of the partition). When used in conjunction with the work space, this table would be excellent for conferences or meetings; at other times, it could serve as a dining table. Both living and work areas are decorated with variations on the same colour scheme – neutral whites and natural colours, with highlights in dusty rose pink and terracotta.*

1

2

3

3   *The work area in this well-planned and well-equipped dual-purpose room is raised up on a low platform and visually defined by the use of grid-pattern sheet-vinyl flooring in contrast to the carpeted living area. The large storage platform suspended from the ceiling echoes the shape of the desk arrangement below. It is softened by a graceful trailing houseplant, and permits a substantial light to hang in a convenient position above the desk. The desk consists of a trestle table tucked neatly into the corner created by an outward-facing, L-shaped group of cabinets: desk clutter is hidden from the living area because the table surface is lower than the cabinet tops. When entertaining, the island desk can be completely screened by lowering slatted white blinds.*

*Although living and work areas are clearly delineated, the room as a whole gains coherence by having counters in both areas — beneath the window of the living area and along the wall of the work area — and cabinet tops occupy the same horizontal plane. The neutral colours of the soft seating and carpets give the illusion of more space.*

For years solutions to seating used to be centred round that ubiquitous set – the three-piece suite. With a more relaxed and casual attitude to living come more interesting alternatives: occasional chairs, not necessarily from the same period, teamed with a three-seater sofa, all covered in different but complementary fabrics, or a pair of two-seater sofas that define the seating space. Platform seating with big comfortable cushions placed upon a plinth is another alternative, since cushion covers in different colours and patterns introduce variety to the line-up.

It is a myth that the small room needs small pieces of furniture. A single big piece, like a giant Chesterfield button-back sofa, or a Louis XVI look-alike upholstered chair, is grander than a lot of small occasional tables and chairs, and more saving in space. Each individual piece of furniture, no matter how small, must be allocated a certain amount of walk-around space, so a group of smaller pieces, such as a pair of armchairs and a table, can sometimes require more space than one large piece, such as a sofa.

Where you place your furniture is an individual choice. In most houses, it is obviously best near the fireplace, or round the window, where light is best. In a more spacious room, there could be two groups of furniture, using an occasional table or a single sofa as a room divider to break up the space. At times, your placement of seating furniture may hinge on the availability of power sockets in the room, or the siting of a television aerial connection point. There are no hard and fast rules – place furniture where it will best suit you and the use you expect to make of the living room.

There is a case for buying a really good piece of furniture as and when your budget permits. Borrowing money from your bank on a personal loan scheme could be one way to start: look upon it as an investment, since cheaper chipboard and melamine really never improve with age, while soft leather and woods age graciously. Just a single piece will bring you more joy. Combine it with other simpler, cheaper items that can change with your tastes and decor, since it is easy to team a classic with anything. There are some really good look-alikes of classic furniture: chrome and leather Bauhaus reproductions, or the earlier Victorian Chesterfield still upholstered with age-old craft button backing, or the wicker-work cantilevered chairs of the functionalists, now in production as dining room chairs. These reproductions bring a distinctive style to your room while avoiding the extremely high cost of the original pieces.

Undistinguished pieces can be covered simply with slip-covers, which last as long as upholstery, can be removed for cleaning and make instantly effective changes. Cushions and bolsters upon a bed or window seat can similarly make an inviting seating arrangement without much expense.

When you start off with a large, elegant, well-proportioned room such as this one, even simple furniture will make a distinct impression. The architectural detail is superb, from the ornately moulded cornice to the deep skirting board and from the decorated fireplace to the magnificent floor-to-ceiling window bay. The furnishings have been designed to make the most of the way these windows bring the garden indoors. The room features a set of Lloyd Loom-style wicker seats painted a deep, matt bottle green arranged in a conversation grouping around a dark hardwood coffee-table in front of the fireplace. Although wicker is generally associated with outdoor or casual furniture, it would be a shame to expose these elegant chairs to the elements. A small hardwood desk with chrome task light is positioned directly in front of the window and surrounded by houseplants and tubbed trees. The liberal use of trees and houseplants in this room reinforces the link with the garden outdoors.

For anyone who favours a sprawling, informal approach to seating, platforms provide the change of level needed if you wish to avoid having people walk all over the cushions scattered on the floor. Simply moving the bolsters and larger cushions up on to a plinth creates one of the cheapest forms of seating available. Such a plinth need not be uncomfortable, especially if a covered foam block is used as the base. A platform should be supported at both ends by shelves or uprights, or it should run along the entire length of a wall to prevent the cushions from toppling off.

1   Whitewashed rough plaster has been used to finish not only the walls, but also the built-in platform, coffee-table and segmented display column in this Greek island villa. The clean, bright whitewash combines with a polished dark ceiling, a dark brick floor and blue accents to create a cool, cave-like and completely Mediterranean retreat.

2   Here, a plain box platform covered in the same jute that carpets the floor provides an informal seating system which, like a stepped terrace, leads to another which doubles as a bed. The pale neutral colour scheme, maintained by using natural fibres – jute, wood, wicker and canvas – is extremely restful.

1

2

3 Headroom is limited in this attic living room, with its steeply pitched ceiling. Low platform seating along the wall beneath the skylight, where there is least clearance, makes intelligent use of the space. A built-in white box serves as a base for foam blocks and bolster armrests covered in a duck-egg blue fabric.

4 Here, the concept of platform seating is applied to modular, free-standing furniture. These three-seater sofas are made up of wooden bases and upright plywood ends topped with flap armrests which house thick foam bases and plump cushions. Elements of this room are purposefully casual: the striped terracotta 'crack' in the area rug, the expensive sound system propped on an upturned beer crate and the coffee-table, apparently constructed from plywood cut-outs and the clever wooden shelving unit.

5 The seating/sleeping areas of this inventive living room sit on a geometric platform which echoes the shape of the table built into a partition. The tiny work space concealed by the partition is shown on page 30.

6 Here, purpose-built sofas are perched atop a raised platform in an ingenious split-level plan which takes advantage of the arched conservatory windows.

*Fabrics bring pattern and colour into a room, and are used in different ways for different styles of decoration. Choice of a particular fabric for a particular purpose, perhaps a flimsy muslin for draping a window or a rich, heavy brocade for re-covering a three-piece living room suite. For example, if you choose a blue-, yellow- and red-patterned fabric reminiscent of an old-style cornfield with poppies and cornflowers growing in amongst the wheatsheaves to cover a two-seater sofa, you can then distribute those colours throughout the room by adding a chair upholstered in wheat and white striped ticking, a plain cornflower blue chair and wheat-coloured slatted blinds made from cane or bamboo. Then use a bold poppy scarlet as an accent colour – for borders, curtains, cushions or trimmings.*

*The elegant Art Deco shape of the plain sofa pictured here lends itself to creating many different types of interiors, depending on how it is upholstered. The fabrics shown on these two pages have been selected from designs produced by Habitat and Laura Ashley and are grouped to illustrate but a few of the effects and combinations possible.*

Blues

Bright primaries

Pastels

Earth colours

Neutrals

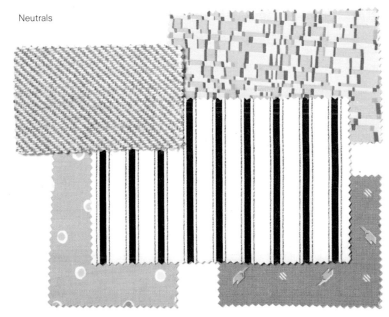

You have the greatest choice when you are purchasing a new sofa or armchair and can select the upholstery fabric when placing the order. It is then simply a question of keeping a large sample of the chosen fabric for planning the rest of the room. Some sofas come upholstered in cream cotton, which will go well with almost any colour scheme, and are supplied with paper patterns so you can make your own loose-fitting covers from the fabric of your choice when you feel in the mood for a change. Likewise, an existing sofa can be given a relatively inexpensive face-lift with a new loose cover.

It is always best to stick with durable upholstery fabrics specially manufactured to withstand hard wear for years, although lighter-weight fabrics need not be ruled out entirely. If, for example, a fairly lightweight fabric unsuitable for upholstery is the only one you feel is right for you, it may well be suitable for loose covers if you take the precaution of lining the cover. Or you may be able to use the design you prefer for some other major aspect of the room – perhaps floor-to-ceiling drapes – and upholster or cover the seating in a complementary, upholstery-weight fabric.

Upholstery can be expensive and, since the fabrics used are chosen for durability, it is not practical to ring the changes too often by reupholstering. But circumstances — and rooms — change. A more versatile approach to altering the look of seating involves using removable slip-covers. Even traditional furniture-makers are beginning to realize the value of the flexibility offered by loose covers. One Italian firm recently launched a range of upholstered furniture where each piece, each sofa or chair, is supplied with two different loose covers, one in cashmere wool for winter and the other in white drawn-thread linen for summer. So long as loose covers are well executed — made from a good strong fabric and tailored to suit the carcass being covered — they can transform furniture.

1  Here, stripes in fine lines and diagonal weaves are combined on cushion covers to bring an original freshness to this platform seating area.

2  A basic canvas and wood chair of the sort usually found in a casual setting, such as the familiar director's chair or the lounge chair illustrated in 3 can be moved into the living room by adding a simple slip-cover. These loose covers are not difficult to make, but it is important to begin by preparing a paper pattern.

1

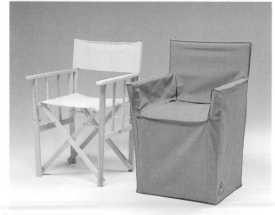

2

3

4

## DRESSING A SOFA

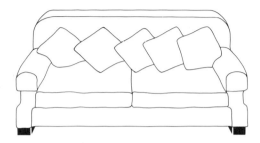

A line-up of small scatter cushions provide accent colour.

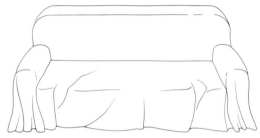

Fabric draped and folded over a sofa adds formal interest.

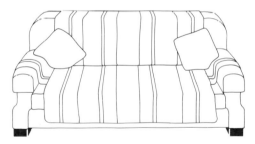

Lightweight throw rugs contribute pattern and colour.

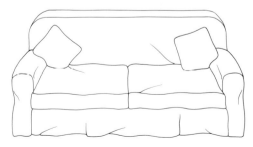

Loose covers transform a sofa without re-upholstering.

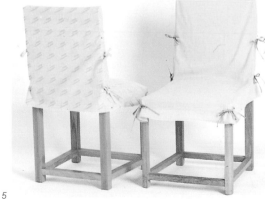

5

4 *Choice of furnishing fabric is always vital to the overall style of a room, although it is not always necessary to use one with a particular pattern or colour. The dramatic effect of this scheme relies on the contrast between the large areas of plain white fabric and the hard, shiny surfaces of the furniture frames, tables and walls. A plump pillow set against the triangular back support of an angular modern chair is covered in the same simple white as the rectangular seating base. This makes for a striking reversal of the theme established by the geometric, platform-style, black lacquer furniture frames and box tables: soft on hard, white on black, matt on glossy. The high-gloss blue-grey walls and ceiling provide a perfect background.*
*This modular furnishing system can be pushed together and anchored by placing the occasional tables in between. The placement of the ceiling-mounted corner speaker and pivoting floor lamp, which tilts up and down to focus light where it is needed most, emphasizes the geometric precision of the line-up.*

5 *Here, an ordinary wooden dining chair has been restyled with a removable slip-cover with neat bows which envelops the chair securely but which can be untied when cleaning is needed.*

1 *The design consultant who owns this penthouse, which occupies the top two floors of an early Victorian north London building, so likes the view that he seldom pulls down the blinds, made of white nylon from a ship's chandler to evoke a ship's sails. His fascination with the nautical life is also revealed by the wooden floorboards, whose natural yellow has been stained silver-grey with printer's ink to resemble faded driftwood. In this large, uncrowded, austere setting, his prized furniture collection acquires the significance of sculpture in a gallery. The low marquetry coffee-table, made of wood with inlaid shell and boat motifs in keeping with the nautical theme, was made by Peter Niczewski. Irish-born Eileen Gray designed the sofa and the ribbed leather and tubular steel chair in the thirties. The slatted wooden reclining chair with pedestal footstool was designed by David Colwell. A four-tier, hi-tech stand houses stereo equipment. The deliberately sparse furnishings are grouped around a woollen kelim rug. Rough, unplastered brick walls provide an undistracting background. The room is illuminated by recessed downlighters and black metallic Italian designer lamps.*

1

2

3

2   *In this restored Edwardian house, the living room blends old and new with its combination of contemporary and period furniture. The room features a large Edwardian sofa, with giant brass castors and scrolled armrests. Its soft velvet twill upholstery matches the grey finish of the low, contemporary coffee-table opposite, whose moulded legs echo the architectural features of the room itself. These features – deep skirting boards, dado rail, picture rail and fireplace surround – are picked out in a lighter matt grey. Indeed, grey is the unifying and elegant ground for the entire room. Diffuse natural light through plain Holland blinds enhances the soft effect of the stippled, rag-rolled grey walls.*

3   *The quality of furniture can be judged just like a horse – the narrower the ankle and leg, the further back its antecedents. This graciously curved little love-seat is given a casual setting amid a jungle of houseplants which echo the garden visible through the large windows and French windows. The atmosphere of this Parisian living room is deliciously provincial: bare floorboards squeak, an elegant mirror enhances the fireplace and antique family furniture takes pride of place. Freed from the elaborate trappings of the furniture's real vintage, this room dances with light.*

1 *Here, as we have seen elsewhere, the principle of the three-piece living room suite – a sofa and two armchairs – is upended by placing an identical pair of sofas opposite each other. The pair of two-seater sofas, one upholstered in amber and the other in burgundy, were made to order, but the tubular steel chair opposite the fireplace is an original Mies van der Rohe easy chair. Old and new mix happily in this room, from modern Italian designer lamps – a 'Teseo' standard lamp by Programma Luce and a 'Candido' table lamp by Porsche – to a pair of antique lyre-back chairs. The fireplace has been newly built between two French windows that lead to the garden, but its mantelpiece is made from antique stone.*

2 *The comfortable Chesterfield, traditionally upholstered in button-back leather, is here covered in a giddy, mosaic-pattern print made up of multi-coloured triangles and bars on a camel background. The colours echo those of the traditional dhurries and kelims laid on wooden floorboards waxed to a golden patina. The effect is to create a warm, reassuring country atmosphere, without sacrificing the stateliness of the Chesterfield sofas. Scatter cushions and drapes pick up the sofas' patterned theme.*

1

2

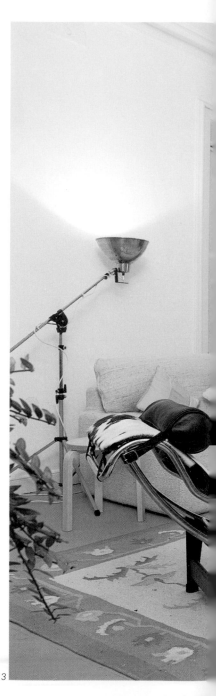

3

3 *This high-ceilinged apartment living room features a tubular Le Corbusier chaise longue which can be adjusted on its chromed steel runners to suit a variety of positions, from sitting to reclining, and Gerrit Rietveld's famous 'Red and Blue' chair of 1918 – both collectors' items. The room is decorated so as to provide a neutral, non-distracting background for these twentieth-century classics with a pair of cream-coloured slub-weave two-seater sofas, a matching flat-weave rug between them whose simple fawn pattern emulates needlepoint, white walls and a cream ceiling. Sculptural lights – including the Fortuny-designed lamp turned to act as an uplighter against one wall – a circular, tubular steel Eileen Gray occasional table and a modern television/video stand are the only other furniture. Aside from the single picture propped up on the mantelpiece, pools of light are the only wall decoration. Even the window treatment is as plain and undistracting as possible, with a plain white roller blind presenting a surface as flat as the wall itself.*

*Classic furniture need not be expensive – enterprising manufacturers have reproduced great chairs, rugs and storage systems from all periods, including this century.*

1   *This Victorian room has been painted a soft grey to act as a background for classic furniture designs of the twenties and thirties. The pair of tubular steel and black leather 'Wassily' chairs designed by Marcel Breuer at the Bauhaus were first publicized in 1925, but are still in production today. The tubular steel trolley is also a Bauhaus design, and the lamp that stands on it is the low-voltage 'Tizio' design created by Richard Sapper in 1978. A plain, charcoal two-seater sofa, Venetian blinds, grey carpet and Eileen Gray-style rug perfectly round out this bold statement of the twenties and thirties. The fireplace, although blocked up and no longer in use, has been retained for its graceful original surround, which has been painted white like the rest of the woodwork. Inside, white lilies arranged in a large grey vase with white speckles enliven an otherwise dull space.*

1

2

3

2 There has been a recent revival of interest in the furniture designs of Charles Rennie Mackintosh, a turn-of-the-century Scottish architect. His ebonized black dining room chairs inspired those illustrated here, around which an integrated range of dining and living room furniture has been designed. Grey speckled walls and grey carpet provide the most suitable background for the strong lines of the round-backed chairs and the unique underframe of the oval table.

3 Just a single, well-chosen piece of furniture can set the style for an entire room. Although a woven cane sofa with white seat evokes the conservatory, the bent beechwood trolley with its black laminate top sets the tone. It is reminiscent of the thirties' designs of Alvar Aalto, the Finnish designer who followed up the Bauhaus development of tubular steel furniture with his pioneering, modern uses of laminated and steam-bent wood and plywood. His designs are classics, and many are still in production.
A floor covered in large, white tiles in 1m (3ft) square blocks echoes the clean lines of the white built-in storage system.

Your first thoughts on storage in the living room should concern the function of the room. This is the place you will entertain friends, relax, talk, watch television, listen to music. Here you will house the objects you have collected to be admired, those personal pieces, whether sea-shells or ceramics, that would be clutter in the kitchen or seldom seen in the bedroom. So your living room storage system should be a showpiece. Secondly, you will keep your electronic equipment here – television, video, stereo sound system have to be stored here and be easily accessible for changing tapes, inserting compact discs or playing records on the turntable.

The point about accessibility will restrict the height of your shelves in a way that does not arise, for example, with bedroom storage. Bedroom cupboards at the top can take unseasonal bedding for six months of the year, while shoes, for example, can be at floor level. This does not apply in the living room. You need wall space at the right height for viewing and reaching. Worse, wall space will be at a premium – every radiator panel, window, large-scale piece of furniture, like a piano or dresser, will limit your storage options. You can circumvent this with a purpose-built storage system that is free-standing, panelled to act as a room divider, but you will find it an expensive alternative. Collections of pretty china or vases for flowers can be housed on tables, maybe making use of a wasted corner, or placed centrally on a coffee-table between seating. Shelving systems with adjustable-height shelves on tracks can be used for books – remember, a wall lined with books can provide extra insulation and soundproofing, since no insulation system is as thick or as effective as paperback books. An alternative to fixed shelving systems is to consider a trolley in tubular steel or wicker, on which you can keep drinks, or plants, or a television set to trundle about when you wish to have it nearby.

Electronics storage is altogether more demanding. The shelving, cabinet, trolley or table which houses a valuable piece of electronic equipment must first of all be stable. There must be a power point nearby, and several sockets are often required when a number of different pieces of equipment are grouped together – which is often the case with stereo systems made up of individual components, such as turntable, receiver/amplifier, tape player and speakers. In addition to the problem of finding enough nearby power sockets, you must also allow for other wiring requirements, such as the length and routing of the cable which connects the television to the aerial socket, or the wire which connects the stereo system to the speakers, which may well be far removed from the source of sound. The wide variety of shapes and sizes of different pieces of electronic equipment, and the different siting requirements of each, makes the problem even more complex.

This library tucks neatly under the stairs and occupies the full width of the adjoining wall, using every available space for books and scattered display items, such as clocks, china, casually propped pictures and an unusual lamp, 'Omega', designed by Gilles Derain. Painting the entire library unit white unifies the random pattern of motley book bindings. The wavy diagonal black and white stripes of the area rug echo the pleated concertina shape of the Eastern paper fans. The three-seater leather-covered sofa converts into a large bed. The contents of the library have been split roughly into two sections. Older books with dark, tooled leather bindings are stored in the portion of the library built in under the staircase. Modern books and paperbacks, with their white and brightly coloured jackets, cover one wall.

1   *Built-in floor-to-ceiling columns of shelves accommodate music scores and a record player in this musician's study. The shelves are high enough to house over-sized scores, to permit the record player lid to be raised and to allow good sound reproduction from speakers placed well away from the record source. A quiet and subdued alcove framed by the shelving system defines the desk area, with a telephone answering machine to prevent unwelcome disturbance.*

2   *This working wall of bookshelves employs special floor-to-ceiling wall-mounted brackets and clip-on shelf supports. The advantage of such a system is that wall-mounted brackets can be closely spaced so shelves are supported at frequent intervals. Otherwise, shelves may sag or bow between widely spaced supports under the considerable weight of books and other heavy objects. The vertical spacing of shelves is adjustable, permitting great flexibility. This all-purpose open shelving system also acts as a drinks cabinet and stereo housing unit.*

3   *This free-standing floor-to-ceiling tubular unit provides a lightweight but non-adjustable shelving system. It comfortably houses everything from a television to a slide projector in addition to ranks of books.*

4

5

6

## SHELVING SYSTEMS

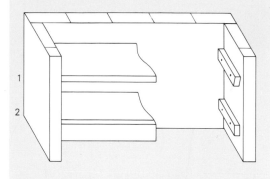

1

2

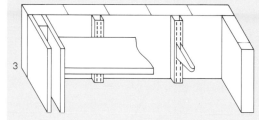

3

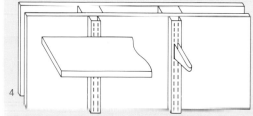

4

When planning a shelving system for a wall or alcove, it is important to consider the type of wall structure. In an alcove with solid brick walls all around, a medium-strength shelf can be supported by battens screwed to the side walls **1**. Use a pelmet or valance on the front edge of each shelf to conceal the battens **2**. If one side of an alcove is a stud partition wall, use a system of adjustable brackets to support shelves and screw the upright bracket supports to the back wall **3**. Such adjustable shelving systems also work well along hollow stud walls so long as the uprights are fixed to the studs, which are usually spaced at 610mm (2ft) intervals **4**. To find a stud behind a plasterboard wall, tap along the wall and listen for a change in sound.

4 *Alcoves flanking a fireplace and chimney-breast make excellent storage areas. This system of wooden shelves is intended for the decorative display of collectables – unglazed terracotta pots, baskets and other objets d'art – as well as for the functional storage of books. There is a neat precision and orderliness about this artful arrangement, from the evenly spaced, glossy white glazed tiles of the fireplace surround to the dappled earth colours of the woven rug and the pair of identical chairs covered in pure, plain cotton.*

5 *Here, two systems of brightly lacquered shelves hold an irregular array of books. This system has been installed in a staggered pattern – against one wall in order to obtain maximum storage space around the window and against another in order to create visual interest.*

6 *This small dual-purpose room demands economic use of every available space. The neat built-in storage system doubles as frame for a plush two-seater platform sofa filled with scatter cushions covered in turquoise, aquamarine and purple satin. Even the armrests and backrest are brought into use as a display shelf for handsome foliage houseplants and decorative china. The design cleverly incorporates storage for every purpose.*

1   *An inexpensive plain wooden
shelf unit with crossed steel
brace supports and wire basket
storage achieves a certain
dignity in this well-appointed
living room, where the forceful
use of amber and silken grey,
leather, an Oriental rug, and
graphics create a stylish,
opulent effect. Shelving
system uprights serve as
clamping points for flexible clip-
on lamps. The stippled brown
wallpaper gives the room a
warm, cheery glow which is
balanced by sophisticated
silvery-grey Venetian blinds
masking the window. The
coffee-table, which juxtaposes
smoked grey glass and natural
wood, topped by an amber and
peach lamp, is in the same
mood. A pair of comfortable,
squashy two-seater leather
sofas half-frame the sand,
earth and ochre Chinese
border-pattern weave rug,
which tones well with the
wooden floorboards waxed to
a golden shine. A wall covered
with mirror tiles creates a
much-needed illusion of space.*

1

2

3

2 *Custom-built storage systems permit an infinite variety of alternatives, from open shelves to as much closed cupboard space as necessary. A manufacturer's modular storage system can offer almost as much flexibility, with diverse units in different shapes and sizes that can be put together in any combination to suit the requirements of the owner. Here, such a system houses an eclectic range of items: a topi, a collection of decanters and stoppered bottles, gourds, wood carvings, tableware and a sound system.*

3 *An attic sitting room tucked away in the eaves, although charming to reflect upon, can be an awkward space to marshall, since such rooms usually lose height at the points where any sharply pitched roof meets the walls or floor. Here, the storage system cleverly follows the natural dictates of this unusual room, with modular boxes stacked in a low, two-level line-up where the room is busiest and stacked in a tall column next to a structural pillar. The natural colours of the room, from the floor covering to the roof beams, permits it to dance with light, enhanced by fresh green houseplants and just a touch of deep apple-red accent supplied by the telephone, the pots and vases atop a shelf and the birdcage.*

1 *This elegant solution makes good use of the space beneath a staircase for storing awkward electronic equipment. Tongue-and-groove timber panelling installed below the dado rail is painted black, with hand-painted white marbling detail that spills over from the panel on to skirting boards, the dado rail and the storage shelf surround. This makes for a clean look that goes well with the reproduction trolley. The wall above the dado rail has been sponge-painted in buttercup yellow, and is enlivened by a black picture rail. The decorative treatment of both the wall and of the tongue-and-groove panelling are a good illustration of the way special paint finishes can contribute to the overall effect of a room. Plain yellow walls with a plain black panel would have created a stark and dramatic contrast. Instead, the treatment is subtle and the result is very elegant. A Bauhaus-design circular tubular steel trolley provides unusual but distinctive storage for speakers and decorative pieces.*

1

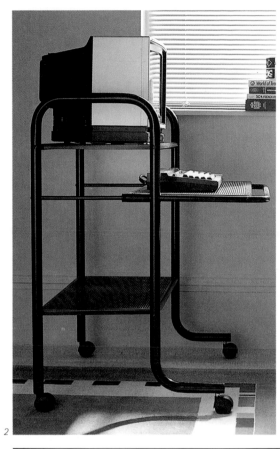

2 *This simple German home computer stand has two perforated metal shelves supported by a tubular frame and a sliding middle shelf to bring the keyboard nearer the operator. In many home computer systems, television sets double as visual display units (VDUs) and so movable stands on castors, such as this one, can be a good idea. Here, the VDU is positioned as it should be, at right angles to the window, to avoid unnecessary eye fatigue caused by light reflecting off the screen.*

3 *Purpose-built computer furniture is not essential. In this work room, a large, generously proportioned table comfortably provides both an area for traditional pencil-and-paper work, a handy range of reference books and a full-size microcomputer with VDU, double disk drives and keyboard. A restful, creative atmosphere is achieved by the combination of butter-yellow walls, grey Venetian blinds, grey carpet and natural wicker basket, rather than the more usual hi-tech look of hard-edged metallic materials.*

4 *Electronic storage must fulfil a practical requirement – that of housing delicate and complicated equipment – and at the same time suit the style of the room where it is located. This skeletal frame achieves both these objectives.*

## STORAGE TROLLEYS

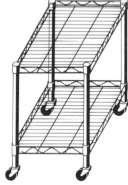

Video trolley with tube frame and metal shelves

Self-assembly trolley with metal shelves and uprights

Trolley assembled from industrial chromed wire storage system

Designer video trolley with television shelf and sling for video recorder

Features are those parts of the room that become focal points, either because the eye is drawn to them or because they suggest the way you should continue your decorative theme. Architectural features can work like this, as when a cornice or mouldings are used to suggest a style or influence the choice of furnishing period.

These focal points in any room can be whatever you select to grab the most attention – a plant, a table sporting a collection of interesting objects, a flamboyant window treatment, a cluster of vases filled with flowers, a well-lit poster, or the fireplace. A fireplace automatically becomes the feature of any room, since chairs are drawn round it for long winter evenings. To make sure it holds centre stage in summer when the fire is out, you need to decorate the fireplace surround. If you are refurbishing an older home, you may find that a boring painted fireplace surround can be stripped to reveal a handsome original made from wood, cast iron or tiles – or a combination of the three. Otherwise, a stripped fireplace surround can be given new life by refinishing it using a decorative paint treatment. Marbling, or a speckled glaze, will brighten a fireplace considerably; then hang a mirror on the wall above and arrange vases or other decorative objects along the mantelshelf. Where there is no fireplace to use as a feature, it is often possible to install one.

Flat-weave dhurries and cotton rag rugs can provide inexpensive splashes of colour and pattern that focus attention on the floor, creating an obvious centre around which to group furniture. Plants are naturally a focal point for the conversation area. Group them for maximum effect, line them up geometrically in identical plant holders or add a single rather grand plant, like a tall palm or an exotic orchid. A small floor uplighter placed below a single tree throws an interesting variegated light upon the ceiling and walls. Even an array of flowers in a simple composition that can be changed daily will make a focal point of a mantelshelf, if your budget and your garden supplies can stretch to fresh flowers on a regular basis.

Groups of posters, paintings and drawings can make a focal point. Throughout this book you will discover different groupings of graphic art in people's houses, either casually propped up against the wall for a changing tableau, or as a montage of formally arranged and well-mounted pictures. Take note of the way pictures are framed to make an undistinguished painting a feature on the wall. The right frame unearthed in an auction job lot of several dusty prints can have the contents removed and be regilded, or painted, then distressed by a brisk rubbing with wire wool.

Features can be created from architectural details. Painting the coving an accent colour to fit in with the scheme, or adding a cornice of polystyrene which, when painted, looks like plasterwork, will make a feature worthy of a second look, as in the room shown here.

Everything in this London house is centred around the decorative details of the fine Art Deco fireplace and chimney-breast. The base of the large inverted triangle which points down from the junction of wall and ceiling has been fitted with an eyeball lamp to wash the wall in light and illuminate the small sculpture on the mantelpiece. Shelving installed in the alcoves to either side is well recessed, allowing the fireplace to dominate, and one pair of shelves visually extends the line established by the decorative fireplace moulding. The design of the fireplace suggests the façade of a classical Greek temple, down to the small statue occupying the upper triangular 'pediment' area. The pretty cast-iron hood frames the original Victorian tiles of the fireplace surround.

1   *This monochrome room shimmers owing to the combination of white vinyl floor tiles, white Venetian blinds and white walls. Against this gallery-like background, the lines of an individual furniture collection become all-important. Here, the high-backed, curvaceous profile of a large white love-seat is outlined in dark hardwood and emphasized at each corner with pale buff cushions. These cushions echo the colour scheme of the room's other furnishings – a tubular steel and buff leather 'Wassily' chair designed by Marcel Breuer and a pair of buff Lloyd Loom-style wicker chairs grouped in the far corner beneath the open window. A glass-topped, angular chrome trolley moves freely around the room. This open, bright room is visually anchored by the low coffee-table, with its sparkling prismatic hexagonal globe vase of sharp palm fronds and white blossom, which becomes the focal point of the table top.*

*In a colourful room full of pattern and light, finding a focal point can be more difficult than in a restrained, neutral and natural background, where a single jolt of colour or a single giant houseplant has the power to attract attention.*

1

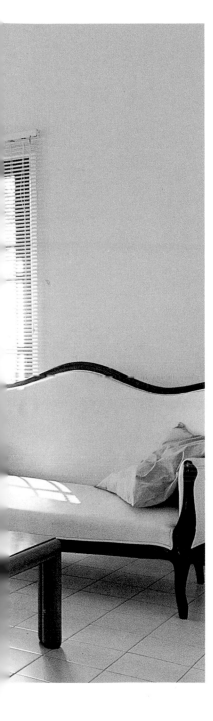

2

3

4

2　*A two-tier coffee-table made from beech-lipped white laminate and topped with a bright turquoise bowl anchors this room of many blues. Aside from this focal point, occasional yellow accents – a bunch of flowers and the rim on the arched coffee-table lamp – provide the only other departure from the blues and greys of this room.*

3　*Here a two-seater sofa and chair are upholstered in a grey speckled fabric that matches the wallpaper and contrasts well with the black ash-veneer coffee-table and shelving. Pictures with narrow black frames, tall black uplighters and black Venetian blinds reinforce the effect. The green ferns growing in the terrarium provide the sole spot of colour – even their growing medium seems to have been chosen to reinforce the neutral tones used throughout the room.*

4　*A pair of two-seater sofas, an armchair and a day-bed – upholstered all in cream – are anchored in this spacious room by the glass-topped nesting tables at the centre. Such tables can be separated so as to provide each seating area with its own coffee-table or, as here, grouped to form a linked stage in the centre. This room also derives a graceful serenity from the placement of a giant tree, a bronze sculpture and casually propped pictures.*

1   *Pictures and posters instantly make a bold contribution to the decor of any room. In this completely refurbished turn-of-the-century Milan apartment, the living room has been painted white, a natural wool carpet installed and a fireplace with a slate seating slab has been built, all contributing to the quiet dignity and restraint of this subdued, elegant room. Four eighteenth-century ink-wash garden plans are arranged in a traditional grouping above a grey sofa. Together, the four pictures form an unframed, glazed square whose dimensions are echoed by the dramatic, low, castor-mounted, glass-topped coffee-table in front of it. Such a large central coffee-table could easily make a room seem crowded, but use of a transparent glass-topped table, whose surface reflects the light, contributes to the bright, open atmosphere created by the white walls and area rug and the pastel accent colours used to decorate this room. The slate hearth of a newly installed fireplace, just visible in the corner of this photograph, is depicted in full on page 61.*

1

## HOW TO HANG CURTAINS

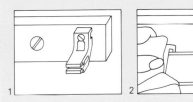

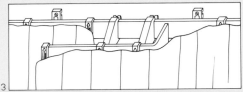

Correct positioning and hanging ensure that curtains look their best. **1** Use a wooden batten to fix the curtain track bracket to a wall. **2** Clip the curtain track to the wall bracket; glider hooks clip on to the track, or can be fed on at one end, and the curtain hangs from the glider hooks. **3** An overlap arm ensures that there is no gap between the curtains when they are drawn.

## WINDOW BAY CURTAINS

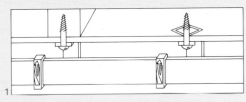

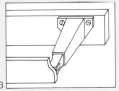

Fix battens above each run of windows in three-sided bays. Fit curtain tracks inside the window reveal or directly to the wooden window frame of a curved bay. **1** Alternatively, fix curtain tracks to ceiling joists or plasterboard. **2** Use a round tin as a former when bending aluminium track. **3** Extension brackets make curtains hang neatly over the sill.

2   *The success of this distinctive monochrome white room depends on a reversal of decorating schemes and a juxtaposition of colours and textures. One side of the room is accessorized in blue — blue ceramic plant holders, telephone and graphic print — and the other in the natural tones of wicker, bamboo and pine. A golden timber beam bisects the white-painted tongue-and-groove panelled ceiling and links the two sides of the room together. The tall palm in the corner gives the decor a tropical definition.*

3   *Decorated all in cream, with full-length pleated cream drapes, cream wall-to-wall carpet, cream walls, cream upholstery with a small repeat motif pattern and blond furniture, this room lacks any definition other than that provided by the low central table. Three carved wooden lidded urns and contemporary speckle-glaze pots filled with gypsophila draw the eye. Otherwise, attention naturally focuses on the view of the garden through the windows.*

4   *This simple piece of furniture illustrates the value of the traditional sideboard, both as a display surface and as a storage place to hide glasses, ashtrays and other items.*

1   *There is a precise and pleasing symmetry about this unusually tall central fireplace. The lower part of the immediate fire surround has been given a matt black finish, the top edge of which visually aligns with the lower edge of the windows which flank it. The rest of the fire surround has been given a hand-painted marbled finish. To reinforce the visual link with other architectural features of the room, the mantelshelf is positioned to correspond with the wide picture rail and the top of its backing board aligns with the top edge of the windows. A glass vase with three irises casually tumbling from it graces the mantelshelf, providing colour and drawing the eye upward.*

1

2 *The golden wood of the Art Deco-inspired fireplace surround brings a comforting glow to this white room, with its neutral fawn wall-to-wall carpet and formal dark mahogany furniture. The wedge-shaped central decoration pinpoints the exact spot to place a tall glass cylinder filled with lilies. The gateleg table, with its silver salver positioned as though ready to accept visiting cards of another era, successfully masks the fact that the fire is not lit in summer..*

3 *A modern fireplace such as this built into a chimney-breast can be an efficient way of heating a room. Today's fire appliances have ducted vents at the back which push more heat out into the room and less up the chimney than was once the case. This fireplace has been given a neat, undistracting brass trim. The position of the elegant Edwardian wicker chairs depends on the fireplace.*

4 *This second view of the living room shown on page 58 illustrates the fire place full-front. Custom-built to warm a small space, its design is rigorously geometric and angled. A small inlaid Eastern mirror is propped against the wall on the extended slate hearth to reflect the firelight.*

## FIREPLACE TREATMENTS

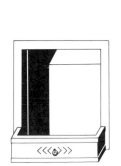

Stainless steel grate and fire surround

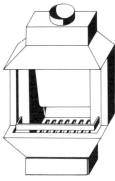

Free-standing stainless steel fireplace

Free-standing cast-iron stove

Free-standing, enamelled iron stove

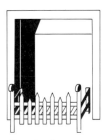

Free-standing cast-iron grate

1  *Reproduction fireplace
surrounds and firedogs and
fenders – accessories of
another age, when fires were
the only way to heat a home –
can be appropriate in the right
setting. Here, an ornately
carved stripped pine fire
surround frames the Victorian
tiles set around the hearth and
sets the tone for the
furnishings and golden woods
that glow as warmly and
welcomingly as any fire in this
living room. The floorboards
are unadorned, the window
shutters stripped and
ornamental, the furnishings all
simple, from the wicker chairs
to the glass-topped table.*

2  *This room boasts a formal
decorative treatment which
begins with the stippled fawn
and amber paint finish on the
walls and the wallpaper border,
which reinforces the line of the
picture rail. A mirror hung on
the chimney-breast effectively
doubles the image of the
picture rail. The fireplace
surround, with its hand-painted
marbled finish, anchors the
entire decorative scheme.*

4

3  A grand cast-iron fire surround with decorative studs provides a black metallic frame to the glowing embers. By contrast, the fireplace is delicately moulded and articulated, and painted a pristine white. The combination is surprisingly successful. The decor of the room works well with the dominant traditional-style fireplace, combining flower-print upholstery, old candlesticks and lamps, knick-knacks and decorative tableware displayed on the shelves of the chimney-breast alcove and dramatic houseplants.

4  Turn-of-the-century ironmongery produced such delightful Art Deco stoves and fireplaces that they are still copied by manufacturers today, such as the reproduction French enamelled stoves which are now fuelled by natural gas rather than wood or coal. This Scandinavian stove is a one-off, its reassuring solidity a reminder of the companionable warmth it brings this essentially summery blue and white room.

1   *The pitched roof of this apartment allows for bold vertical treatments. Here, an original furniture collection, from battered old leather sofas and blanket throws to the modern Harry Bertoia wire mesh chairs and dining table, is completely dominated by the potted palm set inside a white pail. To offset its immensity, the owners have placed a modest hand-picked bunch of black-eyed anemones upon the low coffee-table.*

2   *The ribbons of colour covering this sofa tone well with the brightly patterned drapery fabric, which evokes terraces and palm fronds – a feeling echoed by the potted palm in its large terracotta pot. Bright window-box primulas share the jewel-like colours of the fabrics. A single bunch of pale primroses or spray of catkins would not have been out of place, but would not have made such an excellent foil to the fabrics, both designed by Susan Collier and Sarah Campbell.*

1

2

3

4

3  *Here again, houseplants have been specifically chosen to complement the existing decor. The wallpaper in this little living room is speckled with irregular slivers of colour, and the dappled shade cast by the Ficus benjamina (weeping fig tree) adds to the appeal of this sunny corner.*

4  *Certain plants have associations with places or periods in history and can evoke a particular mood. A magenta-flowered orchid and a large splashy fern grouped under a ceiling fan in a room draped with white muslin will evoke tropical nights, whereas in this illustration, large potted palms set in heraldic relation to traditional leather Chesterfield-type sofas evoke the Victorian era. The floorboards have been whitened and the walls painted a gentle eau-de-Nil blue. Cut flowers pick up the rich red accent of the kelim rugs.*

1  *Houseplants need not be clustered near the windows to be effective. These splendid weeping fig trees (Ficus benjamina) are carefully placed in a room with a high ceiling to give the feeling of living in a leafy glade. The 'planting' occurs on either side of the room, echoing the formal symmetry of the storage shelves in the alcoves to either side of the central fireplace. Those shelves dictate the room plan and the positioning of the trees. Although the effect is decorative, the room is plain and simple, with white walls, an old wooden chest, white Art Deco sofas and a polished parquet floor. The plants in their huge wicker baskets and the gilded nineteenth-century mirror above the fireplace become the focal points.*

*A doorway leads to a small room with good natural light which has been turned into an indoor jungle. Foliage houseplants sit on the floor, and are set along the full height of a shelving system that reaches to the high ceiling. Most plants suitable for indoor cultivation are native to tropical climates and are thus able to withstand the year-round warmth of the indoor habitat.*

1

## INDOOR GARDENING: FOOD AND WATER

**1** Self-watering pots with a wick to draw water from a reservoir are ideal in dry, centrally heated homes and useful for holidays. **2** Grow plants without soil in a pot of silver sand, vermiculite, mica, leca or gravel. Liquid plant food provides nutrients. **3** Group plants in a tray of sphagnum moss with their rims at uniform height. Moisten the moss to provide humidity.

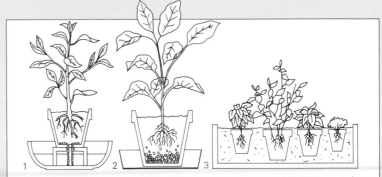

2

3

4

## INDOOR GARDENING: ARTIFICIAL LIGHT

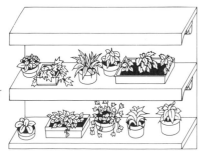

Three-tier stand with lights.

Fluorescent light tubes specially designed to meet plants' growing requirements can be fitted under shelves behind a pelmet.

Rather than blocking off an unused fireplace, fit it with a fluorescent plant light.

A miniature terrarium garden will flourish even in a dark corner if fitted with a plant light.

2 *The beams in this modern wooden-framed house inspired the selection of plants which would either trail gracefully down from them, or which would clamber up over them. Additional trailing plants are grown on a display stand next to the door. The treatment of the decor is well suited to lots of greenery — jute flooring, slatted blinds at the windows and wicker seating everywhere — all in sympathy with the tongue-and-groove panelling of the walls and ceilings.*

3 *Dark-stained timber ceiling beams which run the length of this room define its shape. Their line has been echoed by the formal rank of houseplants, all lined up in front of unadorned windows. Each plant is potted individually in its own terracotta pot and placed upon a ceramic tile in the kitchen that marks its position. There is nothing haphazard about it. Another leafy clump of plants in an old stone trough is framed against a white wall opposite, anchoring the room.*

4 *Plants banked in a hallway, especially when the hall terminates in French windows overlooking a garden, have the effect of linking outside with inside. As it would be difficult to move all these houseplants in their terracotta pots for watering, the floor of the hallway is sensibly tiled with terracotta tiles.*

Surface finishes in the living room can be more fun to choose than in the hall or kitchen, where the determining factor is how durable the finish will be. Now is the chance to be more fashionable, more experimental, less concerned about tough treatments.

Begin with the floor since it makes the biggest impact and anchors the scheme. Floorboards can be sanded, then rubbed with a coloured stain, or whitened to ship-deck freshness with a white emulsion, then sealed with a matt varnish applied in at least five coats. There are flat-weave dhurries from India which introduce both colour and pattern to your room. They have to an extent overtaken the wall-to-wall carpet in popularity, but there are living rooms in apartments or cold country cottages, for example, which will benefit from carpeting, whether jute, ribbed coir matting or the thicker wool, tufted or looped-pile carpet. Wool mixture carpets are the most expensive: cheaper versions come in wool/synthetic mixtures, cut-pile or cord-bonded carpet, which is pile fibre bonded to a backing. Whatever your choice, remember that carpet grades on the back which give the duty areas that match the carpet quality will grade living areas as 'not too tough', though children and dogs can trample any such gradings underfoot. Since coloured flooring makes a bold impact in the room, make sure you add accessories and soft furnishings in compatible colours. Try to avoid uniformity with wall-to-wall carpeting in beige or brown. If you inherit such drab carpets, introduce rugs to interrupt the expanse of floor and bring interest to the room.

Walls can be painted, either with a matt emulsion, which could benefit from stencilling, or with a special paint finish, scumbled, spattered, rag-rolled or marbled. If you tackle hand marbling, add a rail to the wall at dado (chair) height and marble below it so that it looks like panelling. Or you can paper walls with an overall motif pattern, or papers that emulate these special paint finishes rather successfully. Remember, too, that fabrics of all sorts, including bedsheets, can make wonderful wall coverings. The disguising properties of textured fabrics can often make the most of uneven wall surfaces.

If the ceilings are low, you can add height to a room by choosing a striped paper or fabric, the vertical stripes taking the eye visually upwards, or bring light and space to it with plain white curtains, unlined, or pinoleum blinds or Roman battened blinds. If you use white drapes, add colour to the walls. Even in small rooms, the background does not have to be white. Pattern can give the illusion of space, especially if you alternate the pattern in the same room, scaled in different sizes within the same colour range. Try to use, for example, large-scale florals on the sofa, a smaller scale of the same floral on the wallpaper, then matched curtains in a stripe that picks out one of the main colours.

The current fashion for decorative surface finishes has led to the revival of numerous decorative paint treatments, including rag-rolling, scumbling, sponging, spattering, marbling, staining and stencilling. It is refreshing to see a room like this one, where even a plain surface can be unconventional. Here, a black lacquer sideboard is placed unexpectedly against a glass wall, with the greenery of the back garden acting as a backdrop for two abstract drawings, a ceramic plate and a modern chrome Italian designer light. The rug adds pattern and colour, and the cool greeny blue of its border suggests a colour for the tubular furniture frames and large vase.

1  *Wooden floorboards waxed to a pale gold patina always suggest countrified interiors, with rag rugs and pretty pastels, so it is surprising to see this floor used as a background for a contemporary room. The plump black sofas filling carcasses of tubular steel, the black-painted door with red handle, the Venetian blinds – all are uncompromisingly geometric and modern. The rug is the element which pulls the composition together, with its great bands of red and black set on a blue-grey background.*
*Wooden floors can be used to create very different effects, depending upon the type of wood and the width of the floorboards. Pine floorboards tend to be fairly wide. Older pine floors, generally intended to be covered with carpet or another floor covering, can be stripped to reveal the rich, mellow tones of aged pine. New pine floorboards, on the other hand, have a bright, yellow colour when finished with varnish or another sealer. Hardwood floorboards are often narrower. Maple is a light yellow colour, ash has a silvery hue and oak has a more golden tone. Wooden floors can also be stained to enchance their natural colour and bring up their decorative grain.*

1

## HOW TO SAND A WOODEN FLOOR

Prepare the floor by punching in nails which are proud of the surface and by removing all staples and tacks. Hire heavy-duty sanders: **1** an edging sander and **2** a floor sander. Be sure to obtain a range of appropriate grades of abrasive paper for each. To provide a good surface, you may have to sand the floor as many as four times. **3** Begin with coarse grade abrasive and sand the floor diagonally, at a 45° angle to the run of the boards and using a fine grade abrasive. **4** Lower the sander slowly, do not allow it to remain in one position and overlap each sanding by 75mm (3in) to avoid ridges.

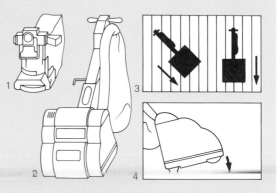

2

3

2 *This unusual floor surface, made up of inexpensive plywood squares, has been varnished many times to produce a highly polished surface which gives a reflective dimension to the room, in keeping with its Art Deco furnishings. The flat texture of the carpet and slight sheen of the leather chair are highlighted in contrast and add to the thirties' theme. Round rugs such as this were more common in the twenties and thirties than today. The choice here of predominant white with blue markings is the perfect anchor for the white chair outlined with blue piping. An entrance to this living room has been boarded up and covered with mirror tiles, a treatment sympathetic to the mood of the room and one which increases its apparent size and brightness.*

3 *This gymnasium-style floor is created by narrow lengths of maple, an extremely durable hardwood. A plain white rug with a fine linear blue border anchors the seating area, which is linked to the desk area by some red books, which pick up the accent colour of the filing cabinet, tulips, lamp, desk-tidy and chairs.*

## HOW TO SEAL A WOODEN FLOOR

Use floor sealer on new, unsealed floorboards or on older floors stripped of all earlier finishes. Before applying either oleo-resin sealer or polyurethane varnish, clean the floor thoroughly with white spirit and allow it to dry. **1** Apply at least three coats of oleo-resin sealer, using a non-fluffy cloth or applicator to work each coat well into the wood. **2** To obtain a good lustre, buff each coat with a soft cloth or floor polisher before applying the next. **3** Alternatively, apply at least three coats of floor-grade polyurethane varnish with a clean brush, always brushing in the direction of the wood grain. Try to apply each brushful with a single stroke. **4** After each coat dries, lightly sand the surface with a very fine grade sandpaper and thoroughly remove the dust before applying the next.

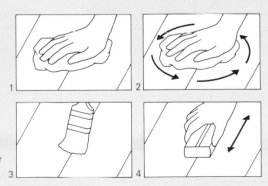

1 It is an old maxim that blue is a cold colour, especially when used over a large area. This room, however, which is painted and furnished in shades of blue, shows that a bold, large-scale treatment can achieve a sophistication that is far from chilling. The portrait above the fireplace suggests yellow as an accent colour, and the radiator pipe above the window is painted yellow to match the piping of the blue footstool cushions.
Colour co-ordination unifies this room, but the use of softly varied shades of blue and green enlivens the monochrome effect. The blue walls are marginally darker than the paler blue sofa and the use of duck-egg blue-green for the handrail beneath the window creates additional surface interest. Strategic touches of white, such as the fireplace surround, window frame and picture mat contribute welcome fresh touches to this exercise in blues and greens.

2 The use of fabric as a wall covering is dramatic, but can be expensive. Here, a pin-dotted charcoal fabric is pleated over a felt interlining and stapled in place at top and bottom for a rich, panelled look.

3  In this subtle room, careful
attention has been paid to
achieving a high-quality finish
on every surface. The glossy
white paint on the woodwork –
radiator grilles, doors, fireplace
and two columns which
support a beam – is in delicate
contrast to the hand-painted
cream and white marbled
walls. The warmth of the
wooden floorboards is
reinforced by the collection of
terracotta jugs on the
mantelshelf, the cheerful red,
green and blue of the Indian
kelim rug and the log basket.
A wall-mounted flat radiator
painted the same cream colour
as the walls is virtually invisible
behind a white screen made up
of widely spaced slats which
permits heat to flow into the
room. Flat cushions on top of
the screen turn it into a cosy
bench where anyone entering
on a cold day can warm
themselves while removing
their boots.

If you work away from home, the chances are that you will mostly view your living room by night. Of course, there are the weekends to relax indoors, but then shopping, visiting or gardening often curtail that time. Consider that fact early in the planning of your living room decorative scheme because you could introduce more dramatic colours, deeper tones, more intense shades than you would choose with sunlight streaming upon them. Red-lacquered furniture, burgundy velvet drapes, high-gloss boldly coloured paints, mirrors and glass shelving are just some of the theatrical additions that can be added to a room viewed by night light. Then you need to ensure that it is lit properly. Reflectors in the bulbs can affect the quality of the light with silver reflectors giving a mysterious cool light, and gold ones warming it up. Light fittings are usually the dullest item you inherit in your home, often no more than a pendant bulb hanging in the centre of the room, or perhaps a lighting track on the ceiling with a few spotlights, and a lamp on the table.

A few simple moves can transform this. In place of the spot, install a specialist downlighter fitting which can be recessed in the ceiling. Most of these downlighters are marketed with instructions for the simple installation of the piece, including a template so you can cut the hole in the ceiling. Then you can extend the flex of the central overhead light to change the direction of the general lighting, putting hooks on the ceiling to loop up the light at different points where you need it most. To stop an overhead light giving a flat glare to the room, widen the shade as much as possible, since shade will diffuse the light. Reduce its dominance with task lights round the room, more lamps with the traditional base with silk or paper shades, or the specialist fittings with low-voltage bulbs that throw direct beams where they are most needed.

Consider uplighters either to stand upon the floor behind a sofa or plant, and highlight the wall, or the slender standard lamps with concentrated beams of light cast upon the ceiling. All these suggestions do not involve any major electrical changes. Paintings could be lit with the new low-voltage clamp-on lights for this purpose, no thicker than a pencil and designed to throw out very little heat, but a strong light.

Houseplants can place unusual demands on lighting, especially if they are used as an integral part of the decor by a dedicated indoor gardener. Plants are not necessarily used to best effect when they are clustered near the windows for light, but plants which have been selected because of their low light requirements may thrive if subject to a mixture of indirect natural light and the right kind of artificial light. Special light bulbs for indoor horticulture – usually either special tungsten halogen or fluorescent bulbs – can be fitted under shelves, inside unused fireplaces or in other places.

## LIGHTING CHECKLIST

- ■ Are you certain enough about the uses and style of the room to install permanent, built-in lights?
- ■ How much lighting is required as a supplement to natural light by day?
- ■ Which activities require specific task lighting?
- ■ Does the room have good features which could be highlighted by lighting?
- ■ Is lighting required for safety when a room is not in use, such as a guiding light on a stairwell?
- ■ Are staircases well illuminated so that the stairs cast sharp shadows?
- ■ If the room is too big or too small, can lighting improve its proportions?
- ■ Do you want to be able to vary the mood of your lighting scheme? *Put all lights on dimmer switches.*

*Night light transforms a room which by day may seem airy and light. In this combination work/living/dining room, the decor is based on light colours. With its combination of spotlights and wall-mounted, standard and table uplighters, the room can be transformed at the flick of a switch.*

1 *This cool, grey-green living room, with a distinctive duo-tone colour scheme held firmly throughout the room, has the feel of the thirties about it. The lamp set up on the storage system casts a pool of light below the sofa, and the mirror tiles around the door bounce light back into the room. A tall floor standard uplighter near the door maintains a balance.*

2 *Uplighters looking like graceful bowls on slender chrome stems cast a pool of light upwards where it is needed most – towards the walls of this graciously appointed apartment. Panel mouldings and an elaborate plaster cornice in this early nineteenth-century room would be lost to view without these efficient, low-voltage halogen lights, which bring out every detail.*

3 *A room with a low ceiling is here given a cool distance with simple but effective planning – the walls are painted blue and eyeball spotlights capable of swivelling and spotlighting have been installed. The gilt frame on the American cabin picture, with its yellow grass foreground, and yellow scatter cushions provide a vivid splash of accent colour.*

1

2

3

4

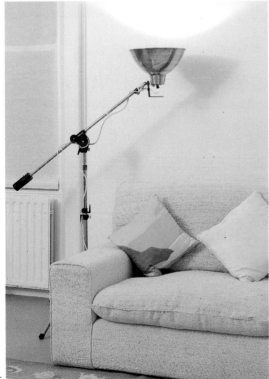

5

## TYPES OF LIGHTING

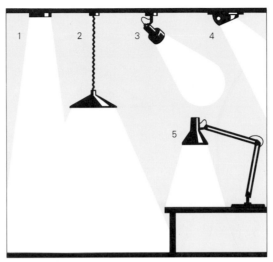

**Downlighters: 1** recessed tungsten downlighter, **2** standard tungsten pendant light, **3** tungsten parabolic spotlight, **4** recessed eyeball spotlight and **5** free-standing tungsten worklamp (also available as a clamp-on worklamp).

**Uplighters:1** tungsten wall washers, **2** tungsten table lamp, **3** free-standing tungsten halogen uplighter, **4** suspension lamp with diffused uplighters and concentrated task downlighter and **5** floor fitting for tungsten halogen light.

4 *French windows are given an elegant treatment with upright brass security rods, a white wooden curtain rail, white drapes hanging from plain wooden rings and a flanking pair of lyre-back chairs. Dish-shaped wall uplighters placed just above the picture rail cast upward pools of light. It is easy to see why uplighters positioned on a wall are so often known as 'wall washers'.*

5 *This theatrical lamp, designed by Mariano Fortuny, casts an effective light from its giant shade and operates like a director's light from a tripod stand. It is most effective in this anonymous cream-dominated corner. Although a lamp such as this is immensely versatile and adaptable to a wide range of conditions and requirements, it takes up more space than most domestic floor lamps.*

Lighting should be intended either for general illumination, or for illuminating specific task or activity areas.

To plan lighting effectively, it is necessary to consider what activities will be taking place in any given room, and at what times of day or night.

1   In daytime, a room like this, with its wall of windows, is filled with natural light. At night, however, task lighting is necessary: the extendable arm lamp and the small yellow table lamp in the corner are back-ups by day.

2   Two urn lamps flank this slanted-side sofa. The white muslin draped over the window diffuses the light and achieves a neo-classical effect.

3   When living rooms double as offices, it is important to use lights to differentiate the areas under review. Here, platform seating has clamp-on lights that can be twisted to highlight the pages of a book or hand work.

The desk is well placed in front of the window where natural light will fall by day. At night, the work area is illuminated by a low-hung pendant light. It drops all the way down to the level of the desk to illuminate any task in hand, in this instance the arrangement of dried flowers.

1

2

3

4 *Mirrors are used to amplify and reflect the light in this sunny but subtly coloured living room. It is small, just the width of the pink sofa and small white table, yet the mirrored panel, outlined and framed in chrome, makes it seem more spacious. The same simple storage boxes below the second panel house the sound equipment and provide a display surface for leafy houseplants. Scale is clearly not an issue here, as armfuls of scented stock spill from an enormous modern black and white ceramic globe. A white low-voltage, small bulb-headed lamp at the left casts reading light above the sofa, while in the corner of the room a slender upright floor lamp can be pivoted to direct light wherever it is needed.*

## LAMPS FOR TASK LIGHTING

Swivelling tungsten halogen desk lamp

Adjustable wall, ceiling or table lamp

Versatile tungsten halogen desk lamp

Polished brass wall-mounted downlight

Table lamp with ceramic base

Urn-shaped table lamp/uplighter

# KITCHENS

Your dream kitchen may be a romantic vision in a rustic farmhouse with flagstone floors, herbs hanging from wooden beams, a smell of baking coming from an old iron range and a bustle of people round a large pine table. If you are a creative cook, it may be an ultra-modern, stainless steel kitchen designed for a professional chef with the very latest gadgetry and every utensil and convenience available. Alternatively you may prefer a narrow, ship-shape galley, with all clutter concealed in laminated fitted units and the digital clock on the microwave giving a countdown for a meal in minutes.

Obviously the reality is rather different. A reasonable budget will rarely stretch to the ultimate dream kitchen. Space is also a severe limitation since you cannot fit a large, airy, country-style kitchen into the average home. Yet, whatever shape or size you have available, and no matter how small your budget, the lay-out, the style and the atmosphere of your kitchen are for you to decide and the possibilities are almost endless. There is no single, universal kitchen lay-out which is right for everyone.

The lay-out must be carefully planned to accommodate the wide range of things which make up the kitchen – bulky equipment such as cookers, storage for everything from frozen meat to those fondue skewers you occasionally use, gadgets and appliances, and probably a place for the family to eat. The lay-out must also take account of power and water supplies, safety, comfort and efficiency.

The style of your kitchen is something only you can decide. The choices are enormous. You must decide on the type of storage units and major fittings you want. You must choose the finish for your surfaces – it could be plastic laminate, natural wood or a subtle paint effect – and when you have made that decision you must decide on the precise colour or pattern. The type of floor you decide on will not only affect cost and efficiency but also style.

The atmosphere of your kitchen will come from the personal details and final touches you give to it, but it is something to keep in mind from the outset. We rarely have the opportunity to build a kitchen from scratch, so this book will help you deal with styles and lay-outs you inherit as well as offering a complete guide to creating the kitchen of your dreams.

## PLANNING CHECKLIST

- What do you dislike about your present kitchen?
- How many adults, children and pets will be using the room?
- What activities will the kitchen be used for?
  - cooking
  - dining
  - laundry
  - ironing
  - home office
  - sewing
- Which meals do you eat or serve in the kitchen?
- What are the storage requirements?
- Which appliances do you require?
  - refrigerator
  - freezer
  - microwave oven
  - oven
  - fume extractor
  - hob
  - cool larder
  - dishwasher
  - washing machine
  - tumble drier
- Do any appliances require special plumbing or ducting?
- Where will you put the rubbish?
- How many electric power outlets will you need for appliances, and where should these be sited?
- Will all working areas have adequate lighting?
- Are your kitchen requirements likely to change over time?
- What sort of atmosphere would you like to create?

*In this bold, small-space kitchen, everyday necessities are treated as objects of interest in their own right. The angular black fume extractor hood is both practical and good-looking and an array of utensils decorates the wall.*

These two views of the same small kitchen before and after decoration show that redesigning a kitchen does not need to be expensive, or to involve major structural changes, in order to be extremely effective.

1 *Before refurbishment, the kitchen was fairly typical of the kind often inherited in housing built or redecorated on a speculative basis in recent decades. The imitation timber doors of the kitchen units, tile-effect flooring and roller blinds are the cheap fitments of the modern townhouse kitchen. Worse, the arrangement of kitchen units and appliances has not been designed to overcome space limitations. The unfortunate placement of the old gas stove, which juts awkwardly into the room, creates a dead, wasted corner space. The dog basket tucked away below is ready to trip up the cook moving from the stovetop with a saucepan full of boiling liquid, and the coffee maker stashed in the corner of the worktop is virtually inaccessible. The display unit for spices and coffee mugs, which might make sense in a larger kitchen, takes up a lot of valuable wall space to store very little. With such limited storage space, appliances and gadgets occupy the worktop area, and some items are stored in inaccessible spots on top of tall wall units.*

1

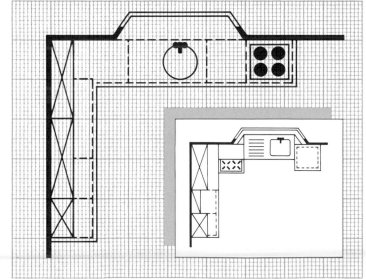

2

2  *This inexpensive but successful transformation is achieved by replacing the kitchen units and the stove. The new design also reinforces the modern style of the room, rather than working against it. To successfully transform the inherent style of a room is always more expensive. Functional self-assembly kitchen units such as those used here are easy to find in a wide variety of shapes, sizes and styles.*

*Kitchen units with cool grey melamine-faced doors and smart 'D'-handles have been fitted according to an ergonomic plan which provides maximum storage — even in the corner — and ample worktop space for preparing food, while minimizing walkabouts between the stove and the sink. No space-wasting spice racks interrupt the block of wall units. Narrow-slatted grey Venetian blinds admit the natural light necessary for a window sill herb garden even as they provide privacy and enhance the clean lines of the large window — the room's best feature. By night, the sink and food preparation area is illuminated by downlighters recessed into the top of the window bay.*

*The white vinyl flooring with fine diagonal stripes, the white plinths of the floor units and the white melamine countertops with their white-tiled splashback all contrive to make this kitchen more spacious.*

*These two kitchens illustrate the way a single modular system of manufactured kitchen units can be used to different effect in different spaces. With a range of units which offers many options, from the usual floor and wall units to finishing touches like space-filling shelves and plinths, it is possible to put together a customized kitchen that suits the individual requirements of a room and its occupants.*

1  *The owner of this small, working kitchen has chosen units with white laminate surfaces and beech edges and handles for a clean, sharp look. Open, easy-access adjustable shelves instead of closed wall cupboards display decorative storage jars and tableware. Everything is stored within arm's reach for the busy cook and, although it is all on view, the result is a warm and welcoming workplace, rather than a cluttered mess. Cupboard doors hide unsightly bulky items at a lower level, and the floor unit plinths, which are usually no more than a decorative kickboard panel, have been heightened and deepened to house drawers and trays for storing infrequently used items. This range of kitchen cupboards includes appliances — a stove and a refrigerator — which fit snugly into built-in units.*

1

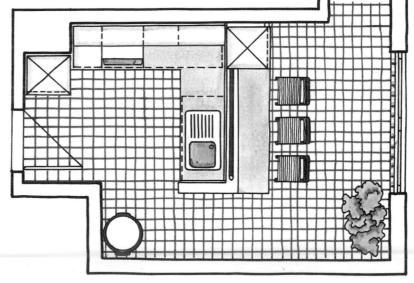

2

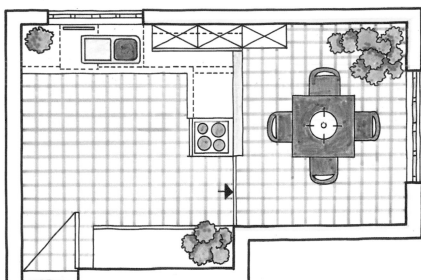

2 *In this slightly larger kitchen/ dining area, the same kitchen units — recognizable by their distinctive handles, drawer fronts and deep storage plinths — are used to different effect. Here, banding with primary colours in parallel stripes — an easy way to brighten a kitchen and make appliances more fun — begins on the free-standing stove and refrigerator, and goes on to provide a strong visual link between cooking and dining areas on the ceiling. There are many ways in which changes in surface finish detail can be used to introduce colour or revamp old units. Drawer handles, rails, peel-off adhesive colour strips and coloured tile grout are a few of the many ideas for improving a kitchen without replacing the units. Both the kitchen and dining areas of the room feature large, many-paned windows with louvred shutters outside and use houseplants to focus attention on them, against the natural-looking background of easy-care doors faced with beech-effect laminate to match the beech trim. Open display shelves enliven a corner of the dining area and one corner beneath the long white countertop. This lay-out accommodates free-standing appliances and makes good use of the modular kitchen system, which includes the neat shelf below the wall cupboards.*

1  *Small, narrow galley kitchens pose a challenge. There is the obvious problem of how to accommodate all the required appliances, as well as sufficient work space for food preparation and cooking, and storage for ingredients and utensils. Safety is another consideration: saucepan handles projecting past the edge of the stove top are especially dangerous when floor space is cramped.*
*This long, narrow kitchen is dominated by the off-centre positioning of the window at the far end. A food preparation area has been created along one wall, where a deep countertop houses a built-in stove. To make the room seem as light and spacious as possible, everything is white. Lights under the wall cupboards cast light on the worktop.*

2  *A very basic kitchen can be fitted in a space not much bigger than a walk-in cupboard. Here, inexpensive self-assembly kitchen units with white melamine doors have been teamed with white worktops, walls, tiles and grid-patterned flooring to make this tiny, windowless kitchen as light as possible. Bright blue 'D' handles anchor a blue and yellow colour scheme introduced by small details, from the blue wall socket to the collection of yellow plastic sink accessories.*

1

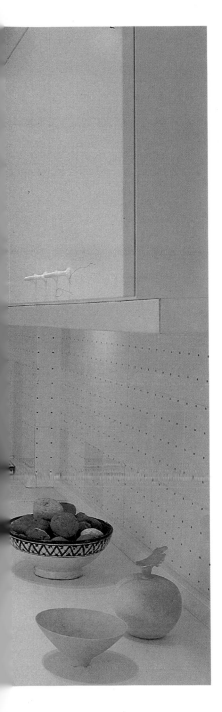

2

3

4

3 *This imaginative treatment unboxes a basic box of a kitchen. Curved open shelving and a curved worktop at one end of the room add much-needed interest. White tiles, which unify the overall scheme, are laid in an unusual and effective stepped pattern to form a splashback against the painted concrete block wall. Carved and painted shelf brackets are as decorative as the storage containers and utensils they display. Two large skylights in the slanting, lean-to roof of this tiny extension ensure plenty of light.*

4 *Long, narrow white tiles highlighted by black grout improve the proportions of this difficult room. Laid horizontally across the floor, they visually widen the narrow room; the rhythm of vertical tiles along the side walls seems to shorten the distance to the far wall, making the room seem more square than rectangular. Even the pattern of the latticed diamond-pane windows contributes to the effect by drawing the end of the room forward. Double sinks fitted in the very small work area below the window have an oval shape which complements the geometric regularity of the tiled surfaces. As in so many small kitchens, plain white units have been chosen to avoid a dark, cramped effect.*

Medium-sized kitchens offer more scope for adopting a preferred lay-out than small ones, where planning is often a question of making the most of a kitchen along a single wall or at best a narrow galley kitchen with units lining opposite walls. When planning a kitchen for a medium-sized rectangular room, consider a U-shaped plan, especially for an open-plan room with a kitchen area. An L-shaped kitchen plan also works well if the kitchen is combined with a dining area.

1 One end of this graciously proportioned room has become a kitchen, partitioned from the rest by a built-in peninsular counter that houses the cooker top. Below, glazed cabinets and open shelves stocked with attractive tableware face into the living/dining area. A counter along the wall opposite the U-shaped work area ends in a similar open-shelf unit, with a curved edge to make a swift entrance into the kitchen from the adjacent door a great deal easier. The high ceiling permits a tall column unit to house a double oven.

2 This workmanlike kitchen is basically designed along an ergonomic L-shaped plan which minimizes walking to and fro between the stove, sink and refrigerator. A narrower counter tucked into a wall alcove extends the worktop to make a U-shaped area.

1

2

3

3 *Where there is enough space, and a large enough budget, an island unit in the middle of the room adds extra work and storage space. The high, pitched ceiling of this A-frame house provides an interesting shape for a spacious kitchen. The generous floor space is broken by a long island work station in the centre whose marble worktop, with access from both sides, allows the cook to enlist several helpers. There is a desirable change of levels in the work surface which is difficult to achieve except with an island unit. The worktop around a sink should be about 75mm (3in) higher than the usual work surface to allow for reaching down into the sink. Heavy tasks which employ the back and arm muscles, such as kneading bread, are best carried out at a slightly lower level.*

*On the far wall, a tall built-in structure includes cupboards for brooms, ironing board and the hot water tank, along with open alcoves designed to house a double oven and a large refrigerator/freezer. Plenty of space has been allowed to encompass the opening of doors. A stainless steel stove top is sited close to the oven to avoid carrying cooked dishes a long distance to brown or grill in the oven. Appliances which require plumbing are lined up along the outer wall of the room, with access to water inlet and outlet pipes.*

The farmhouse-style kitchen is most often associated with a big kitchen: a large old-fashioned iron stove throwing out steady warmth, a huge central table that doubles as work space for baking, a dresser that displays blue and white china and a low window sill, with a cat asleep beside the geraniums. So often the kitchens built in modern houses are small, or, at best, medium-sized and they may share space with the living room or dining room. It is rare to find a big kitchen furnished with modern laminates and technologically advanced appliances. The three examples illustrated here are planned to incorporate modern labour-saving innovations, but still present comforting charm.

1  This large kitchen revolves around a central island work station with a cooker top and chopping board. A wine rack and a rubbish bin with a bottom-hung door flap are built into one side of the island unit. One side of the kitchen houses a refrigerator and a freezer, each hidden behind a burnished metal door framed with black.
The same black outlining technique highlights the unscreened narrow window, making it a feature of the far wall. Since it is the outer wall, the washing machine, dishwasher and sink are plumbed in there.

1

2

3

2 *A square kitchen of ample dimensions is given a fairly conventional treatment with a U-shaped work area defined by the units lining three walls, and a dining table area in the foreground. The cast-iron cookware upon the worktop is at hand for use in the double oven. A double refrigerator and separate freezer are housed in special units away from the warmth of the oven.*

3 *As the concept of the fitted kitchen has become dominant, with its emphasis on long, unbroken worktops, it is easy to forget that kitchen tables provide useful work surfaces. They have the advantage of doubling up for casual dining once the meal is cooked. This scrubbed pine farmhouse table, bleached over its years of use as an additional worktop surface, has an impressive array of cook's equipment suspended within an arm's reach. With its turned-up, tray-like edge, the counter is clearly not intended as a food preparation area. Every detail contributes to the quaintly old-fashioned air of this kitchen: the Delft-style tiles of the splashback, the white-painted tongue-and-groove boards, the dark wooden worktop with its unusual edge, even the brass hinges and handles. Nonetheless, the modern kitchen equipment — the large stove and the refrigerator — are perfectly at home.*

Cooking equipment is the most fundamental part of the kitchen – the very reason for its existence. So your kitchen plan – and style – will be influenced by the type of cooker you need and the placing of the appliance. The kitchen where a commuter cook speedily thaws and heats pre-cooked convenience foods in a microwave is different in every way from the kitchen where a cast-iron cooking range is steadily warm all day and used to cook the produce from a country garden. Country kitchen or hi-tech streamline, these labels are determined as much by the oven you choose in the first place as by the fittings in which food and equipment are housed. Today, the latest technology does not necessarily mean a space-age design. Behind dark enamelled fronts with brass towel rails there could be an ultra-modern fan oven which cooks faster at lower temperatures. Even the timer that allows you to cook at your convenience does not have to be a digital design but could be a traditional Roman numeral clock face that fits perfectly into an old-style wood kitchen.

Never has the cook had more choice. Eye-level appliances can now combine hot air ovens or conventional convection ovens with an adjoining microwave and a grill. One hob fitting can include both electric and gas rings with an adjoining deep fryer, charcoal barbecue or warming plate. Separate ovens and hobs can be slotted into a fitted kitchen so that they merge completely with the overall design. Ceramic hobs can be as little as 30mm (1in) in depth and be powered by tungsten light elements, called halogen heat, which produce a bright glow of light but are as efficient and easily adjustable as old-fashioned gas burners.

Alternatively, your preference may be a free-standing cooker which is available with many of the latest innovations in oven settings, timers and with eye-level grills and revolving spits. Microwave ovens can be built into a kitchen wall unit or can be added to an existing kitchen as a free-standing unit which sits on the worktop or a trolley. There is a wide variety of other countertop cooking appliances to supplement or upgrade traditional large appliances: coffee-makers, toasters, sandwich/waffle-makers, electric woks and frying pans, rice steamers, slow cooking pots with timers, portable ovens and grills, deep-fat fryers.

Air and fume extractors are also available in an enormous range of styles and sophistication – from the basic wall extractor fan to ultra-modern, slimline hoods on push-button control or ornamental extractor hoods chosen to complement your kitchen style.

Before you choose your appliances visit every available display of kitchens and appliances so that you can judge not only the best type of cooker but how it looks in a kitchen setting. Consider if it is practical for your kitchen in terms of size, style and, most important, the way you cook.

This very professional cook's kitchen is designed so that a busy chef can produce vast quantities of food with the minimum of fuss or clutter. Gadgets, pots, pans and utensils line every available surface, ready to be put to work: kettle, food processor, coffee-maker, waffle-maker, bread-slicer, scales. Open, easy-access shelves line the room so that no one need rummage frantically through the cupboards.

At the heart of this working kitchen – the central island work station – everything is at hand to keep the cook from dashing to and fro. There is ample worktop space around the built-in cooker top. An enormous fume extraction hood is designed to remove the significant amount of steam and vapour generated in a large, active kitchen. The extraction unit is covered with a wire grid which provides a handy storage place for skillets and ladles within arm's reach of the cooking area. A pair of large double ovens are easily accessible from the island work station.

*How do you cook? Not so long ago you had to choose between gas or electricity, but today appliances are designed to cook with both. You can buy a stove with both electric and gas burners or a double oven with an electric unit below and a microwave or gas oven above. Perhaps you prefer to cook on a large, old-fashioned, cast-iron stove which burns wood or coal. Modern models of traditional stoves can also be oil- or gas-fired.*

*The most striking change introduced by advanced kitchen planning has been the separation of the stove top from the oven. The newest hobs are ultra-slim, 30mm (1¼in) deep, so that an appliance can be fitted beneath. Microchip technology has revolutionized the way ovens and burners work, too. For example, an electrosensor ceramic cooking surface – so flat that it fits firmly into the worktop – can bring a saucepan of liquid to the boil, then the heat can be instantly reduced to a pre-selected simmering temperature and maintained exactly.*

1 *Here, a pair of double gas burners have been set into a custom-built low-level recess in the marble worktop of an island counter. Varying the levels for different tasks is attractive as well as practical. A fume extraction hood above removes steam and cooking odours.*

1

2

3

4

2 *Here, a combination of three independent panels chosen from a matching range form a customized, versatile cooking area in a small-space kitchen. Gas burners have long had certain advantages over regular electric ones: cooking rings heat up almost instantly, their temperature can be finely adjusted to the exact cooking heat required and the heat cuts off as soon as the burner is turned off, which is especially useful in a kitchen with limited counter space. In this kitchen a double gas ring sits beside a panel with two electric burners, which are best for economic cooking where an even heat is more important than accurate cooking temperature. The third panel is a deep-fat fryer with a stainless steel lid that doubles as a hot plate.*
*Other types of panel are available, such as barbecue grills or rotisserie spits with efficient fume extractors built in.*

3 *The electric burners of this inset cooking area are virtually flush with the surrounding worktop, an ideal arrangement for a cook who works at the stove.*

4 *Certain ceramic glass stove tops have tungsten tube burners which produce a special kind of light — sometimes called 'halogen heat' — that responds to temperature adjustments instantly, like a gas burner.*

1 *The oven you choose from the immense variety available will determine — and depend on — the kind of food you serve and the sort of kitchen you plan. If you know that your stay in the house is to be a short one, you may prefer to have a familiar free-standing stove that incorporates both cooker top and oven which you can take with you when you move. These can be quite simple or very elaborate, with double ovens, built-in grills and storage areas for pots and pans. Separate, built-in ovens, on the other hand, blend in with the kitchen units and can be sited wherever it is most convenient, preferably at waist height or above to avoid bending over to lift heavy pans. Built-in ovens can also fit into a small space. Kitchens with island or peninsular units are often designed so that gregarious cooks are not isolated from family or guests while they work. A free-standing stove, which must have its back to the wall, would defeat this purpose. The solution adopted here is ideal: a cooker top is dropped into the work surface of the island unit and an independent split-level oven is sited along a nearby wall as close to the stove as possible. Double ovens often combine two or more types of appliances for maximum flexibility: often a conventional oven below, supplemented by a fast-cooking microwave above.*

1

## COUNTERTOP COOKING

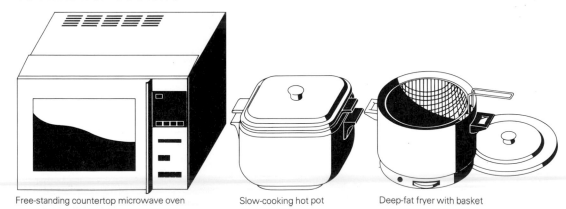

Free-standing countertop microwave oven

Slow-cooking hot pot

Deep-fat fryer with basket

2 *Older farmhouse and cottage kitchens may retain their original wood- or coal-burning cast-iron stoves which may also heat the hot water supply. A handsome modern version, such as the one illustrated here, comes with a bright enamel finish which is easy to clean, and is fuelled by oil or natural gas, not solid fuel. It also requires a great deal of space, a sound floor that will bear its considerable weight and a big kitchen, since it throws out a lot of heat.*

3 *In many kitchens, the conventional free-standing stove, with cooker top above and oven below, remains the best option. This kitchen combines the ergonomic advantages of a conventional stove with the clean look of a built-in unit.*

4 *You can update a kitchen by adding any of a number of small appliances which sit on the countertop.*

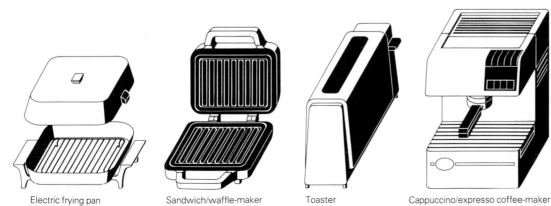

Electric frying pan        Sandwich/waffle-maker        Toaster        Cappuccino/expresso coffee-maker

1 *This purpose-built fume extraction hood has been designed as an integral part of a decorative storage system which seems to be suspended from the ceiling. Extraction hoods above island units must be ducted to an outside wall, and require careful planning. Rails fitted to the hood and the worktop keep equipment and utensils within easy reach.*

2 *Here, the stove has been placed against an outside wall, which makes the installation of an extraction hood and ventilation ducting a simpler and less expensive process. The narrow flue links with a wide hood to form a cap above a cooking area which combines electric and gas burners.*

3 *This imaginative solution to the problem of ducting in fume extraction over an island cooking area is in keeping with the overall decorative treatment of this small kitchen. Paintings of the sort usually associated with grand, showpiece rooms appear on the ceiling – an unusual treatment for a small working space. Above, a projectile bird floats in a windswept sky, and below is a pearly marbled floor. In such classical surroundings, it is particularly important not to introduce ungainly appliances. The angled flue of this extraction hood solves the problem of fume extraction from the middle of the room.*

1

2

3

## VENTILATION AND EXTRACTION

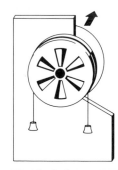

Window ventilator with air pressure rotor

Electric window fan with automatic shutter

Electric wall or window fan with automatic shutter

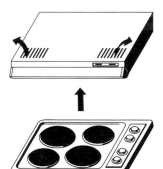

Recirculating extraction hood with renewable charcoal filter

2

2 *Despite the advent of steel sinks enamelled in all colours of the rainbow, many kitchens are fitted with one of the innumerable stainless steel models available. Stainless steel is more hard-wearing than vitreous enamel, although even its surface can become dulled in time from myriad tiny scratches. To retain the original smoothly burnished look, the sink and drainer should be buffed with a cloth after use. Stainless steel sinks are appropriate in almost any decor, from countrified kitchens with wooden cabinets and quarry tiles on the floor to rooms decorated in flowery pastels. The minimal, almost industrial style of this kitchen could easily have been inspired by the eminently practical double stainless steel sink fitted into the matt charcoal countertop. The kitchen is decorated entirely in shades of grey, with unusual perforated aluminium doors which echo the steely grey of the sink.*

*Unlike more homely arrangements, with cooking utensils hanging from the walls and appliances lining the countertops, here everything is stored away out of sight. A drainer basket for clean dishes can fit into one of the deep rectangular bowls, eliminating unsightly countertop clutter, and a spray attachment on an extendible hose has been fitted in alongside the swivelling mixer tap.*

## TAPS AND ACCESSORIES

Hot rinse spray with hose

Pair of traditional stand-up taps (non-mixing)

Designer mixer tap with swivelling spout

Liquid soap dispenser

Mixer tap with built-in extractable spray and cleaning attachments

1 *At first glance, this appears to be a traditional china sink with old brass taps. It is in fact entirely modern, right down to the mixer tap and cross-head faucets, and is made from enamelled steel. The enamel finish is five times thicker than usual, which gives a deep, chip-resistant gloss which looks like an old-style ceramic finish. A closer look at its gently curving lines reveals its modern manufacture.*

2 *Although sinks are most often associated with the tedious chore of washing up after a meal, they are also the focus of much food preparation. Modern sinks have numerous optional accessories to assist the shift from one activity to the other. Here, a single sink with a fitted drainer basket, a small central sink with a fitted vegetable strainer and a counter-level drainer may make better use of space than a double sink. For maximum utility, a waste-disposal unit can be fitted to the small central sink.*

3 *This elegant white-enamelled bowl and drainer sink is designed to be extremely practical. A built-in inset drainer sufficiently recessed to prevent water from seeping on to the surrounding worktop is useful both for drying dishes and for washing vegetables. As with so many modern sink sets, a matching designer mixer tap is an optional extra.*

1

2

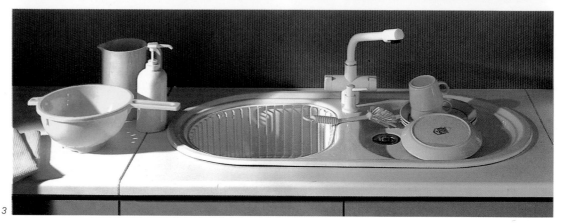
3

## DISH DRAINERS

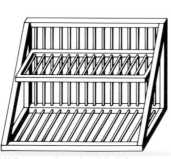
Wall-mounted wooden dish drainer

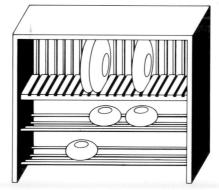
Wall-mounted wooden dish drainer/display

Wire drainer basket to fit sink

Wire drainer basket for counter

4

5

6

7

## WASTE DISPOSAL

Waste disposal units are especially valuable for urban apartment dwellers with limited space to accommodate the rubbish which can build up between weekly collections. They are best installed in kitchens with at least a double sink, or with a sink unit containing a large single sink and a half bowl to the side for the waste disposal unit as shown here, which is particularly effective in association with a dishwasher. Waste disposal units occupy a good deal of under-sink storage space, but will take care of all organic rubbish. If hard waste disposal is also a problem, you should consider a waste compactor, which compresses everything that cannot go into the waste disposal into manageable units.

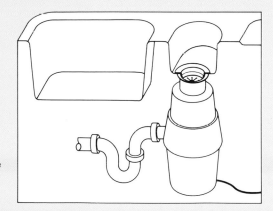

4 *The cupboards below a sink generally disguise its plumbing requirements, which can occupy much of their storage potential. The best use for the remaining space is to house cleaning materials and a rubbish bin. Kitchen manufacturers have developed ingenious systems for making garbage disposal as handy and space-saving as possible.*
*This rubbish bin is designed to be mounted on the inside of a cupboard door. When the door is opened, a special mechanism lifts the dustbin lid.*

5 *Here, a panel which matches the cupboard doors, hinged at the bottom and fitted with a guard chain, drops open to reveal an attached rubbish bin.*

6 *This pull-out bin is an ideal solution for under-sink rubbish. A deep tray mounted on easy-sliding runners is fronted by a panel which matches the kitchen cupboard doors. The narrow garbage bin attached to the inside of the panel is as large as it can be without interfering with the plumbing.*

7 *The drainer portion of this commodious double sink incorporates a hole for dropping rubbish through into the garbage bin below the counter. The circular, solid beech cover doubles as a small chopping board. Behind, a matching block keeps knives accessible without dulling their blades.*

Storage needs vary enormously from household to household. To discover your needs, a professional kitchen designer would ask the following questions: how many people live in the house or apartment, how many meals do you prepare a day, what sort of food do you like, how much cooking equipment do you use, how many sets of crockery do you own, do you eat in a separate dining room with its own storage facilities? Once they have approximately calculated the amount and type of storage required, it is said, they usually double it.

Obviously, the large family with a double oven, dishwasher, crockery and equipment that has accumulated for years and a tendency to buy basic foodstuffs in bulk, will require substantially more storage space than the single person who grabs one hasty meal a day at home and does not want a life cluttered with unnecessary possessions. You already have a very useful guide to your needs, namely your present storage system and how well it works.

The amount of equipment, gadgetry, glasses, cutlery and china you possess is not difficult to quantify and plan for, but you have to decide whether you want it hidden behind attractive fitted units or on display. Another important consideration is ease of access – remembering to place heavy objects at lower levels and things which are in constant use close at hand. Bending and searching for everyday pots and pans becomes a nuisance, which is why busy cooks often hang them from hooks where they can be easily reached without getting in the way. Whether shelves are open or behind doors, they must be planned so that they are not too deep at higher levels where objects at the back cannot be seen or reached. Safety is another factor since young children will find knives and glassware endlessly fascinating if they are within reach.

The same is true of potentially dangerous cleaning products. Dishcloths, sponges, dustpans, brushes and larger brooms and vacuum cleaners can create chaos if not properly stored.

Canned and dry foods are usually easy to plan for, but fresh food is the ever-changing item in the kitchen – expanding after shopping expeditions and shrinking quickly after a family feast. Versatile ventilated larder units and smaller food storage units with fitted wire baskets for vegetables and compartments for bread are now available. Refrigerators and freezers – either separate or combined – offer a very wide choice in terms of size and function and require as much research as cookers do in order to ensure the right choice.

Whatever the size of your kitchen, whether it is a small galley dedicated to cooking or an all-purpose family room, your storage requirements will compete for space with the working equipment of the room. Fortunately, modern kitchen systems are designed to incorporate every convenience you can imagine – from cooking appliances to laundry facilities – so as to maximize storage space.

There was a day when separate rooms fulfilled many of the storage functions of the modern kitchen: the galley-like butler's pantry between the dining room and kitchen was lined with shelves and drawers for tableware, glasses and linens; a naturally cool walk-in larder was reserved for foodstuffs; a separate laundry room kept the washing, drying and ironing of clothes out of the cook's way. Today, in addition to its traditional food-preparation function, the kitchen often has to be a dining room, pantry, larder, laundry, wine cellar and even play room – all rolled into one. The more efficiently you can store things, the better.

Kitchen storage is all about organization. Equipment, accessories and ingredients should be stored nearest to the place where they are likely to be used. Pans or utensils in frequent use should be within easy reach, somewhere between eye and knee level. Open-shelf storage systems, like the one illustrated here, are suitable for an organized cook with naturally tidy instincts.

1   *The numerous fitted cupboards of this sophisticated kitchen provide more than enough storage space for most purposes. Items stored in full view or behind glazed doors are those whose colour or shape contribute to the overall decor, where subtle natural tones predominate. Perfect pigeon-hole rows of cups and bowls look extremely elegant against the cool natural textures and colours of sand and pure white. Even the wall cupboards, which are glazed with wire glass, display tableware which contributes to the overall theme. Major appliances which do not fit in with the scheme are fitted with decor panels that match the cupboard doors. The white façade of the built-in oven, a fan-assisted model which cooks faster at lower temperatures, is featured as part of a white theme that embraces some cupboard doors, tableware, storage jars, saucepans, the countertop and even the taps. The unusual panes of the Japanese-style window throw soft pools of light on to the work area near the sink.*

1

2

3

2 *When is a kitchen not a kitchen? An un-kitchen appearance is especially important where kitchens double as living rooms. It is possible to house kitchen requisites without installing storage units specially designed for the kitchen. In this tiny living area, the tile-covered open storage shelves serve admirably.*

3 *Designers of modern kitchens have developed something of a fetish about dish drainers, which they would prefer to see banished for ever from sight. The practical reality for most of us is that dishes dry more hygienically and with much less work on their own, in purpose-made drainers exposed to air circulation. In this tiny kitchen with limited space for wall cupboards, the problems of draining washed dishes and of storing them once dried are both solved with a single space-saving and decorative open-shelf system. It is unusual to find the sink sited any place other than on an outside wall, where the water supply is usually located. Because this sink is fitted into the peninsular worktop-cum-breakfast counter, the three-tier dish draining rack suspended from the ceiling helps to visually screen the kitchen area from the living area while retaining a light, open atmosphere.*

Cunning fittings inside cupboard doors make each kitchen individual, even when it is made up of standard units. Explore the most basic kitchen and you will discover that the act of opening the door also opens the lid of a rubbish bin fitted inside. There are countless possibilities.

1 Corner space is often wasted, since the contents of deep corner cupboards are generally inaccessible. These half-round plastic-coated wire carousels make it easy to find whatever saucepan or implement is required without rummaging in the dark depths of the corner cupboard. The lower carousel swings out to reveal its contents when the door is opened.

2 This corner unit is designed to make the most of wasted corner space. A double-hinged door permits three-quarter-round carousels to spin around and out, so that any item stored inside is within easy reach in seconds.

3 An imitation door pulls out to reveal a heavy-duty trolley which fits below the counter when not in use. A protective rail and attached basket keep contents firmly in place.

4 These pull-out shelves store all the appliances and attachments you could ever want to use with the food processing unit built into the worktop above.

5

6

7

8

5 *This tall larder unit makes good use of a narrow corner for storing food supplies. At its lowest level, a round carousel shelf provides easy access to dry goods, with reserve items stashed on shelves above. A sliding roll-down door conceals this clever treatment of a difficult space.*

6 *Often it is more sensible to keep china behind closed doors, rather than displaying it on the shelves of a dresser, which takes up more space than stacking. China can be astonishingly heavy, and needs to be stored on secure shelves. The sturdy adjustable shelving fitted in this wall cupboard wastes no space. Stacks of plates and soup bowls require shallower shelving than cups and jugs: shelves can be adjusted to accommodate the maximum amount of china. The hinges, developed especially for laid-on kitchen cabinet doors, prevent doors from snapping and swinging shut abruptly.*

7 *The space below a built-in cooker top is ideal for storing saucepans and baking tins. Even the plinth at the floor can house shallow cake pans.*

8 *To save bending over and searching through lower cupboards for a saucepan stored at the back, consider instead these pull-out shelves on easy-sliding runners.*

Refrigerators and freezers are now available in shapes, sizes and colours to suit every requirement. Some are free-standing, and others are designed to be housed in built-in units and concealed by decor panels which match the kitchen cupboard doors. Some can sit on top of the counter, and others fit underneath it, pulling out on smooth slides like deep drawers. It is possible to find everything from a simple refrigerator with a small freezer compartment, to stacking refrigerator and freezer units, to side-by-side combination refrigerator/freezers, to large independent freezer chests. Only you will know which of the many fittings available are essential to your requirements.

1   The owner of this comfortable family kitchen has painted the built-in units a warm, glossy cream colour which looks good with the bleached boards of the old stripped pine table. Incorporating large white appliances such as this combination refrigerator/freezer into an integrated kitchen decor poses a difficult challenge. However, its ample capacity is ideal for someone with limited shopping time who must nonetheless get a meal on the table every day. The ice cube dispenser built into the freezer door adds a touch of luxury, and is useful for entertaining.

1

## STORAGE TIMES FOR FRESH FOODS

| | Refrigerated | Frozen | | Refrigerated | Frozen |
|---|---|---|---|---|---|
| Bacon, packed for deep freeze | – | 5 months | Butter, salted | 3-4 weeks | 3 months |
| Bacon rashers, green | 7 days | 1 month | Casseroles with bacon | 2 days | 3 months |
| Bacon rashers, smoked | 7 days | 1½ months | Casseroles without bacon | 3 days | 6 months |
| Bacon rashers, vacuum-packed | 7 days | 3 months | Cheese, hard | 7 days | 6 months |
| Beef, large roasts and joints | 3-5 days | 12 months | Cheese, soft | 4-5 days | 3 months |
| Beef, steaks and small cuts | 3-5 days | 8 months | Chicken | 1-3 days | 12 months |
| Beef, minced | 3-5 days | 3 months | Duck | 1-3 days | 4-6 months |
| Bread | 3-6 days | 2-6 months | Eggs | 3 weeks | 1 month |
| Bread dough | – | 3 months | Fish, cooked | 1 day | 2 months |
| Butter and fats | 2-3 weeks | 6 months | Fish, raw | 1-2 days | 4-6 months |

2

3

2 *This small refrigerator, designed to be built in under the countertop, manages to incorporate a great deal of storage capacity and would be good for a kitchen with limited space. It has a small freezer compartment at the top, plastic-coated wire shelves with hinged flaps to accommodate large bottles and two lower bins for vegetables or other odd-shaped foods. Door fittings include a compartment for butter and cheese, a lipped shelf with an egg rack and a bottle rack with retaining rail.*

3 *This three-part built-in refrigerator illustrates the immense versatility of modern food storage systems. The upper portion incorporates a large freezing compartment. Although it would probably be insufficient for a green-fingered vegetable gardener with vast quantities of fresh produce to preserve, it would certainly do for a busy cook who wants to keep a moderate stock of frozen food on hand. The shelves of the main food storage area are adjustable, which minimizes wasted space above shallow items and makes it possible to accommodate unusually tall bottles when necessary. The lower portion is a pull-out, 'cellar-cool' storage cabinet, ideal for chilling fresh fruit, vegetables and beverages.*

| | Refrigerated | Frozen |
|---|---|---|
| Fish, smoked | 3-4 days | 3 months |
| Fruit, soft (without sugar) | 1-5 days | 6 months |
| Ham | 2-3 days | 2 months |
| Lamb, large joints | 3-5 days | 8 months |
| Lamb, chops and noisettes | 3-5 days | 6 months |
| Lamb, cubed for stews | 3-5 days | 4 months |
| Leftovers | 1 day | – |
| Milk and cream | 3-5 days | – |
| Offal | 1-2 days | 2-3 months |
| Pastry, uncooked | 2 days | 3-6 months |

| | Refrigerated | Frozen |
|---|---|---|
| Pork, large roasts or cuts | 2-4 days | 6 months |
| Pork, chops | 2-4 days | 4 months |
| Sausages | 3 days | 3 months |
| Shellfish, fresh | 1 day | 2 months |
| Shellfish, defrosted | use at once | never refreeze |
| Soups, stocks and sauces | 3-6 days | 2-3 months |
| Turkey | 2 days | 4-6 months |
| Veal, large roasts or joints | 2-4 days | 6 months |
| Veal, chops or cutlets | 2-4 days | 3 months |
| Vegetables, green | 1-5 days | 12 months |

*Before the advent of refrigeration, foodstuffs were stored in the larder, a cool, ventilated room or cupboard located on an east- or north-facing wall. For many, a cool larder is still the preferred place to store many foods whose flavour is diminished by excessive chilling. In modern homes with no ventilated larder, a 'cellar-cool' storage cabinet like the one illustrated on page 113 is another option. Although the refrigerator has replaced the larder for cold foodstuff storage to a great extent, most modern kitchens will still require a special storage facility for those foodstuffs which do not require refrigeration.*

1 *Fruit and vegetables can be stored in well-ventilated, deep, plastic-coated wire baskets on easy-glide runners in a cool, dark cupboard.*

2 *These shallow plastic-coated wire racks, which slide forward to make items stored in the back easily accessible, are ideal for hard-to-store goods.*

3 *This pull-out storage rack is intended for tall objects, such as bottles and French bread.*

4 *Dried goods such as salt, spices, flour and sugar can benefit from storage in wooden boxes. These pigeon-hole stacking drawers provide easy access to perishables.*

1

2

3

4

5

5 *The storage fittings developed by the manufacturers of standard kitchen units make best use of every inch of precious space, but are of little interest when it is not feasible completely to rebuild a kitchen, since they are generally designed to fit inside the manufacturer's own units. When it is not possible to adopt purpose-built food storage systems, there are many imaginative options. Dry foodstuffs can be decanted into decorative storage jars and displayed on an open shelf, rather than being stashed away, still in their original plastic bags, in a tray like the one illustrated opposite (2). This modern wood dresser bridges the gap between the modern kitchen, where every element is built in, and the older kitchen, with its motley assortment of free-standing furniture and appliances. Instead of the usual rank of treasured plates, the glazed upper cabinet displays a colourful assortment of home preserves and storage jars containing dried foodstuffs. It is all too easy for the work of preserving fresh fruits and vegetables at their prime to be forgotten months later when the jars are stuffed away in an inaccessible cupboard. This unusual solution contributes to a homespun atmosphere, with its combination of traditional-style furniture, natural wood and array of foodstuffs.*

1 *A room dedicated to laundry – from washing and drying to ironing – is a luxury few modern homeowners could contemplate. But sooner or later most people will add at least a washing machine to their list of essential appliances. The kitchen, with its water inlet and outlet plumbing, is the most logical location for home laundry facilities. Front-loading washing machines fit below the worktop or extend its surface. Combination washer-dryers which do not require outside ducting are ideal for a small apartment kitchen. For larger rooms, consider stacking washing machines and dryers, or commodious free-standing appliances.*

*In this spacious utility area, a stacking washing machine and separate dryer have been installed in special units manufactured for the purpose next to a large sink near an outside wall. Full advantage has been taken of the range of special units available to provide a superbly equipped laundry/utility area for a big family.*

*The roller ironing machine, operated by a treadle from a comfortable chair, makes ironing sheets and tablecloths a relatively painless process, even in a busy big household. It folds up and rolls into a tall storage cupboard which also houses mops, brooms and other tall objects – including a conventional ironing board.*

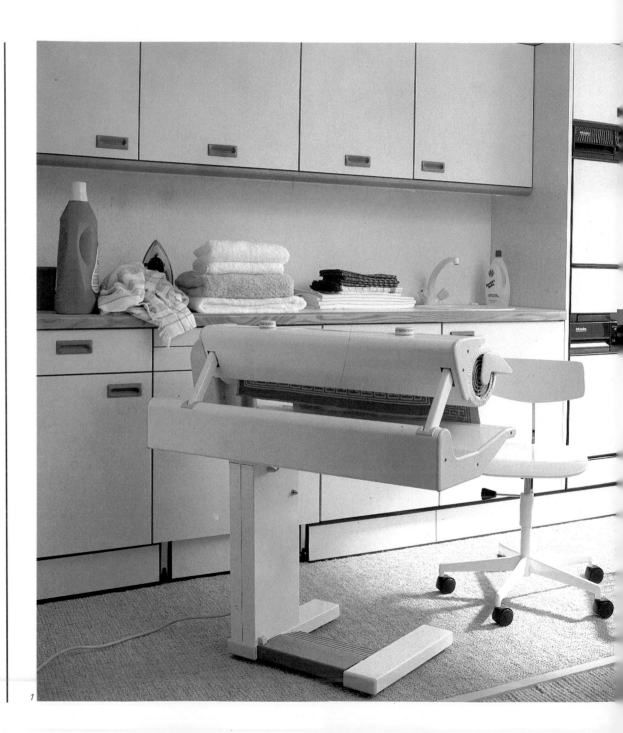

1

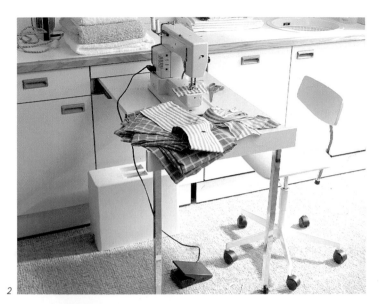

2 *When planning laundry and other utility storage, modern kitchen manufacturers have not forgotten the number of odd-shaped and bulky items to be accommodated in connection with washing and cleaning, from laundry and ironing gear to everyday cleaning fluids, mops and brooms. Special storage cupboard fittings allow for the awkward shapes and sizes. This close-up view of the utility area shown opposite reveals a stable hideaway work table. Here, it is used as a sewing table when the portable sewing machine stored in the cupboard below is needed.*

3 *The unit next to the sink in the utility area shown opposite opens to reveal a cupboard front panel with an attached trolley. A feature of many manufactured kitchens, this one is fitted near the laundry machines, with a plastic-coated wire bin to act as a handy laundry basket.*

4 *Plumbing beneath the sink can be a hindrance to storage. This plastic-coated wire storage rack attaches to the back of the cupboard door, and maximizes use of an often cluttered area.*

5 *All-purpose, tall utility cupboards provide an intelligent solution to most ordinary utility storage. The combination of hooks and shelves keeps cleaning tools and appliances ready for use.*

Kitchen surfaces take more battering and scrubbing than any other surfaces in the house. If kitchen surfaces mark easily this creates more work because of extra cleaning and more expense because they will not last. Surfaces also play a large part in determining the style and visual impact of the kitchen, so when choosing them it is vital to think in terms of durability and not be entirely seduced by appearance. Good looks are important, but so are strength and quality. Fortunately, modern kitchen surfaces are made from such a wide range of natural and man-made materials that it is always possible to find something which will suit the style of your kitchen decor, your working requirements and your budget.

Surfaces for cupboard doors are directly related to the cost of units. The cheapest are doors made from chipboard with a paper-thin laminate finish. In the middle range are solid laminates and wood veneers; and then combinations of laminate with wood trims and solid wood. Shapely doors with moulded panels or specialist finishes such as staining, lacquering and hand painting, including effects like dragging or marbling, all make the price go up significantly. Fashion influences finishes – golden pine is popular one year and grey laminate the next – and technology does too. The latest immensely durable and resistant surface being used by German kitchen manufacturers uses car-factory techniques of dipping whole units in polystyrene colour which is surface sealed and then baked to a really hard, tough consistency.

Worktops need to be even more wear resistant to take sharp knives and hot pans as well as messy stains and constant scrubbing. Few modern alternatives can compete with the traditional worktops of solid marble or hardwood, such as beech, which clean easily and age graciously. They are also among the most expensive options. Tiles are attractive but the grouting between them usually stains – always use heavy-duty non-porous grout and high-quality tiles. Marble-like materials, such as Corian, can be hard-wearing. Laminates are not usually so successful unless chopping is always done on a board and hot pans are placed on mats. Laminates vary and the most expensive are usually the most hard-wearing. Other alternatives include luxury burnished steel, granite or slate.

Having assessed the quality and durability of a surface you then have to choose the colour, pattern, wood grain and any decorative details or other options. Remember that you will have to live with your choice for some time so try not to be too heavily influenced by sales talk or fashion considerations. Bright red may look stunning in a well-lit open area where it is on display but would be overwhelming in a small city kitchen galley. Even the most spacious and well-planned kitchens are busy, cluttered places, so a neutral background is usually an advantage.

Kitchen surfaces need to withstand a lot of hard treatment and still look good. For this reason, durable laminate countertops and other surfaces have come to feature in many kitchens.

Unlike older laminates, with their thin veneer of coloured plastic laminate, newer products consist of several layers compressed under immense pressure to produce a thicker surface with solid colour throughout. Layers of different colours can be compressed together so that the cut edge of a single-colour surface reveals the different coloured layers like a geological drawing.

Here, a variety of solid-colour core laminates are used: solid white, solid white sandwiched between wood veneer and solid navy similarly sandwiched. The exposed edges of most materials used in kitchen surfaces — the end-grain of wood or the edges of laminate-veneered composite boards — must be protected from moisture, if not concealed.

1 *Worktops vary to suit each cook's particular speciality – and budget. Serious pastry and pasta chefs prefer to work on a white marble top; anyone whose food preparation involves frequent chopping of vegetables for salads, soups and casseroles will use a wooden surface. Slabs or boards made from any material which is especially desirable can always be added.*
*The worktop surface which unites your entire kitchen lay-out should be as practical and hard-wearing as possible. Marble, for example, is extremely handsome and prized by pastry cooks, but is neither stain-resistant nor chip-proof. This warm, wooden, country-style kitchen has been entirely fitted with heavy butcher-block worktops made from maple, a handsome hardwood used for the cabinets as well. One drawback to wooden worktops is that standing water can tend to warp the wood or raise its grain. Here, a double stainless steel sink with an ample integral draining board has been fitted to minimize water damage. With use, the smooth surface of this new wooden worktop will become chipped and scratched, but it is best not to consider refinishing it, for evidence of wear will be in keeping with the warm patina which should develop as it ages.*

1

2

3

## HOW TO TILE A WORKTOP

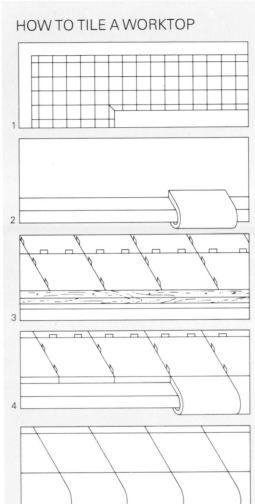

1

2

3

4

5

**1** Plan worktop tiling so that the cut tile will be next to the wall. **2** Use an edge tile placed in position to mark a base line. **3** Nail a batten to the base line. Spread adhesive and lay the first row of tiles working back from the batten towards the wall, using spacer cards to ensure even spacing between individual tiles. **4** When all the tiles have been laid, remove the batten and spread adhesive on the worktop and on the undersides of the edge tiles. **5** Remove spacer cards. Grout the spaces between the tiles, compacting the grout to finish level with the top of the tiles.

2 *Portable boards for particular jobs — wooden chopping boards, marble pastry boards, stainless steel or plastic draining boards — are indispensable, especially to save wear and tear on all-purpose laminate worktops. Appliances which do the chopping, grinding, blending, slicing or grating save on labour as well as preserving worktops. Unfortunately, electric appliances can easily become wasters of counter space. This well-designed work station solves the problem by housing appliances and their attachments in a shallow cupboard fitted with a handy electric socket where they are easy to reach. With the addition of a wooden chopping block, it becomes a very versatile food preparation area.*

3 *Ceramic tile work surfaces are a favourite in country-style kitchens, although they are not ideal for chopping and their surfaces tend to be uneven. Nonetheless, they are solid, durable and easy to clean so long as they have been installed with impenetrable, water-resistant grout. Here, warm wood and terracotta tiles are juxtaposed over large surface areas — floors, worktops and ceiling — to unify an irregularly shaped kitchen. Large ceramic tiles form an attractive pattern when cut diagonally to fit the sharply angled shape of the worktop.*

1 *The wall area in any kitchen above the worktop and below the wall-mounted cupboards – known as the splashback area – needs to be protected from greasy stains, liquids and other spatters from vigorous mixing, stove-top cooking and dish-washing. The splashback area can be covered with any surface finish that is durable and easy to wipe clean. Even painted plaster with several coats of protective varnish withstands a lot of scrubbing – yacht varnish provides the heaviest-duty protection, as it is designed to hold up against corrosive sprays of salt water. Although it occupies only a small area of wall, the splashback area visually defines the kitchen's work space, providing a link between the lower cupboards with the worktop and the upper cupboards, and it is often given a colourful or patterned treatment. If you inherit a tiled splashback you do not fancy, think twice before you remove the offending tiles, as this will probably lead to replastering the wall. Rather, sacrifice a few millimetres of space and tile over the existing ones using a special adhesive.*

*This unusual splashback surface is made from industrial aluminium sheeting with a raised pattern. Its burnished metallic surface softly reflects the lights mounted behind pelmets on the underside of an extended window sill.*

1

2

3

## HOW TO TILE A WINDOW SILL

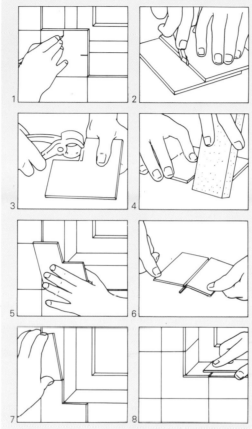

**1** To measure a tile for cutting, hold it up to the wall and mark the area to be cut away **2** Score the glazed surface of the tile along the marked line. **3** For an L-shaped tile, use pincers or tile cutters to remove unwanted waste in small pieces. **4** Use a carborundum stone to clean and smooth the cut edges of the tile. **5** Fix the cut tile so that any spacer lugs are against those of the adjoining tiles. If the tiles you have chosen do not have spacer lugs, use spacer cards to ensure an even gap between tiles. **6** To prepare a tile for breaking, follow steps 1 and 2 above, then place a matchstick under the tile along the scored line for a clean break. **7** Clean the cut edges as in step 4, and fix the cut tile in place. **8** At external corners, make allowance for the tile edge to be covered.

2 *Ordinary wallpaper, which is not washable, only makes a suitable covering for wall surfaces in kitchens equipped with efficient fume extraction systems, and even then it is unsuitable for splashback areas around the sink and stove. Durable, vinyl-coated wallpapers, on the other hand, can be easily wiped clean, although they are more expensive. Here, a dark brown vinyl-coated wallpaper with a white grid pattern echoes the grid pattern on the kitchen cupboard doors and makes a dramatic backdrop for the striking, sculptural extraction hood above the cooker top.*

3 *Ceramic tiles, a traditional favourite for kitchen wall surfaces, present the most hard-wearing, stain-resistant and waterproof option, and are ideal for splashback areas, especially around sinks and stoves. Here, a broad splashback area is covered in ceramic tiles with a small navy and white chequerboard pattern which visually defines the work area against the deep navy cupboards, white worktop and white stove. When unpatterned tiles are used on every available surface, a kitchen can seem cold and clinical. Here, the homy chequered pattern of the tiles in the limited splashback area introduces a warm, enlivening touch in an otherwise sophisticated room.*

1 *Natural wood brings a welcoming, reassuring sense of solidity and familiarity to a kitchen. Unfortunately, the cost of a custom kitchen built entirely of solid wood, such as the one illustrated on page 120, can be prohibitive. Affordable wooden kitchens are produced by using a mixture of solid wood and wood veneered board for the visible façade, with the inside cabinet carcasses made from less expensive composite board with a washable melamine surface. These economies make it possible for manufacturers to offer a wide range of woods, finishes and styles. Each timber has its own characteristic wood grain pattern, texture and colour, and these qualities can be enhanced by the finish applied. New pine has a bright, clear yellow colour, and for rustic-style kitchens boards with prominent knots are often used. In its natural state, ash has a lovely silvery colour, although it is sometimes more prized for the beautiful pattern of its distinctive grain, which is subtly highlighted when ash is stained black or a clear bright colour. Traditional hardwoods, such as oak, maple or cherry, may be given a transparent protective finish to seal the wood so that the natural colour shows through, or may be stained before sealing.*

1

2

3

2   *When it is not feasible to install new wooden cabinets, the warmth of natural wood can still contribute to a cosy, friendly atmosphere. This small, family-style kitchen features a hardwood butcher-block worktop which complements the style of the painted cabinets, with their traditional glazed wall cupboards. Butcher-block tabletops and work surfaces are generally made from close-grained hardwoods, such as beech or maple, which are considerably more expensive than softwoods suitable for painting. The addition of wooden furniture reinforces the theme. The owners have also made the most of original timber floorboards by stripping them down to reveal the mellow tones of older wood and applying a durable clear finish.*

3   *Those who favour laminated plastic surfaces, for whatever reason, can still introduce wood to the kitchen by mixing the two materials. Some manufacturers produce cabinet doors whose frames are made from solid wood, but with laminate-faced board instead of wood-veneered board as the panel. Here, the wooden edges of cool blue laminate worktops and shelves work well with a timber-panelled ceiling. Where uneven walls require replastering, tongue-and-groove timber panelling can cover a multitude of sins.*

1  *The great advantage of wood over plastic laminates as a material for cabinet construction is that it can be shaped and moulded into an infinite variety of forms. If this gracious floor-to-ceiling kitchen had been built primarily from laminates, it would have presented a flat facade. Instead, doors and drawer fronts have raised, coffered panels and are set in frames with richly moulded edges. Open display racks are screened by miniature balustrades made from turned wood. By staining the oak cabinets white, the distinctive wood grain remains visible, but a traditional timber kitchen is turned into a light and airy one.*

2  *There has been a revival of interest in specialist paint finishes, which use colour mixtures and texture variations, rather than great blocks of flat colour, to enliven surfaces. Paint or glaze can be added over a background colour with a sponge or by spattering, or a second coat of paint glaze can be partially removed with crumpled rags (called rag-rolling) or special combs (called dragging). The result is a subtly broken colour surface with highly individual effect (depending on the colours and technique used), which gives a charming and distinctive finish to manufactured wooden kitchen cabinets, as in this heavenly blue kitchen.*

3  *The combination of pale blue and white with natural wood is a favourite for kitchens, where it works particularly well. Here, this familiar, informal colour scheme is given a more sophisticated tone by the use of black as an accent. The design takes full advantage of wood as a main material, with slatted door fronts, decorative miniature balustrades on the display shelving and built-in pigeon-hole storage boxes. Cupboards have been custom-built to bend around the difficult corner area. Aside from the natural wood worktop and the main framing of the kitchen – which is white – everything has been painted a refreshing pale blue, from the hinged flap of the extraction hood, to the small spice and salt cellars fixed to the white tiled splashback, to the blue decor panel covering the dishwasher. The warm natural fibres of the sisal carpet echo the wood tones of the worktop, and areas of black are skilfully picked out for emphasis: black stove, black cooking pots and black lacquered bentwood chairs. The pleasing combination of black and white with areas of cool blue demonstrates the importance of distributing colours and accent colours around a room. When painting a new kitchen, or refurbishing an older one, it is best to choose a paint which will withstand washing and wiping.*

1 *Hard-wearing, easy-to-clean plastic laminates are made by bonding layers of resin-impregnated paper together and coating them with plastic. Sheets of plastic laminate are then bonded to chipboard, blockboard or plywood for use in kitchen construction. Improvements in laminate technology have made this practical, relatively inexpensive material even more flexible. A variety of printed, patterned and textured surfaces is available, in addition to a wide range of colours. The edges of plastic laminate worktops can be post-formed so that they are curved, eliminating sharp counter edges. Here, crisp and functional kitchen units made from matt white plastic laminate provide the main structure of a small, friendly kitchen. A treasured rag rug and a collection of bright enamelware displayed on the shelf above the countertop introduce a cheerful, primary colour scheme. Great care has been taken to ensure that all accessories contribute to the theme of red accents, from the trim on the kitchen units, to the Venetian blinds, taps, sink, draining board, hob and shelf uprights and brackets – right down to the floor cupboard plinths. A wooden pine floor and stripped pine door create a warm golden background and enhance the countrified air of this room.*

1

2

3

2 *A chic effect is achieved here by combining pale grey with white trim and appliances and bright yellow accessories. A somewhat different effect could be achieved simply by using red or blue accessories. With subtle shades like grey and white it is important to create some visual contrasts for interest. Here a tablecloth with a bold black and white pattern has been introduced.*

3 *Although plastic laminate surfaces are often chosen because they provide good value for money, they can also play an important role in achieving an elegant interior. Here, intelligent design and planning have teamed ordinary white plastic laminates with more exotic materials – wood and chrome – to create a kitchen which is both stylish and practical. A large wooden peninsular counter extends from the white façade next to the stove, doubling as worktop and table for impromptu dining. Chrome drawer and door handles are echoed by a chrome draining board with built-in circular knife storage block and refuse disposal chute. Special storage compartments house bread, herbs, spices and even a foldaway stepladder in a plinth panel drawer.*

Refitting a kitchen from scratch is an expensive business. Sometimes a change of colour and attention to detail can create all the difference to standard kitchen units. Colourful lipped handles, 'D'-handles and knobs with coloured laminate trims can be added to doors, drawers and panels to brighten up dull units. A more profound change can still be achieved by replacing only the doors and drawer fronts of an existing kitchen. Some manufacturers supply doors in a range of colours which fit standard kitchen units. Or create an eye-catching new look at minimal expense by staining or painting old kitchen units. A bright finish in a new colour can transform a kitchen. Surfaces can be textured with a specialist paint finish, such as rag-rolling or sponging, or decorative patterns can be painted on using a stencil cut for the purpose.

1 The moulded edges of the frames of these doors and drawer fronts have been deepened and highlighted by a finely painted line. Ceramic knobs and pulls look good with the dragged paint finish.

2 Here, a more baroque treatment of door frames has elaborately moulded edges on both frame and raised coffered panels.

6

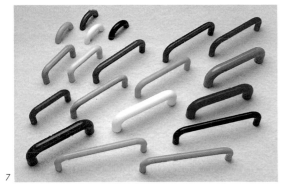

7

8

## SPECIALIST PAINT FINISHES

**Rag-rolling** creates an attractive two-tone 'distressed' paint finish. Roll a wadded cloth over a wet glaze which you have brushed on top of a dried first coat of paint.

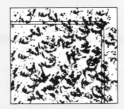

**Sponging** produces a two-tone variegated surface. Dip a natural sponge into a pan of wet glaze and then sponge the glaze over a dried first coat of paint.

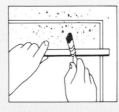
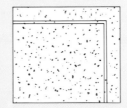

**Spattering** produces multicolour patterning. Fleck droplets of glaze on to a dried first coat of paint by passing a metal ruler over the glaze-filled bristles of a paintbrush.

**Stencilling** adds figurative interest. Make a stencil from waterproof paper and use quick-drying paint and a stencil brush to paint the pattern on to a prepared surface.

3   Natural wood lends itself well to the design of these doors and drawer fronts. The deep frames and raised inner panels have a curved shape which is highlighted by their elaborately moulded edges.

4   The D-shaped plastic handles on this simple white laminate drawer front and door continue as a dramatic line stretched across the surface, which adds not only a splash of colour but also dynamic interest.

5   The edges of these white plastic laminate doors and drawer fronts have been angled and finished with chrome to provide very stylish detailing, which is reinforced by the handsome chrome handles. The angled edges of raised panels or frames are often outlined or picked out by a contrast in colour. Here, an unusual effect is achieved by a similar use of contrast in material.

6   Plastic handles, pulls and knobs, such as the small selection illustrated here, can be chosen to co-ordinate with a range of other accessories to brighten a room.

7   Some manufacturers let buyers of their kitchen units choose which colour they prefer from a range of 'D'-handles.

8   Plastic door and drawer furniture can take any shape.

The kitchen floor needs to be the toughest in the house because of wear from the constant movement of feet and chair legs and also because of spillage, scuffing, heat and the occasional heavy knock from a falling frying pan or bottle. It must be easy to clean, non-slip for safety and water-resistant. It is not an aspect of the kitchen that can be chosen on looks alone, but looks are important and the floor you select must complement the style of the room. Always seek professional advice about laying floors if you are not experienced, since a potentially excellent floor can be ruined if it is badly laid, the wrong adhesive is used or the sub-floor not adequately prepared. It is often necessary to put down a flat layer of board to even out irregular concrete or floorboards which can create dents and may not be a suitable base for the flooring you have selected.

The least expensive and most flexible choice is usually sheet vinyl, which can be applied to most floor surfaces and is available in a wide variety of qualities and strengths, with cushion backing, and every kind of colour and pattern from fake marble to stylish modern grid and chequered designs. Vinyl tiles are similarly varied and easily extended or replaced provided you buy in excess rather than try to match existing tiles at a later date.

Treated cork is warm, resilient and does not show the dirt. Like vinyl, it has the advantage of causing fewer breakages if china or glassware is dropped and it is a quiet surface. Terrazzo, a surface composed of marble chips, quarry tiles or marble slips set in concrete, is rather cold and hard, but extremely hard-wearing and attractive. The same is true of ceramic tiles, which also have the advantage of creating colourful or unusual designs, depending on the pattern in which they are laid.

Linoleum, available in sheets or tiles, has been much improved by new technology and is no longer the brittle substance it once was. It is now available with a durable, non-scuff plastic finish and in designs of great sophistication. It is not cheap and some of the most attractive designs are among the most expensive options for your kitchen floor. Other luxury surfaces include slate and traditional flagstone, but they must be laid on a solid floor that can withstand the weight of these materials.

Polished wood is warm and long-lasting but needs regular polishing and frequent resealing in areas of heavy wear. Painted wood and carpet are not advisable for kitchens. There are several ways to achieve a polished wood floor, depending on your kitchen decor and budget. For a country-style kitchen in an older home, simply refinish existing floorboards by stripping off existing tiles or sheet flooring, sanding the floorboards back to clean wood and applying a hard-wearing sealer. Otherwise, lay new hardwood floorboards or wood strip tiles which emulate elaborate parquet flooring.

A black and white chequerboard floor is in bold contrast to the clean lines and quiet restraint of this large kitchen, but perfectly in keeping with its styling, which is that of a turn-of-the-century dairy. The kitchen units, with their homy tongue-and-groove timber panel doors, have been painted with a glossy cream-coloured paint. A wooden worktop below a long row of many-paned windows follows the A-line of the roof. Despite its old-style atmosphere, full advantage has been taken of available space to install large modern appliances. Large chequerboard patterned floors can also work well in smaller rooms. Vinyl or linoleum tiles can be laid in alternating colours. Sheet vinyl or linoleum with chequerboard patterning is also available.

1  *A pattern of small white diamond insets against a rich navy blue makes a bold flooring to anchor a relatively casual alignment of pine kitchen units with sliding doors and open shelves in three widths set above. This treatment draws the eye to the kitchen and provides a dramatic backdrop for a simple pine kitchen table. The fresh colour combination is echoed in reverse by the fine blue floral motif on the white tiles of the splashback.*

2  *Polished wooden floorboards make both a good foil for a fine tapestry rug in the living room and a handsome, practical kitchen floor in this comfortable open-plan house. The eye is drawn from the wooden farmhouse table and ladderback chairs to the deep, glossy green of the kitchen units. The rocking chair and dresser are in keeping with this theme of natural forest colours and woods.*

1

2

3

3 *This subdued grey floor, made up of synthetic rubber floor tiles, is eminently practical and provides an ideal backdrop for the fresh look of this white plastic laminate self-assembly kitchen. The tiles echo the colour of the stainless steel sink and drainer and the grey-painted slatted blinds. Deep green 'D'-handles are matched by green accessories and objects: a Perrier bottle, apples, bottle lids, laundry basket, bucket and dish draining rack. A simple unplastered brick column which reinforces the wall in this open-plan kitchen also screens the laundry area, providing a niche large enough to house appliances and utility cupboards.*

*Although this relatively large kitchen area incorporates a convenient laundry centre and plenty of storage space, its design takes advantage of relatively inexpensive components.*

*Simple, self-assembly kitchen units can cost considerably less than a kitchen installed by specialists. Synthetic rubber floor tiles represent good value for money, especially when covering a large floor area such as this one.*

1 *Glazed ceramic floor tiles, which are sold in packs with laying instructions, can be a great deal more stylish when they are laid with a border pattern. Here, black tiles interspersed with the primary white floor tiles to form a pattern give definition to the outer edge of a large room. Tiles can also be laid diagonally, point to point, or smaller tiles can form a houndstooth pattern. Frostproof ceramic tiles can form a continuous floor surface for a kitchen with a door opening on to a patio garden.*

2 *Vinyl sheet flooring is immensely practical and easy to install. The simple diagonal line pattern of this vinyl sheet flooring visually extends the eye, making a room seem slightly larger. This material is ideal for both kitchen and laundry room floors, since it is easily cleaned with a mop and water. Its smooth, cushioned surface is warm and comfortable for bare feet. Vinyl sheet flooring can be laid loose with double-sided tape at doorways and seams, or it can be firmly stuck in place with tiling adhesive.*

1

2

## HOW TO LAY CORK OR VINYL FLOOR TILES

Mark the centre of the room by stretching a chalked line taut between pins tacked into the floor or skirting in the middle of facing walls about 25mm (1in) above the floor. Snap the chalked line to leave a chalk mark on the floor. On long lengths, press the centre of the chalked string on the floor and snap each side in turn. If you wish, substitute any light powder for chalk.

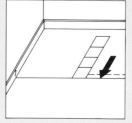

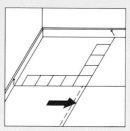

**1** Mark the centre of the chalk line and lay a 'dry' row of tiles out to an end wall.

**2** If the end gap is 75mm (3in) or less, snap a new line half a tile width from the first.

**3** Repeat the procedure with a chalked line and row of tiles at right angles to the first.

3

4

5

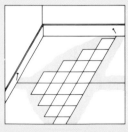

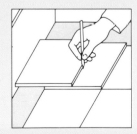

**4** Spread adhesive over the lines and snap fresh lines when it is dry.

**5** Lay the first tiles in the corner of the lines, then lay tiles to form a pyramid shape.

**6** Lower each tile into place, butting it tightly against the adjacent tiles.

**7** Score edge tiles with a knife and then bend sharply to complete the break.

3 *Warm cork tiles add natural colour to any room and are appropriate in a kitchen so long as they are well sealed. They are available in different shades. Pre-sanded cork tiles must be sealed with polyurethane varnish – preferably several coats – after they are laid. Some can be bought already sealed with polyurethane varnish, and some have a vinyl skin surface which is extremely durable. The fine diagonal lines on these sealed cork tiles transform this everyday flooring into a bold definition of space. They can be used to create a pattern in one area, say in the centre of a room where furniture is grouped, with plain cork tiles occupying the rest of the floor area.*

4 *Terracotta-coloured floor tiles and quarry tiles are traditionally a favourite for country-style and farmhouse kitchens.*

5 *Synthetic rubber floor tiles, with their characteristic raised circular pattern, first appeared in hi-tech kitchens and interiors, borrowed from the industrial settings where they were first used. Even the lighter-duty tiles now made for domestic use, which are available in a vast range of colours, have superb wearing properties: they are easy to lay, comfortable to walk on and easy to look after. Try laying tiles of two or more colours for a patterned effect.*

1 *Task lighting is a rather intimidating phrase which simply means what it says: lighting which illuminates the task in hand. In the kitchen, this particularly refers to the worktop area. The advantage of wall-mounted cupboards is that they present a surface area at precisely the right height above the worktop for a light to be fitted, shielded by a narrow pelmet. Manufacturers often build lighting strips into the base of the wall-hung cupboards, but you can also fit them yourself to an existing kitchen. Fluorescent light is the favoured source, since it lasts longest for the least money. This is the light of the supermarkets, a rather cold light above food – which is why the new tungsten halogen sources are finding favour. Solid wooden worktops are illuminated from above in this practical line-up of appliances. Notice how there is space allocated for each task: first, the food preparation area, then the stainless steel hob and lidded deep-fat fryer, followed by an area for stacking the dishes before washing them up in the spacious sink. Below the worktop is an array of good labour-saving appliances.*

1

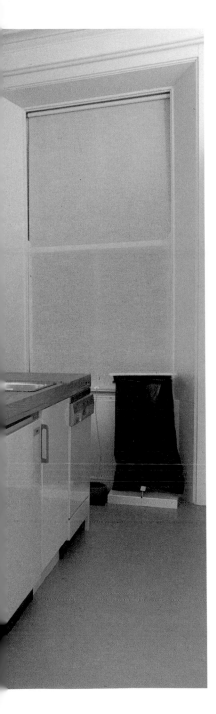

2

3

2  *There is an orderly marshalling of light sources in these flamboyantly shaped light bulbs, which are fitted simply in rows along the high glossy painted ceiling without shields, shades or protectors. A false ceiling has been lowered over the kitchen area to bring the light source nearer to the worktops. The use of glossy paint on the ceiling and high-gloss varnish on the teak worktop on the central island all help to catch and reflect the light. There are areas of dark, from the terracotta floor to the wooden shelves and island, which are contrasted by the white kitchen units. The mosaic made up from pieces of broken tile in primary colours on white makes an interesting splashback that is easy to reproduce at home.*

3  *This stylish kitchen contrasts dark matt blue units with chrome rails for the cook's equipment and with the stainless steel sink. Since the ceiling is lower, and in interesting stepped levels, it is painted white. Downlighters are suspended from it at strategic points to throw light on the blue. These lights have the same shape as the spotlights attached to the wall.*

Many people prefer to make the kitchen the centre of the house where the family congregate and enjoy casual meals and friendly entertaining. Increasingly, homes are designed or converted so that a dining area is provided adjacent to the kitchen rather than in a separate dining room. It is practical for the cook and washer-up as well as indicative of a change in the way we live, with less demand for formal rooms. With good planning, careful lighting and adequate ventilation, eating in or beside the kitchen need not mean eating amidst the debris and smells of food preparation.

If possible, screen off the food preparation or cooking area from the dining section. Create a lay-out which incorporates a divider in the form of an island which extends into the room and contains cupboards and a work surface or breakfast bar or a form of screen. It is sometimes possible in a smaller area to have a built-in screen which hides clutter behind a blind or doors.

Properly planned lighting which uses the correct type of fittings can be extremely effective in highlighting eating areas and dimming the food preparation area when necessary. It is essential to have dimmer switches for the flexibility they offer in a room with two separate functions – working and relaxing. Make sure you have two circuits so that each area can be separately controlled.

Spotlights are particularly effective in kitchens for highlighting specific areas. Low-voltage tungsten halogen spotlights give intense beams of light and provide a particularly attractive form of illumination, both in terms of the light they give and the style of the fitting. Small fittings or strip lights can be hidden below units. Fluorescent tubes create a cold, unattractive light but are economical. A good alternative is a tungsten strip light. Adjustable-height pendant lights for placing directly over a table are available in a wide range of styles. Whatever you choose, plan for flexibility.

Space will determine the lay-out of the kitchen/diner. People seated round a table take up a lot of space so allow plenty of room. Consider also the ease of serving food and removing dirty plates and place the table where it will not hinder a passageway. An advantage of a dining table in the kitchen is that it can double as a surface for food preparation or for another purpose such as a desk area for work or study.

Kitchen dining furniture, unlike the fine polished table and matching chairs of a formal dining room, needs to be easily washable and sturdy. Elaborate shapes, complicated mouldings or delicate finishes will be difficult to maintain in a busy, greasy kitchen environment. Also remember that the style of the table and chairs should be in keeping with that of the kitchen units. Although it may not be possible to match worktop or door surfaces exactly, choose furniture to harmonize with the kitchen decor.

A separate dining room may be maintained in large houses, but most homes today combine the dining area with another room: either it is part of the living room or it is an extension of the kitchen. This delightful kitchen/dining area is divided by a peninsular unit with an elaborate roofing structure. This creates an open, informal atmosphere where the cook is not isolated from the guests, but where diners do not have to look at the aftermath of food preparation while eating. The marble-topped cast-iron Art Nouveau table is pushed against this partition so that the alcove created beside the chimney-breast leaves room for a chair to be pushed back. Above the open brick fireplace, bookshelves and an abstract modern painting with bright splashes of colour create a casually charming area, while the fire burning in the hearth adds a comforting glow.

1 *The bay windows in this kitchen/diner suggested a shape for the working peninsula which separates the cooking from the associated dining area. Floor units with appliances and sink are grouped to form a U-shaped curve which makes full use of corner space. The outward-facing side of the peninsula has been tiled in an attractive fresh blue and white chequerboard pattern, which is easy to mop clean of any spills which occur while handing food over the counter. Once the food has been prepared, the worktop acts as a natural serving counter.*

2 *Nowhere is the principle of lighting the dining area separately from the cooking and food preparation area better illustrated than with this divided room. The kitchen, with its cool line-up of long vertical cupboards and granite worktops, is illuminated by a circular ceiling light whose bright light is useful when working. The dining area is given a different, more atmospheric treatment, with an overhead pendant light whose white shade casts a diffused light upon the round beech dining table.*

1

2

3

4

3  *In a small space, a central island unit can be as important for casual meals as it is for food preparation. Here, a slatted false ceiling is suspended above a beech table to define a combination work area and dining area.*

4  *Sometimes, as here, a dining table can add a sculptural and architectural grace to a kitchen. It would clearly be a mistake to spoil the main feature of the dining area – the full-length window – by blocking it with a table and chairs. The slender dining counter, with a matching shelf seemingly suspended from the ceiling, creates a natural barrier and makes the window even more of a feature. The worktop nearby provides an efficient base for serving plates and tableware.*

1 *The severe restraint of this kitchen and separate dining area makes a bold architectural statement. The kitchen is still visible, seen through the big windows framed in stained wood. The dining area has a sculptural quality, with its large square white table mounted on a black plinth and black lacquered folding chairs set against white tiles. The table is cleverly laid so as to enhance the geometry of the room and its furniture. Curved oval black place mats reproduce the cut-out shape of the chairs' backrests. The dramatically angled form of the lighting fixture over the dining room table is appropriately unfussy and modern.*
*Although this kitchen/dining area began as two separate rooms, the installation of interior windows in the wall between them makes each room seem larger. An arrangement such as this would suit someone who likes to escape from the kitchen when dining, but who prefers a less formal setting than the traditional dining room.*

1

2

2 *Plants make good room dividers, and work quite well when separating a kitchen and dining room so long as they are stable enough to permit access without being knocked over. Uplighters concealed at the base of tubs holding vertically growing houseplants, such as the weeping fig (Ficus benjamina), can cast a dappled light on the ceiling, as though you were picnicking in an indoor forest. Here, a conservatory-like indoor dining area has been created with a skylight, windows and glass doors. The kitchen, with its cool marbled worktop and white drawer units, can be seen from all sides. Lemons in hanging supermarket sacks and fruit in hanging baskets make an attractive link between the two areas. The floor is made from vinyl sheeting, which is more practical than tiles when carrying china and glass back and forth, and easy to keep clean, even when watering the numerous houseplants which decorate the area.*

# DINING ROOMS

Dining rooms are disappearing with the advent of open-plan living. When space is limited it is often the first room to be sacrificed for the sake of an extra bedroom, guest room or study. Yet there is a nostalgia for that once elegant and formal setting for dinner parties and family meals. Sideboards are back. The newest kitchens include units angled and shaped like sideboards and set upon recessed plinths which perform the traditional sideboard function of storing glass, china and cutlery. The flat counter is the place for carving meat, keeping condiments and displaying salads, desserts, fruit and cheese – a feast for the eyes and the palate.

Dining tables can be truly elegant and beautiful pieces of furniture and the latest designer versions are particularly attractive. Designers have long sought to create the perfect dining chair to accompany them and as a result the choice is wide. There are Bauhaus-style chrome chairs with wicker or leather seats, shapely bentwood forms seen in restaurants, spindly black lacquer designs, simple pine and types with many other finishes, including paint and upholstery. Finally, you may wish to add a free-standing sideboard for storage.

You may prefer, or find it more economical, to search for old pieces in antique shops if you want a room with the style of a bygone age. Ensure that the accessories in the dining room are chosen to combine with the dining suite in terms of style. This can be carried through to your choice of china, glasses, condiments, place mats, serving dishes and cutlery. Creating an attractive table setting for a meal is a pleasure in itself.

Lighting should be planned to highlight the table. Unless it is a pendant which directs light on to the table, a central light will not provide a good atmosphere. Attach a dimmer to the switch for greater flexibility and use candles to create the perfect atmosphere for a special occasion.

The window in a dining room is important for daytime meals. If it provides a good view, then do not obscure it with fussy festoons or heavy curtains, which will also keep out welcome natural light. Your dining room can double as a study or home office provided you ensure there is adequate storage for equipment and papers so they can be hidden with ease before a meal.

## PLANNING CHECKLIST

- How many people usually eat in your dining area?
- Do children take their meals there?
- Which meals are usually taken in the dining area?
- Do you only use the dining area infrequently or for special meals?
- Could you eat elsewhere?
- Do you wish to eat outdoors?
- Is the room used for other activities?
- Can the dining area be extended to serve a larger number of people?
- Is it easy to move between the kitchen and the dining area with food, cutlery and dishes?
- Do you wish to store tableware and cutlery in the dining area?
- What other items must be stored in the room?
- Is the dining area used most during daytime or at night? Or both?
- Do you need to be able to switch between bright task lighting and more atmospheric lighting? *Consider installing lights on a dimmer switch.*
- What atmosphere do you wish to create in the dining area?
- How much are you able to spend?

*Those fortunate to find enough space for a separate dining room can create a peaceful, relaxing haven where it is possible to sit and eat and talk with friends and family. Dining room decorations do not have to be ornate or terribly formal. This restrained room is lit with a comforting glow.*

1 *The furniture of a dedicated dining room generally differs greatly from that of a combination kitchen/diner. When the dining area competes with food preparation and storage for space, chairs – and even tables – may fold up for storage when not in use. Tabletops, which are likely to be pressed into service as work areas, need to be as tough and as durable as worktops. In a dining room, however, the furniture is more solid and purposeful. Honest lines, good craftsmanship and unpretentious solid oak give this dining table and six chairs a certain dignity expressive of old-fashioned values. In this dining room, one would expect to be served hearty, tasty home cooking in generous helpings, rather than artfully arranged Japanese-style or nouvelle cuisine delicacies. The rich colours of the rug, created by vegetable dyes, complement the mellow wooden furniture. The atmosphere of familiar warmth is reinforced by the alcove bookshelves, with their decoy duck, plain bowl and books, and by the bold abstract painting on the wall.*

1

2

3

2 *A craftsman was commissioned to produce this marquetry tabletop, made from blond beech inlaid with teak. Its richly patterned surface calls for extremely plain tableware and glasses of the sort visible through the glass-fronted cupboard doors. All other surfaces and finishes in the room are natural and unpretentious: exposed timber roof beams, sisal flooring, basket chairs, solid wood cupboards, a collection of wicker baskets and a gallery of framed botanical prints. The simple and unassuming decor relies on the single stunning tabletop to make a bold decorative statement.*

3 *In this long, narrow dining room, it was essential to find a table of the right shape and team it with a sideboard. A round table in this setting would leave awkward spaces at either end of the room. A glass-topped table was selected which would seem as light and as airy as possible. An ordinary wooden table would only have emphasized the shape of the room. The room is simply decorated, with great precision and an eye for geometry. Modern Italian chairs are gracefully slender.*

1 *You do not need to acquire yet another bulky piece of furniture if you want the storage and decorative benefits of a dining room dresser. You can create your own in a chimney alcove or, as here, by mounting wooden shelves above a chest of drawers. These have been given a specialist paint finish with combed colour on the carcass and sponged swirls of turquoise and white on the drawer fronts, which makes a pretty, dappled background. The wall behind is painted lemon yellow to provide a sunny complement to the blue and white china plates and platters displayed on the shelves. Jugs of fresh flowers and the weathered wood of a farmhouse table reinforce the country house look of this decor. Never be tempted to refinish a battered table top such as this. The warm patina it has developed over the years would be destroyed, and a bright finish on the newly sanded wood would only highlight surface irregularities which are difficult to remove without skilled planing.*

1

2

3

2 *It makes sense to store tableware and glasses in the dining room when possible. There has been a recent revival of interest in the traditional dining room sideboard, a piece of furniture purpose-built for storing tableware that looks as good in its setting as the table and chairs. In more casual dining rooms, dressers can perform the same function. A dresser can be decorated with a handsome china collection to create a still life which is as functional as it is pretty. Here, a round dining table, which can be more difficult to place than a rectangular one, and four traditional chairs are set against a wall that partly screens the friendly little kitchen glimpsed beyond, leaving the opposite wall for storage. Rather than install shelves which would detract from the charm of the furniture, a traditional dresser has been mixed with a line of bookshelves above to house tableware, glasses and drinks.*

3 *A little sideboard with a protected dresser top and shelves supported on ornate brackets creates a small still life. The top, lined with a marble slab, throws the collection stored on the shelves, which includes everything from decanters to old-fashioned white ceramic storage jars, into relief. Hunting in antique markets often unearths useful kitchenware bargains.*

1 The lighting requirements for a combination kitchen/diner can differ greatly from those of a separate dining room. When a free-standing dining table is part of a large kitchen, it helps to have kitchen lighting controlled by a dimmer switch independent of the dining table lighting. At mealtimes, kitchen lights can be dimmed so that clutter created while cooking recedes into a shadowy background, as only the dining table is brightly illuminated. Sometimes an overhead light hanging from the ceiling is a nuisance in a busy kitchen/ diner, where it is an obstacle to be avoided. In a separate dining room, a pendant light can hang low over the table without obstructing vision or traffic flows through the room. In this dining room, a skylight provides lots of natural light by day, while the two decorative pendant lights hung at different heights throw their pools of light upon the table. Two wall washers which direct light on to the pink walls create a rosy glow of illumination. The patterned oilskin table cloth catches the light and glows in warm earthy terracotta colours. Light which streams in through the skylight is reflected back upwards by the white ceramic tile floor, making this dining room even brighter by day.

1

2

2 *This room reverses the balance of light and shade seen opposite. Here, warm brown cork tile flooring and a wooden table firmly anchor the room in mellow natural tones. The ice-cream pastels used elsewhere in the room – from the cream-coloured walls to the pink or white outlines painted on the woodwork, to the very pale pink blind – lighten the backdrop. The lighting for the room is all supplied by downlighters. A swivelling recessed eyeball downlighter pours a ring of light down the column which separates the dining room from the living room. Above the table is a modern Italian pendant light fitting hung on chains, with an opaque semicircular globe of light reflected in the metallic shade. Reflectors are often fitted to shield the naked bulb and can change the intensity and quality of light. Spotlights have golden reflectors built into the bulb for a warm light, or silver ones for a more mysterious light. Even on the traditional light fitting, the paper or silk shade acts as a reflector, and deflector, of the light source. Consider the change in a room's atmosphere if you were to shield the lamps with red silk, rather than white paper.*

# BEDROOMS

The bedroom is your personal retreat. Here are kept old teddy bears, soft toys, crumpled clothes – and laundered ones – family photographs, guises and disguises, all revealed to those who enter. Or, if you choose, hidden behind closed doors. Today's bedrooms may be lined with fully fitted cupboards and furniture like a kitchen, or more traditionally furnished with free-standing items such as wooden chests, apothecary drawers, lidded trunks or giant wardrobes. Sometimes these bulky pieces from another age can be updated in the most dazzling way with elaborate paint finishes. Whatever your inspiration, plan your bedroom around its dominant feature – the bed.

Any scheme you envisage must be based on the bed style – a box-spring bed offers a different theme to a four-poster. There are lots of alternatives. You can have a zipped-together double bed that converts easily back into singles (space or partners permitting). At simplest, you can place a mattress on the floor, or on a raised platform. A Japanese futon, a cotton mattress, can be rolled up into a giant bolster by day.

You spend up to a third of your life in bed, so unless you want to become an insomniac, you need a well-supported, comfortable mattress with a firm base. Extra-firm orthopaedic mattresses will suit those with back ailments, and beds that tilt to drop the head lower than the feet are made for those with circulatory complaints. A high-quality foam mattress can be as good, and as expensive, as a sprung mattress, but foam can be hot to sleep upon and must be well ventilated. A futon can be damp unless it is aired every day. Sprung mattresses are heavy and the pocketed-spring varieties are more expensive than interlinked-spring types.

Do not feel inhibited about jumping on to the mattress you have selected before you buy. Lie down upon it, eyes closed, and see if it is comfortable and accommodating. When you lie on a bed, the weight of your body is not evenly distributed across the mattress – your shoulders and pelvis are heavier than your wrists, for example. A good mattress is supple enough to adjust, supports your body weight evenly and makes a firm, flat surface for your back. When buying a double mattress, two people should lie on it side by side to see how firmly it will support two bodies.

## PLANNING CHECKLIST

- What size bed suits you?
- Where will you place the bed to leave corridor space and room for opening doors?
- Is the room to have another use? *Consider a sofabed.*
- What are the storage requirements for clothing, linens, luggage, etc:
  - large cupboards
  - drawers
  - hanging rails
  - shelves
  - laundry hamper
  - shoe racks
- Do you prefer built-in or free-standing storage?
- Is the bedroom sunny? *Cooler, north-facing rooms need warming up with decoration.*
- Is the bedroom overlooked? *Curtains also cut down noise.*
- What do you need near the bed:
  - reading light
  - telephone
  - alarm clock
  - radio
  - tea/coffee maker
  - TV/video
  *When watching TV, a 355mm (14in) screen should be viewed from at least 1.2m (4ft) away.*
- Will you need sockets and space for other activities:
  - sewing machine
  - hair drier
  - typewriter
  - computer

*This open-plan bedroom with gallery contrasts traditional with modern styles and natural with primary colours against plain white walls. A bright abstract wall tapestry is set against a stone Regency chimney and the Louis XV armchair is covered with a bright green chintz.*

Combination bedroom/work areas in which you entertain, once a symptom of impoverished student times, now may be a sign of freelance work. When furnishing any dual-purpose room, select furniture or design built-ins which will be space-saving and convertible as well as practical. If you need to entertain or conduct business in the room that houses your bed, either use a convertible sofabed or dress the bed to make it a feature of the room.

Good-looking sofas that open up into beds incorporate simple mechanisms that mean you do not have to be an athlete to produce a bed easily when you do want to rest. More elaborate foldaway beds unhinge from the wall, where they pack flat in the best tradition of a James Bond movie. Others concertina outwards, once they have been unscrewed or unbolted.

You can dress an ordinary bed with a fitted cover by day, bolstered with cushions that make it into a deep-seated but adequate sofa. Or you can dress a rather large, dominant bed in such a manner that it is eye-catching. Even a four-poster bed works in a living/dining area: with a kelim rug pinned to the headboard area, canopied in a vivid Bedouin stripe, it looks unusual and essentially nomadic in theme, so it discourages any associations with the boudoir. The satin-sheeted look with its frills and furbelows, which suits some private bedrooms, establishes an embarrassing intimacy, best avoided in combination bedroom/work rooms.

Geometric pinstripes or zany modern designs can be used to good effect on bedcoverings. The patchwork quilt of yesteryear could be revived in the country-fresh interior of an inner-city apartment, designed around simple features like a rag rug, stained floorboards, a stencilled cornice and soft, washed colours.

Platforms provide a change of direction between sleep and work areas. Emphasize this change with different floorings and colours on each level. Bookshelves placed along one side of a platform can double as both a dividing screen and handy storage area for reference works and bedside reading. A desk can also serve as a partition. Or place the desk in a bay or alcove – or even wasted corner space if you can provide adequate light. When the work-load is not so great as to occupy the worktop constantly, consider a foldaway, hinged-top desk that packs flat when you are not working. If you need storage for files, a filing cabinet in new fashion colours can double up as a bedside table.

Constraints of space and budget may dictate your choice of bed to some extent. Within the work environment few other items of furniture meet such a wide range of individual requirements with such diversity. Whatever your bed style, whether a self-indulgent four-poster or a practical built-in platform, it will reflect – and affect – your life style.

1

2

3

1  In dual-purpose bedrooms where there is little space, Japanese futons provide an attractive solution to sleeping and seating, both spacious activities. By day the bedding is rolled or folded so as to become a seating system. Here, a slatted ash double-bed base with red-stained legs supporting two cushioned futon mattresses is converted for daytime use to a low-backed sofa with bolster seating and two coffee-tables.

2  Convertible sofabeds are practical in any room which is used for sitting as well as sleeping. This metal-framed sofabed is upholstered in foam and has a removable quilted cotton cover. It enables this spare room to be used as a studio for a seamstress and also as a guest bedroom and extra sitting room.

3  A restful Japanese-style interior with ivory and eau-de-Nil walls using a futon mattress laid in the traditional way on the floor and a second, rolled-up futon, with a cushion as a back support, used for seating. The only other furniture is an Alvar Aalto stool, an impromptu bedside table for the miniature television. Notice how the light positioned behind the indoor plant tub casts a pool of dappled light and shadow upon the ceiling.

*A mattress becomes a bed simply by backing it with cushions or raising it on a built-in platform, or with more traditional bases, headboards and footboards.*

1  *The vibrancy of the brilliant bed-linen and high-gloss red storage unit in this low-level bedroom contrasts with the plain white bath visible through the black, glazed doors. The convertible sofabed has a soft yellow backrest for scatter cushions. The storage unit is a good height for watching television in bed.*

2  *This double bed has a sprung base topped with an eighty per cent cotton mattress and a quilted headboard. Co-ordinated detailing makes this conventional bedroom more stylish: the Madras check quilted bedspread matches the drawer fronts and lampshades.*

3  *This unusual attic bedroom combines plain white plasterwork and quarry tiles with black lacquered box shelving and ceiling and brilliant blue bed-linen. A solid concrete slab forms the platform for the double foam mattress. Single Continental quilts allow for individual sleeping habits in a shared bed. The upright concrete slabs of the floor-to-ceiling shelving system and concrete bedside boxes make original built-in furniture.*

4

5

6

4   A pine four-poster bed can be draped to different effect; either with traditional curtains using a fabric such as Bolton twill plus ribbons or sashes, or with sheer muslin draped more simply like a tropical mosquito net. The accessories are suitably Eastern — the Indian dhurry and the ikat design of the bed-linen.

5   A wooden bed, inspired by the simplicity of Quaker design, would fit as well in a smart townhouse interior as it does in this country-style bedroom with its matching sprigged Victorian bed-linen and wallpaper. The curved headboard and footboard are built from traditionally steam-bent solid ash. The bedside table and the chest of drawers come from the same range of furniture as the bed.

6   Different levels, whether sunken or raised, can make a room more attractive. Here, the height of the bedroom floor has been built up to create a platform for a sprung mattress covered in scarlet with a boldly striped extra-large Continental quilt and matching pillows. These can be stashed away by day in deep pull-out drawers at the front of the platform. The fine red architrave line and multicoloured line between white floorboards emphasize the bold stripe of the bedding.

Open-spring mattresses consist of rows of upright wire coils sandwiched between wire frames with padding on top and bottom. The gauge of the wire indicates the resilience of the springs – the higher the gauge, the more giving. This, combined with the number of springs, determines the comfort and durability of the mattress. A double one has about 350 springs.

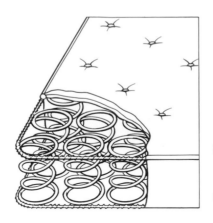

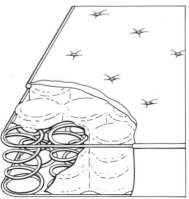

Pocketed-spring mattresses are similar in principle to open-spring mattresses, but each spring is sewn under tension into its own fabric slot or pocket. Because the springs move independently, the mattress is more flexible. Such mattresses incorporate about three times as many springs as open-spring mattresses, so they give more support, but are considerably more expensive.

Foam mattresses vary in quality: the best ones combine layers of foam of different density. A bottom layer of firm foam provides the necessary support, while a softer top layer conforms to individual contours so there are no pressure points. A third outer layer quilted into the mattress cover gives extra cushioning. Foam requires a ventilated base, rather than a solid one.

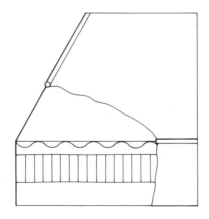

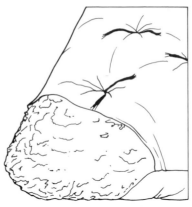

Futons are Japanese mattresses which consist of layers of natural or synthetic fibre, such as cotton or polyester, held in place inside a thick cotton cover with tufted ties. They are available in different thicknesses – generally from 76mm (3in) to 152mm (6in) thick – and some are filled with a mixture of fibres. Futons can be rolled or folded up by day.

1 Traditional brass bed frames are now reproduced in lacquered woods
2 Pocketed-spring mattress on a sprung-edge base
3 Trundle bed with open-spring mattresses and pine frame
4 Bunk bed (stacking twin beds) with open-spring mattresses and solid pine frames

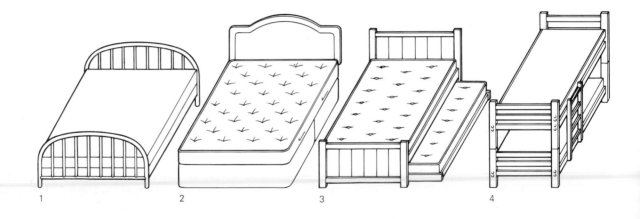

1          2          3          4

Slatted wood bed bases are formed by securely fixing simple softwood slats to a bed frame. It makes a very firm base although it can be quite flexible, as here, where the bed frame is hinged to fold away. A 102mm (4in) foam pad, supported by this slatted wood base, can be folded up when the bed is stored behind a middle cupboard, making a lightweight, space-saving bed.

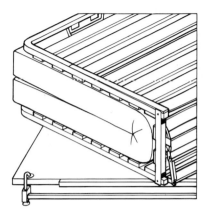
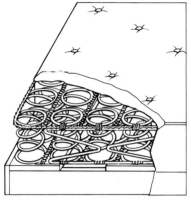

Sprung-edge bed bases consist of rows of upright wire coils supported on a wooden frame, all upholstered with durable fabric. This is the most expensive bed base you can buy. Because the coiled springs extend right out to the edge of the bed base, it is as comfortable to sleep near the edge of the bed as it is in the centre, and there is no tendency to roll inwards.

Sprung slatted wood bed bases, like ordinary slatted bases with firmly fixed softwood slats, tend to be very firm and require an appropriate mattress. An extra degree of give is introduced by sprung hardwood slats held in special flexible fixings. Such a base is not so deep or bulky as a box-like sprung-edge bed base, but is more complex than the ordinary slatted bed.

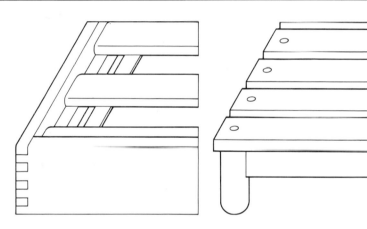

Futon bed bases usually consist of wide wooden slats fixed to a simple, low frame. The slats are closely spaced to prevent the futon from sagging, but narrow gaps are left between the slats to permit air circulation so that it does not become damp or stuffy. Futon bed bases which double as sofa platforms are easy to build, or self-assembly kits can be purchased.

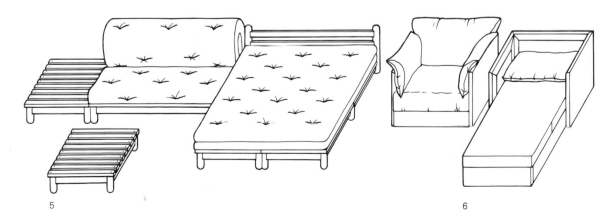

5 Futon sofa made up of two double futons on a platform with two matching side tables converts to a double bed by moving the side tables next to the platform to form a bed base, unrolling the futons and laying them out on the base
6 Convertible armchair with upholstered wooden frame opens into single bed

5          6

The bed occupies more space than any item in your house, including the bath, so how you dress it will determine the style of your room: tailored or casual, quilted or counterpaned, the choice is yours. Only you can decide between the security of familiar sheets and blankets, and the freedom from bed-making that a Continental quilt and fitted bottom sheet brings.

Be it plain or patterned, the top covering will introduce the biggest single jolt of colour to your room. Choose colour schemes wisely for your bed-linen to make a positive statement against the right background. Designer bed-linen provides pattern contrasts: one pattern for the base sheet and a variation for the Continental quilt cover, which is often reversible, with a different yet co-ordinated pillowcase pattern. Use geometric patterns for new angles, with stripes extending the eye visually along the length of the bed or broadening the area in a corridor-like room.

The minimalist who hides clutter behind cupboard doors and prefers to sleep simply upon a floor mattress will choose the purest bed dressing, without intricate patterning and many colours. The simplest is the futon – a Japanese mattress made from tufted cotton wadding layered inside a pure cotton cover. For a modern look, cover a futon with graphic-patterned fabric and top it off with two bolsters akin to Japanese headrests rather than pillows; for a softer effect, choose a pastel futon cover with traditional pillows covered in complementary colours as back- and armrests.

Futons and similar roll-up bedding often fill dual roles, doubling by day as a sofa. Sofabeds themselves seldom provide any daytime storage space for the pillows and coverings, unless you roll and cleat them like yachtsmen's sails to form a bolster. The more expensive convertible sofabeds are upholstered with detachable quilted covers that become the night-time Continental quilt. Or you can take a tip from an architect whose lightweight foam-block mattress is covered in tough but flimsy spinnaker sail fabric made up in all the colours of his studio bedroom. By day, it hangs from the wall and looks like an abstract painting.

The traditionalist will prefer sleeping upon a box-sprung bed raised fairly high from the floor. This bed could have a pleated valance to conceal the legs, and the formality of a fitted bedspread.

Dressing the bed does not end with the bed-linen. You can drape fabric on posts at the four corners or, more simply, create a canopy above with an interesting fabric design to reflect upon when lying in bed. It is possible to make a four-poster bedroom without an actual four-poster bed: hang lightweight curtains from a ceiling rod that matches the bed base in size and shape, or suspend a simple length of fabric, perhaps a hand-blocked Indian sari, between two ceiling rods. You will see many examples on the following pages.

The bed is the centrepiece of most bedrooms and the largest object of furniture, so the bed-linen and coverings are very important to the finished effect of the whole room. Here, the simple effect of a neatly folded blanket emphasizes the lines of the bed against the curves of the unusual arched windows. The blue and yellow tones marry beautifully with the hazy blue walls and silk Indian rug. Dressed in this simple way, the bed can be easily matched with plain and inexpensive furniture such as these small tables and foldaway chairs for a casual breakfast or informal study area.

Bed-linens can determine both the colour scheme and mood of a room. Frills and flounces with valances and counterpanes say something individual about you. When the colour scheme has already been established, with painted or papered walls, and floor coverings laid, take colour samples with you when choosing bed-linen. If you start from scratch, the range of sheets, covers and pillowcases makes it possible to plan the room around the bed-linens you like best, distributing the colours of the linens across the background.

1 A cool blue lightweight cover with neatly mitred corners around striped sheets suits this restful room with little for contemplation but some collectors' ceramics and two abstract paintings. The low-level bed, with its curved black tubular headboard and frame, blends with the black lacquer furniture to give the room style.

1

2

3

2 *In this theatrical Japanese bedroom dressing, the double scale of small chequerboard pillowcases and Continental quilt cover set against giant squares dramatizes the black and white theme. The Japanese style is carried through the paper and wooden panelling at the windows, the tatami matting used on the bed platform and the Japanese Noh theatre puppets strung up on the walls.*

3 *Here adventurous bed-linen transforms a basic box-bed. Geometric stripes, cleverly combined in changes of colour, direction and weight, are mirrored to make a double image. Red and white stripes anchor the box-springs, mattress, bedspread and pillows, all covered with the same width yellow and white stripes, and they are balanced by the fine-line blue and white horizontal stripe on the twin chairs standing against the facing wall.*

Three types of bedcover, all set against plain flooring and walls, traditional wooden furniture and simple window treatments, suggest ways of capturing country style in a town or country bedroom. Country style depends upon a certain understatement in design and an honest, undisguised admiration of form and handicraft to achieve its freshness and charm.

1 A traditional American quilt turns the bed into the decorative centrepiece of this room. The quilted pattern of green leaves and red flowers is picked up by the red scatter cushions, small potted geraniums and decorative frieze on the white blinds. Next to the beautifully inlaid old headboard stand tall wicker baskets, which make unusual bedside tables.

2 This simple room quaintly mixes a floral print with unfussy stripes. The patterned fabric gathered into a valance for the bed is also used for a tablecloth and the cushion on the white rattan chair. The fine muslin cotton quilt is striped in the same warm colours, and the floral motif appears again in the painting used as a fireplace screen, the old embroidered tablemat framed above the fireplace and the jugs or vases of flowers on every surface.

1

2

3

3 Even a Continental quilt and pillowcases with a relatively modern, abstract line design can look serenely countrified on a wooden bed. The soft colours tone with the rug, tiles, and walls painted a creamy pink. The country feel is followed through in details: the framed sampler, candlesticks upon the pine surround, the pitcher with flowers and the wooden stationery box on the little dresser under the window.

Continental quilts (known as comforters or duvets) are an alternative to sheets and blankets, which simplify bed-making. Channels filled with a natural or synthetic insulating fibre comprise the quilt within the cover, made from cotton or sheeting fabric to complement the pillowcases and bottom sheet. Natural fillings are light and warm: goose down is the most luxurious filling, although a mixture of duck down and feather is cheaper. Synthetic fillings are easy to launder, hard-wearing and suitable for those who are allergic to natural feathers.

Using fabric drapes over a bed makes the bed the focal point, as elaborate and eye-catching as any decorative window treatment or drape.

1 This wooden four-poster bed with a lattice-work bed base is built around a recessed window, using a fringed Turkish bed hanging embroidered in silver for drapes. The bed is painted in the same traditional pale blue used for the built-in furniture, wooden frames and stair-rail.

2 A generous length of a delicate material like muslin, voile, cambric or even window netting makes economical but theatrical drapes, with a touch of fun added here by the loosely tied red ribbons which attach the material to the ceiling and allow it to fall into a canopy. The covered headboard and quilted bedcover are patterned in the same colours as the rag rug.

3 A luxury bed has been created in a small bedroom by hanging sumptuous modern drapes from the ceiling and placing an eighteenth-century headboard against the wall. The ruched backcloth, canopy and self-lined curtains are suspended from an upholstered tester with no posts. The matching, broadly quilted bedspread and crewel-work cushions are in silk cambric.

1

2

3

4

5

6

4 This bed drape with a colonial air is achieved by splitting a mosquito net two-thirds of the way up its circular shape so it can be drawn back and the ends knotted around cleats at either side of the bed. The unadorned wood panelling is offset by the plain bed set in a white box and by the window frames. The style of this tropical bedroom can equally be used in northern climates with central heating – a ceiling fan circulates warm air around the room.

5 This small four-poster bed in a mountain inn in the French alps was built by local craftsmen. Its broad border fringing the poles is pulled taut to show the frieze-like pattern of lace flowers. The plump Continental quilt is covered by plain white bed-linen.

6 A curtain swathed over poles at the head of the bed, here enclosing two lacquered rattan bedside tables, lends a classical touch to a modern bedroom. The squared silk moiré scatter cushions lift the richly patterned apricot fabric used for the bedspread, headboard and drapes.

Many of us actually live in the bedroom – or should we say, sleep in the living room? Such a room can be variously known as a studio, a bedsit, a one-room apartment, or an open-plan space – depending on its size and grandeur. These rooms by their very nature contain the whole range of activities of their occupants' lives, and must be much more carefully planned and decorated than any other type of interior. Organization is the key to one-room living.

The average bedroom is often used for dual purposes since few can afford the luxury of a separate room for every activity. The bedroom is the obvious place for study, exercise, hobbies, mending, for TV viewing in luxuriously comfortable surroundings or even a professional home office.

A clear principle for a room with multiple functions is to ensure that it may be cleared of one when you wish to do the other. The one-room home must contain a bed that disappears from sight when not in use, or doubles as a sofa. The popular folding sofabed, which comes in a wide range of styles and prices, is a good solution for one-room living, guest rooms and those bedrooms which serve as a home office. Some fitted storage walls include a pull-down bed behind a panel, with shelves on either side.

Another essential element in the dual-purpose room is efficient and adequate storage so that the room does not become cluttered and unmanageable. Storage can be an integral part of the room's style – an attractive free-standing wardrobe can look charming in a period studio and, similarly, a filing cabinet will not look out of place in a modern room with a tubular steel platform bed. Plan for co-ordination as well as function.

It is worth listing all the functions of the room and with them the accessories, equipment and items to be used or stored there. This list will make it easy to draw up a detailed ground plan for the room on graph paper so that each object is carefully positioned. Make a clear distinction between different activities, so that one does not intrude upon the other. Flexibility is the key word. Objects or fittings which themselves have double functions are both useful and space-saving: if, for example, you choose a desk select one which can serve as a dining table.

Window dressing and lighting must be flexible, too. A bedroom requires privacy from the outside world and shade from intrusive early morning sunlight. But ensure that the windows can be fully revealed if the daytime room is a home office or a living room with its full quota of possible sunlight. After consideration of bedroom lighting, remember that other activities and products have their own requirements, such as home computers where light must not shine directly on the screen, or into the eyes of the operator, or studio entertaining where seating and tables must be subtly illuminated.

A practical space-saving bed can become a design feature: by day, the base slides away on castors under a large seating platform with cushions. The platform is deep enough to hold the Continental quilt and pillow in the wooden bed frame, with a smaller adjacent drawer for bed-linen and space for general storage.

The room is made light and spacious for daytime living by the colour scheme — with white and cream walls, floor, ceiling, print and unlined curtains. Reflected light comes from mirrored wardrobe doors and a sleek swivel pivot chrome lamp gives electric light wherever it is needed. Plants use the height of the room to full advantage while occupying very little precious floor space.

*Any sleeping space which doubles as a private work or general living area, either relaxed or formal, needs clever design and furnishings so that the room can move between day and night use.*

1   *One-room living often requires bed-linen which breaks with traditional bedroom cosiness to make the right daytime effect. Either hide the bed-linen by day, transforming the bed into a more formal day-bed, or choose bed-linen that looks discreet. Here, the formal restraint of the neatly striped covers, set against a black valance and pillow support, links perfectly with the modern severity of the leather chairs, coffee-table and lamp beyond. The thinly striped grey curtains, exotic plants and modern table and light used at the bedside also help to unify the room.*

1

2

3

2 In this imaginative conversion of a small space into a bedroom with work area the neat twin desks, with a clip-on photographer's light, are supported by the bed frame, which also contains a slide-out storage drawer. A deep wall-to-wall shelf around the side and back of the built-in bed makes a surface for television, plants and ornaments and another above the bed at ceiling level provides storage. The floor-to-ceiling wall mirror and uniformly white decor, with the Venetian blinds echoed by horizontally striped wallpaper, create the illusion of more space.

3 The most effective, but also the most expensive, solution to the problem of space is a bed which folds up behind a wood-finish door as part of a wall shelf and storage unit. The bed closes away with mattress and bedding, and the spring mechanism and lightweight frame make it easy to use.

*Careful planning can turn cramped dual-purpose bedrooms into comfortable and efficient studio-style workplaces.*

1 A large drawing table and a work desk are fitted into space released by lifting the bed to a height that also accom-modates a large storage cabinet in this teenage room. The matching red filing cabinet under the desk, the red anglepoise lamp and quilt form links between the sleep and work areas, standing out against the neat white walls, shelving and window shutters.

2 This screened desk on wheels provides a large, mobile writing surface that can be rolled around on the hard-wearing jute floor. The easily enclosed corner with bedside table also gives access to a neatly designed storage cupboard with sliding doors that need no clearance space. The dual purpose of this room is reflected in the conical wall lamp giving a soft bedroom light and the supplementary reading light on the desk.

1

2

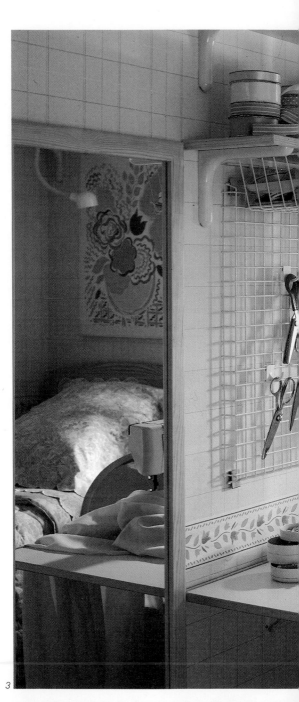

3

## FITTING FOLDING SHELVES

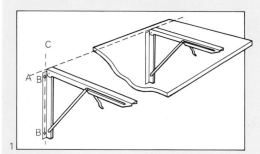

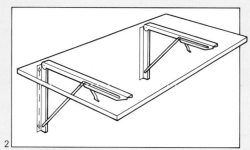

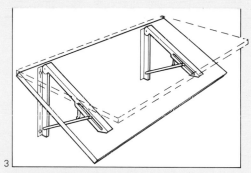

A shelf which folds against the wall can be immensely useful in a small bedroom which doubles as a work room, and is easy to install on folding brackets: **1** Use a spirit level to ensure that positions A, B and C for the brackets and shelf are correctly marked. Holes B should line up vertically. When they are marked, drill and plug the wall and screw on the brackets. **2** Screw the shelf or table on to the brackets. **3** The special brackets lock into an upright position when the shelf is lifted for use.

3  *A bedroom can also double well as a sewing room: the hinged sewing table folds flat against the wall when not in use, with sewing equipment stashed away in wide white shelves, in undershelf baskets and hooked on a wire board, all compactly arranged on the upper wall. The full-length pine-framed mirror is also useful for dressmaking. The shuttered windows and lamp with flexible neck provide plenty of light, for working by day or night, and the stencil border picks up an embroidery motif.*
*Visible wall-mounted storage, such as a hook-and-pegboard system or wire-grid system like this, can be immensely versatile, since hooks, clips, shelves and trays can be added to hang almost any tool or utensil within easy reach. Hiding clothes is a priority; transforming the large space taken up by the bed into an unobtrusive area is another. Planning the worktop – be it draughtsman's board, sewing table or just a plain desk – to be both readily available, yet not a nagging or challenging feature, is the next.*

Bedrooms in modern houses are seldom larger than 3m × 3.7m (10ft × 12ft) yet they contain an enormous amount. Personal belongings, winter and summer clothing, shoes, valuables and bedding are all kept in bedrooms, behind the closed doors of fitted units, or in free-standing furniture.

Fitted bedrooms look smart, but do not necessarily save space. When built-in furniture lines an entire wall length, that amount of floor space narrows the room dimensions accordingly. By comparison, a free-standing wardrobe or a chest of drawers takes up less overall space, but requires more free floor space in front for opening doors or pulling out drawers.

Free-standing wardrobes and chests of drawers in the generous sizes of another spacious era are often inherited. Unconventional storage solutions come from designers who use shop-fitters' furniture, from fashion-shop swing rails to garage mechanics' tool-box trolleys. Extendable arms used in hospitals have been re-employed as domestic bedside tables so the telephone, TV or books can be brought quickly to hand and as swiftly replaced when needed.

Lidded wicker baskets, old school trunks and pull-out boxes on castors that roll beneath the bed are just some of the more solid pieces that can house bedding, providing a linen chest for winter blankets and Continental quilts in the hot months.

When not used for seating, a chair or a day-bed can serve as an impromptu clothes support and blanket throw. A three-panel screen, covered with fabric or paper scraps, offers privacy for dressing as well as somewhere to hang clothes.

To assess the need for a working wall of fitted furniture, use chalk to mark out the spaces along the wall for wardrobes and drawers to the measurements specified in a manufacturers' catalogue. Marketed in pack-flat kits, these units can be self-assembled, though the more expensive ranges on adjustable plinths need specialist fitting. Features like corner carousel racks, stacking shoe racks, containers for storing out-of-season clothes in the inaccessible upper parts, concertina doors that save space, built-in lighting or even a safe for valuables can be housed inside.

The façade presented by fitted furniture doors will determine the look of the bedroom, depending on the finish you choose, whether rustic pine, limed oak, bold lacquered colours or scumbled, dragged or spattered fashion-paint finishes. The more expensive door fronts feature detailed mouldings – make your own by glueing on painted picture-frame edgings or split bamboo bought by the metre. Interior designer John Stefanides uses sections of ordinary garden trellis, painted and tacked to massive cupboard fronts, then given a moulded edging, as a way of cheaply breaking up a façade of faceless door fronts.

This loft bedroom combines rural simplicity with a careful attention to architectural detail. The furnishings and furniture — tapestry headboard, old painted metal console and loosely draped armchair — are simple but decorative. The panelling and chimney-alcove cupboards have moulded fronts, picked out in white against the grey stippled doors, and a black keyhole motif.

*Unfitted storage requires space, but need not dominate the room if properly spaced and highlighted to blend or contrast with the period and decorative scheme of a room.*

1  *This steely grey and charcoal monotone room relies largely on an unfitted storage system, but remains visually uncluttered. The versatile trolley, which can be pushed around, here becomes a television table with a lower version used as a bedside table. The tall tubular steel tower with fixed perforated shelves has space for books or tall ornaments. The only fitted storage – the blocked-up fireplace shelved for a stereo system and speakers – and the bare hanging rail are left open to complement the unadorned steel frame furniture, but they could be covered with curtains or slatted wooden blinds.*

2  *A free-standing coat rack provides unconventional but space-saving hanging space. It becomes a decorative feature in an otherwise conventionally furnished bedroom. The wigwam-shaped rack makes a good use of alcove space and links well with the black-painted grate surround of the old fireplace.*

1

2

3

3 *An advantage of using free-standing storage is that it introduces some attractive items of furniture into the bedroom. These bentwood chairs would not look as good in a room of wall-to-wall cupboards, but they are very much at home with the old wooden chest of drawers. In a room such as this, with an atmosphere and charm of its own – resulting from the fact that it is an attic with a sloping ceiling, old window and wooden ladder up to a skylight – a modern, stylized, bedroom system would spoil that charm. However, such considerations must be weighed against the storage requirements. No bedroom will please the eye if it is constantly cluttered with objects that have no home.*

*Fitted storage units neatly house clutter behind old-fashioned panelling suited to period rooms, spartan hi-tech metal from a gym, or sliding white doors. It is important that the interior fittings accommodate everything you need to store – shoes, socks and underwear, hanging garments, folded clothes, even spare suitcases – as it is to select a system to complement the decor you have chosen.*

1 *Floor-to-ceiling storage such as this leaves stored clothes easily viewed on heavy-duty shelves built from standard lengths of vinyl-coated steel wire shelving. The clothes rack, built in under the top shelf, and the shoe storage unit provide the other necessary components for a highly flexible unit that fits inside a cupboard recess or alcove, protected by a louvred door or a more conventional door. You could screen it with a curtain.*

1

2

3

## FITTING ADJUSTABLE SHELVING

**1** Hold upright supports to wall and mark fixing hole.
**2** Using spirit level and straight-edge, mark identical fixing holes for adjacent uprights. **3** Drill, plug and screw at each mark. **4** Make sure upright is vertical. Mark other fixing holes. Loosen screw, swing upright sideways, then drill, plug and screw marked positions. **5** Slot brackets into uprights and position shelf on top. Screw shelf to bracket (uppermost shelf first), or **6** mark through brackets, remove to screw shelf and bracket together, then slot back into upright in one piece.

2  *This fitted storage unit combines cupboards with beaded panelling and glass doors custom-made to complement the cornice and moulding of the eighteenth-century room. Painted in pale apricot and white, with pleated fabric matching the wallpaper, the small open-shelving islands at either end of the unit give it a decorative touch. The bed base is also hand painted in the same pale apricot, emphasized with white mouldings, but the hand-marbled panelling lends a variety of colour and texture that tones with the sky-patterned carpet and striped wallpaper.*

3  *Ventilated gymnasium locker cupboards make an unusual domestic storage system that fits perfectly in this modern bedroom, stripped to bare essentials. It has sanded and waxed floorboards, a mattress with black and white paned covers simply laid on the floor and four spotlights on wires extended from a central lighting point along a line across the cupboards. One wall is mirrored like a gymnasium, and another has been speckled with cream and a grey-green paint to match the cupboards.*

*Wall-to-wall storage, varied in both form and style, is used like an extended plan chest as a platform under a bed, built into awkwardly angled walls to make use of dead space or ranged behind Japanese screens. It provides the extended storage space often needed for dual-purpose bedrooms, leaving space around the bed and creating an open, uncluttered atmosphere.*

1 *The awkward shape of an attic has here been emphasized by the storage system rather than treated as a problem. The unit was assembled at home from a system made of individual components varying in shape, size and colour. It combines tall full-length cupboards and vertically stacked shelving that follows the slope of the eaves with an L-shaped bar of cupboards and shelves which double as a headboard and room divider. The shape of the room is further highlighted by the grey carpet following the line demonstrated by the lower storage unit and the muslin cover battened to the recess of the skylight.*

1

2 Custom-built storage need not be prohibitively expensive. It offers an opportunity to create an unusual and stylish element in the room. These cupboards are based on Japanese room dividers. They demonstrate the importance of building such structures from floor-to-ceiling as well as wall-to-wall because they then create a complete wall rather than a fussy or irregular section in the room. Another clever device here is the screen on the window which matches the paper 'screening' on the cupboard doors and further unifies the room. Natural wood floors, bamboo table and plain walls are the perfect accompaniment to the Japanese style.

3 Since a bed does not need any great depth of ceiling, the floor level may be built up even when there is no high ceiling. This arrangement creates a large deep-drawer storage chest and clearly defines the bed area as a spacious place, suitable for daytime relaxation and sleep. The quilted fitted bottom sheet and Continental quilt, with its reversible cover that matches the bed base and sheet, lend a luxurious touch, while the platform space around the bed allows everything necessary to be at a convenient level alongside, while providing drawers underneath.

General bedroom lighting involves creating atmosphere with fittings that complement the decorative scheme. To find the right level and quantity of light for bedroom activities, you need a dimmer switch to control the level of intensity. Otherwise, lighting may be too harsh, without softness of play between light and shade. Although pendant or hanging lights are often used, they are obtrusive and flatten shadows. Wall washers will give a less intense light than down-lighters, which should be used sparingly in the bedroom. An awkward placing can glare. Unlike most other rooms, here you will be viewing the lights from flat on your back and you should therefore site them accordingly.

Bedside lighting is crucial and can prove problematic. Whether you are gripped by a spine-chilling thriller or catching up on the Sunday paper, you do not want the page you are reading plunged into shadow when you change position. You may wish to dim the reading light at times so it can double as atmospheric background illumination, and will certainly want to be able to switch it on and off easily from the bed and find the switch in the dark. Free-standing lamps provide numerous small light sources, while purpose-built fittings direct the light exactly where it is needed, with a shade diffusing the light. Avid late-night readers who do not wish to disturb the sleep of others can also try the ultimate in personal reading lights – a very small, high-intensity lamp mounted on a large clip which clamps on to the book itself to illuminate each page.

More than most windows, bedroom windows need to be well protected against any passerby's gaze. Privacy is vital. Just as dimmers control the intensity of light by night, so blinds filter daylight. By lowering or raising them, you change the intensity of the light. Window treatments of every conceivable type are possible: from lined drapes to light-filtering nets, from shirred festoons to trimmed Roman blinds, from louvred shutters to paper panels.

Desks in the bedroom are often placed at the window, so keep windows clear with an efficient window blind that rolls away by day. Anyone living in a high-rise apartment with a small child and outward-opening windows should consider installing vertical window bars for the first few years of the child's life, which are less likely than horizontal bars to become a hazardous climbing frame. In a child's room, light on desktops is essential to focus on the work at hand, but trailing wires should be avoided. Colourful clip-on photographers' lights which can be moved at will, clipped on to work surfaces and set at right angles, are a popular choice, as the illustrations of the real-life rooms featured in the book show. Track-mounted spotlights above a pinboard or mirror provide light where it is most needed. Safety lights and low-level light switches are helpful for young children who may be nervous of the dark.

Bedroom lighting requirements vary. General overhead light is a basic requirement to replace daylight by night or when drapes are drawn, while additional task lighting for dressing, making-up, hairdressing or reading – even working – needs to be considered. A dimmer switch which controls the intensity of light to suit the mood can be invaluable in a bedroom. Simply, shades can vary the direction and intensity of light. One solution to reading in bed without sufficient light is a metal hospital light specifically designed for bedridden people so it can be extended, angled and adjusted as required. Created to last and work effectively, it has been given a high-quality metal finish in a simple design.

1 *This room is impressive for its sheer size, original architectural details and abundance of natural light. The bed is placed to take full advantage of unusually large bay windows. Discreet, narrow, fitted Venetian blinds do not interrupt the fine frames or detract from the generous proportions of the bay. They allow for maximum sunlight and enjoyment of a leafy view, but also give sufficient privacy when necessary. The moulding on the cornices and the geometric lines of the parquet floor can be appreciated against bare walls and simple furniture. Blocking off a corner behind the bed creates a headboard and provides a neat shelf for personal mementoes.*

1

2

2 *Another bed area has been created in a spacious room, this time a dark alcove rather than a sunny bay. It has the quality of a private, cosy retreat, screened from the room and its battered day-bed by a full-length white curtain. Lighting for the alcove adds to its peaceful seclusion because only low-level fittings are used, rather than glaring overhead illumination. Two small lamps on the bookcase and bedside lights provide a warm glow against the deep ochre shade of the walls. This colour also separates the bed area from the main room and assists the intimate warm atmosphere. Red chair seats enhance the wall colour as does the deep tone of the bedspread.*

Bedroom windows pose particular problems for the decorator. Nobody wants their bedroom overlooked, yet excessive privacy with muffled or screened windows is stifling. Window dressing needs imagination.

1   Rich, embroidered fabric, elaborately styled, provides a grand feeling in this traditional bedroom. The curtain and pelmet form a decorative frame to the windows. Privacy is provided by net blinds which gather into festoons when raised. The bed is also framed with drapes in a heavy plain pink material; the use of decorative fabric is repeated on the bedspread and with the floral print of the bed-linen. Every object has been chosen for its traditional dignity – the gilt mirror, table lamps, silver boxes and candlestick, old polished wood tables and a small, ornamental wall table below the mirror carrying an antique china dog and a small print of a cherub.

2   This cottage bedroom has matching sprigged wallpaper and blinds and a pleasing design which props the blind away from the window so that it forms an awning over a traditionally styled chest in natural wood finish.

1

2

3

4

3 The recessed window in an old cottage has been used to create a pleasant study area in a bedroom where the view can be appreciated. By choosing a table which fits the recess, the work area is clearly defined, flooded by natural light during the day and lit by a simple table lamp at night. The floral curtains are in keeping with the cottage atmosphere and frame the area attractively.

4 Roman blinds in plain white cotton give a fresh clean style to windows. They are not formal or fussy but provide a neat finish to the room, particularly where there is a large expanse of windows. The blinds gather, when raised, into large folds and, when lowered, look similar to roller blinds detailed with battens. The white backdrop against which the bedspread, the greenery of the plants and the leafy garden beyond can be viewed provides texture and colour. Blinds are used in the same way as the plain white carpet and walls.

More than in any other room of the house, lighting in the bedroom must be specific. You need light for reading, for dressing, for applying make-up – and a single overhead general light will not do the task. Most people buy bedside reading lights, usually a pair of standard table lamps with a white paper shade, perhaps pleated or border-trimmed, whose deflecting cone shape casts a wider light. Some beds have built-in reading lights attached to the headboard which save reaching out for cords and switches. Or two overhead wall lights can be fixed at the top two corners of the bed, each with its own switch, and angled to illuminate the page. Make sure you attach any such light high enough so that it does not pose a hazard for someone sitting up in bed. Some of the newest low-voltage halogen lights which burn brightly for hours from a single small bulb are so tiny that they can fit on to a book page, a bedside tray or on to a headboard clamp.

Another area which requires specific lighting is the mirror. This is notoriously difficult, and is hardly solved by the traditional manufacturers' inclusion of a strip fluorescent light above vanity mirrors. Actors' dressing rooms have naked bulbs ringed around the mirror, which light the sides of the mirror and reflect a more flattering appearance.

## BEDROOM LAMPS

Solid brass wall light with
swinging arm and paper shade

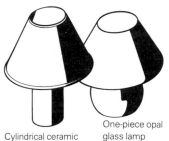

Cylindrical ceramic
lamp

One-piece opal
glass lamp

Polished brass
wall bracket

Spring-clamp lamp can
clip on to book or shelf

Unshaded opaque round wall lights

1 White on white classic bed-linen decorated with lace and embroidery and a bedspread with a woven pattern is highlighted under a low-level table light at night. The windows and walls are unified with matching wallpaper and fabric for the blind, co-ordinated by the green window frame and matching trim to the blinds.

2 In a very simple room, a pair of brass and glass wall lights provide reading light as well as general illumination for the room. They are a feature in themselves because of the prominence they are given by the bare walls. It is important to consider whether a light fitting is to be a prominent feature in a room because it must then work in harmony with other objects. These lights are well matched by the painting in a wooden frame and the wooden side table.

3 In this artist's bedroom a very special shade of blue has been used on the walls and in the choice of fabric for the curtains. It is warm rather than cool and gives an inviting glow to the room when lit by a small bedside lamp.

A child's room may require many special features: open floor space for games; built-in worktops for homework and crafts; adjustable shelves; good lighting; washable, durable surfaces; sturdy beds that can survive the transition from crib to open bed; stacking bunks or trundle beds for shared rooms.

Beds for young children need firm mattresses that are lightweight and washable, such as foam blocks. Webbed slats offer a suitable, ventilated, inexpensive bed base – lightweight, too, for stacking bunks. For a baby, you can find a big cot with detachable slatted drop sides which converts into a single bed. If you start with a standard cot, upgrade to stacking bunks, since children usually enjoy having friends to stay overnight. A Continental quilt and fitted bottom sheet supply an easy-care bedding option: polyester-filled Continental quilts are washable and non-allergenic. When choosing the bed-linen and wall coverings for a child's room, resist the temptation to launch a theme bedroom that its occupant will outgrow sooner than you intend to redecorate. Parents' enthusiasm for sci-fi or cartoon characters may not be matched by the child's, so provide plain walls on which they can place their own decorations.

Walls should be finished with washable paint rather than wallpaper, since few small children can resist the temptation to peel off paper. Posters can be replaced as interests change.

Firm base flooring must be tough and smooth. Stained and sealed floorboards make a good surface for games, as does the heavy-duty cord carpet which is bathroom-rated to withstand splashes. Scratchy but durable floor coverings like jute or cork are appropriate for a teenager's bedroom.

Space is important for people of all ages: play-pens for toddlers, play areas for school-age children, work space for older ones and room for teenagers to entertain. Folding chairs stack away to clear the floor. Rather than investing in special wardrobes for children's clothes, many of which do not need to hang, find good toy and equipment storage systems which will keep toys tidy but accessible.

Learning through sight and sound is basic to this generation so do not underestimate the wiring requirements: supply enough sockets for a television (which doubles as a VDU for the home computer), a video recorder beneath the television, a music centre or stereo, a radio, a clock and any lighting required for work areas. Ensure that all wall sockets have safety shields to prevent a toy, or worse, a finger being experimentally fed in. For electronic equipment to work in harmony and look good, allow for space to house records, tapes and computer gear and a means to keep the tangle of wires under control. There are many alternatives, from purpose-built desks to trolleys for moving the television to the computer keyboard when it is needed as a Visual Display Unit.

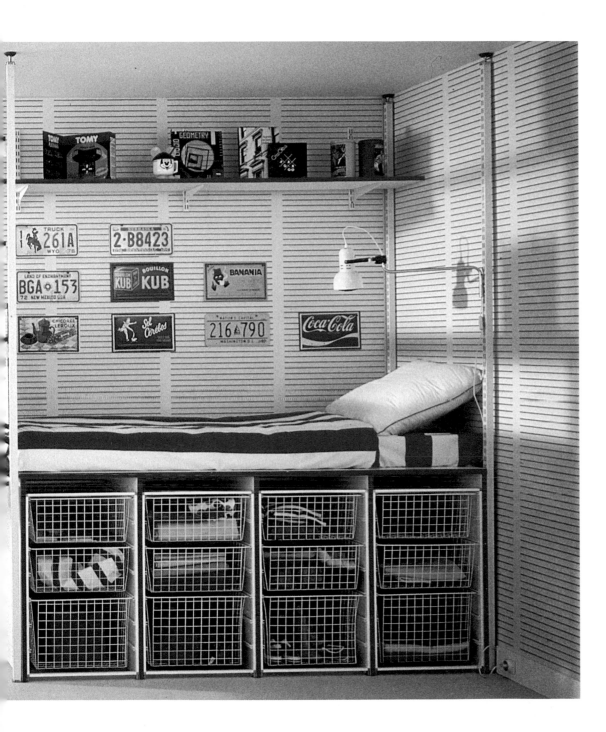

## SAFETY CHECKLIST

- Enclose exposed radiator panels with fireguards.
- Never keep portable heaters or fires in a child's room.
- Use wall-mounted lights in a toddler's room.
- Shield all socket outlets with safety covers.
- Use reinforced thick panes in low-level windows.
- Remove keys from any locks on nursery doors.
- Fit a gate or barrier to restrict access to staircases.
- Select fire-retardant materials for soft furnishings and mattresses.
- Find sturdy, stable furniture without sharp edges or splinters.
- Free-standing furniture likely to topple if pushed or pulled should be bolted to the wall.
- Baby chairs or bouncers must stand on the floor, never on a tabletop.
- Fit a safety rail across an under-five-year-old's bed.
- Top bunk beds need a safety rail and a ladder bolted on.
- Any painted surfaces should be washable, durable and lead-free.

*Although this bedroom is small, it appears spacious because of the wallpaper in white with fine red lines, open wire baskets and red detailing on shelf edges. The biggest single block of colour lies on the bed with broad vertical and horizontal bands of scarlet and white.*

The nursery is the one room where purpose-built furniture is needed, possibly for as little as four years. So there is an advantage to be gained in buying furniture systems that are designed to make the transition from babyhood to toddler with your child, matching changes in both size and needs. The nursery has to house the crib or cot, the child-size wardrobe, pint-size desks and chairs, and toys. Storage systems must be tidy yet easily accessible to the child. Avoid furniture that topples or is too cumbersome.

1   In this spacious nursery, maximum floor space is freed for play, with sanded and sealed floorboards left plain to provide a smooth area. It is more practical for the small child who often plays on hands and knees than prickly jute or unevenly furry carpet. Blocks of foam covered in starry fabric provide alternative seating and impromptu housing, while the little yellow tubular steel chairs pull up at low-level desks. Open stacking boxes that will not topple house childish amusements against the wall, while the same shapes in deeper boxes are given a base and used for toys, to stack away at the end of the day. The same furniture system adapts from babyhood to the toddler's bedroom.

1

2

3

4

## MAKING A TOY STORAGE BOX

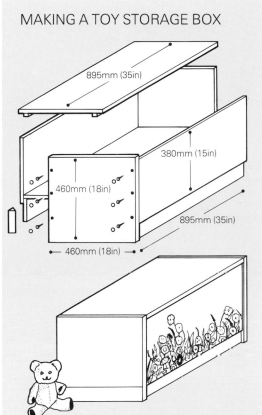

895mm (35in)

380mm (15in)

460mm (18in)

895mm (35in)

460mm (18in)

This toy chest is easy to make from panels of plywood or blockboard, or any sheet material which can be drilled and screwed. **1** Cut four side panels to the dimensions indicated in the drawing, making sure to cut them squarely. **2** Mark and drill screw holes as illustrated. **3** Glue and screw the side panels into place. Check diagonals for squareness. **4** Cut four bottom bearer pieces from a piece of wood. Glue and screw into the corners of the side panels. **5** Cut the bottom piece to fit and glue in place, resting on top of the bottom bearers. **6** Cut the lid to fit, allowing for the top edge of the side panels at each end. Mark hinge-fixing holes, drill and screw hinges into place. **7** Decorate the box with bright paint and adhesive cut-outs.

2 The cot, cupboard and small changing area above the wardrobe offer all the requirements of a nursery: a safe and protected sleep area, somewhere to store clothes behind closed doors and an open shelving system for quick access that supports a plastic-covered foam block for changing and bathing the baby. The heavy-duty flat weave cord carpet is rated suitable for bathrooms since it can withstand splashing.

3 Once the slatted sides from the drop-side cot are removed permanently, the cot becomes a bed. Without its foam top, the worktop is transformed into a practical desk, and the storage system pulls out to become a bedside table that holds the books. The stool swivels to different heights as the child grows.

4 Since the furniture in this nursery is not adaptable, it is feasible to decorate it with stick-on cartoon characters and stencils that an older child will outgrow around the same time as the furniture. Toys are tidied away into the big lidded wicker basket.

*Beds take up a lot of space in the child's room where floor area is at a premium. There are many solutions, ranging from the stacking bunk bed to the platform bed above a cupboard, shelves and worktop. Stacking beds are invaluable when young children share a room, or invite friends home. But such beds need to be shelved when the child is between ten and twelve, so those that separate into two are useful.*

1 This room, shared by two brothers, will grow up with them, though they need not grow apart when the beds do. Easily changed into two singles, the bunk bed does not have a base that is too weighty. A webbing roll or wooden slats will support a light but firm foam base, covered with fitted sheets and the easy-care Continental quilt. Stacking boxes on castors for bed-linen or toys can fit underneath the bed. Here, fabric pockets pinned on the wall provide extra storage for lightweight possessions.

2 In this ship-shape bedroom, the platform sleeping area is reached by a ladder built into a structural wooden frame with muslin drapes like sails above. The modular unit comprises storage shelves with sliding doors like those in a ship's cabin. Lights are suspended on chains, alongside a yacht.

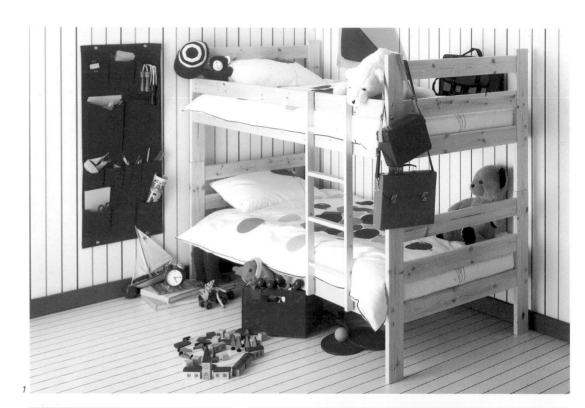

1

2                3

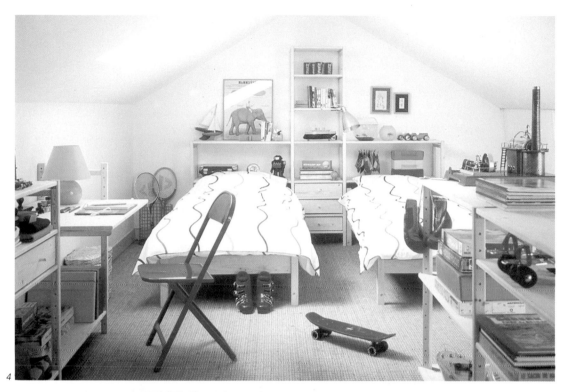

3 This custom-built stacked bed offers space below for a worktop area, with cupboard and bookshelves, and a ladder. Children's cupboards can waste space since their clothes are much smaller and hanging rails should be set lower than usual.

4 A shared room that allows for differing interests, from tennis and skiing to skate-boarding and model-building, even goldfish-minding. With so many divergent interests, lots of work and storage space is essential. It has to be adaptable. The pine shelving system has adjustable pegs to support shelves at differing heights. The addition of a laminated top makes a simple but workmanlike desk. Jute flooring at this stage in a child's development is fine since it offers a practical, hard-wearing surface at a stage when the occupants have stopped playing on their knees and need worktops and shelving.

5 The children who share this playroom have separated a stacking bunk bed into two sofabeds – the peg top at each corner of the bed reveals its origins. A fitted base sheet and patterned cushions like bolsters make these beds into daytime sofas for listening to music and talking to friends, while bulky Continental quilts are stacked in the centrally placed blue blanket box.

*As the child moves towards his teens, basic furniture and furnishings need to allow for individuality. Now the child's personality can be imprinted upon the space, and personal tastes are reflected in the possessions. These are rooms for single occupancy – no longer shared with siblings.*

1   An attic bedroom has a treasury of portraits, both photographic and painted, even postcards, framed and hung like a Victorian collection. An old washstand is given a fake marble top of adhesive paper. Other theatrical touches include the embroidered shawl draped over the bentwood chair, the collection of film star pictures, a ceramic bust and a dressmaker's model. The cast-iron brass bed dressed with a plain white antique lace and crochet cover and old crochet pillow slips gives this room an 'olde worlde' charm.

2   This splendid iron bed has enclosed sides to stop the small child from falling out. Now the occupant is older, that safety frame painted blue becomes a trellised frame for soft toys. In the small alcove behind the bed an unusual collection of costumed dolls of many nations gains importance. So a simple space, as small as a child's bed, doubles up by day as a display case for the child's interests and hobbies.

## SUPPORT SYSTEMS FOR SHELVES

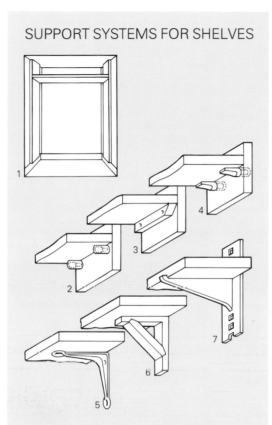

**1** Strips of wood 12-18mm (½-¾in) thick fixed to the walls can support short shelving systems. Shelves are supported at each end. **2** Holes can be drilled into upright wooden standards for metal or plastic dowels which act as shelf end supports. **3** Narrow 25mm (1in) battens screwed into upright standards also act as shelf end supports. **4** Long plastic- or rubber-sleeved screws make decorative end supports for glass shelves, which are particularly effective for displaying houseplants in window bays. **5** Pressed steel brackets are strong enough to support heavy weights when used along the length of a shelf, rather than at the ends. **6** Home-made triangular wooden brackets are suitable for areas such as sheds or garages. **7** Wall-mounted bars with special slot-in brackets form a flexible, adjustable shelving system (see page 31 for installation instructions).

3 New angles on a bedroom where even the wall surfaces are banded geometrically in eau-de-Nil upon white, delineated with a border. Broad bands of these colours are used in the bedspread. The outline of the simple white modern bed is softened with a very tall drape, simple to attach to a coronet or ring fixed to the wall, with the fabric stapled round it. A specially designed corner storage unit takes full advantage of double display windows to house a collection of toys.

4 Bridging the gap between childhood and teens is a furniture system that is flexible, neither too babyish nor too grown up. Here are some basics which can adapt to individual tastes and spaces. A simple wooden desk that can be tilted to become a draughtsman's slanted worktop has a pegboard back to the desktop on which work can be posted and which stops pencils and books from falling off if the desk is not placed against a wall. A screen that is also a blackboard provides a foldaway partition for a work area; a painted trunk offers storage space for clothes; bins house games and artists' materials. Simple wooden poles, fitted with pegs that adjust, hold shelves at varying heights as well as wardrobe rails and drawers.

1 Until now, platform beds featured in children's rooms have been adventure playgrounds reached by rope ladders and rigging. Now, the platform bed in a teenager's bedroom uses stacking boxes at the right height for records and books as a base for an informal bed. The mattress is covered in a zany colourful print, with solid colour cushions scattered upon it to form the backrest. Black framed prints propped against the wall, and two simple tables with solid acrylic tops, in primary colours, provide practical surfaces. The little slanted bedside lamp uses a low-voltage halogen bulb to give an intense beam of light for bedside reading.

2 A bed frame of tubular chrome clamps together in various combinations. Here, a bed raised upon a platform base has the bed area delineated above with a netting top while the clamped side sections form a desktop for the screen and computer keyboard. A scarlet tractor-seat stool provides simple seating. The only other item of furniture is the black lacquer trolley which can bring a TV screen nearer the keyboard, or house the video. Bed lighting is provided by spotlights which clamp on to the tubular frame.

1

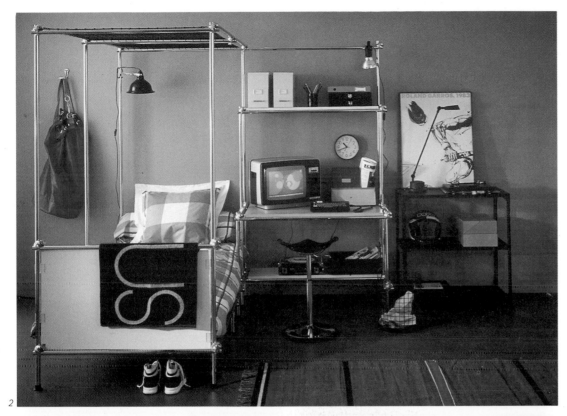

3 The privacy of an alcove retreat is achieved very simply with wooden battens fixed to the ceiling to which curtains are stapled. The room, painted pale yellow to that point, becomes a peaceful pale grey in the alcove. The bedding is an ikat flat-weave quilted counterpane which determines the colours for the pink, green and blue cushions. Beyond the screen, the work area is delineated by a roll-top desk. The work table slides back to be concealed beneath the top. An angled floor lamp throws light where it is needed most.

4 Just as the last room was a peaceful retreat, this room is a vigorous, imaginative area. At the base is a bed, above it another floor, the awning shielding the playhouse area. Within the basic framework there is endless opportunity for imagination; areas can become a crow's nest aboard a ship, look-out posts, or camps. More practically, within the framework is incorporated a rail for clothes — and Kermit the frog.

*Wall-mounted or surface-mounted lights are recommended for children's bedrooms since lights are easily knocked over in pillow fights or any rumbustious activity. But the new low-voltage lights set into lightweight plastic fittings can withstand knocks without shocks. They are fun as well as functional. Many of them can be left on all night in rooms where children are unsure about sleeping in the dark. Adequate lighting at worktop areas should be provided from special clamp-on lamps that alter position as required, since young eyes are easily strained. In teenagers' bedrooms you will need lots of socket outlets for hair driers, record players, computers and televisions.*

1 *Balloons tethered to the wall: their strings are the leads which link the low-voltage bulbs with the socket outlet.*

2 *Small children's favourite, the windmill, in a simple paper shade that conceals a small bulb. The lead is concealed in the stick-like lamp base.*

3 *Lights encased in durable plastic trainer shoes are low voltage so it matters little if they topple over as here, in this studied set piece.*

4 *A paper bag filled with toy cut-outs becomes a 'carry home' night light for small children.*

1

2

3

4

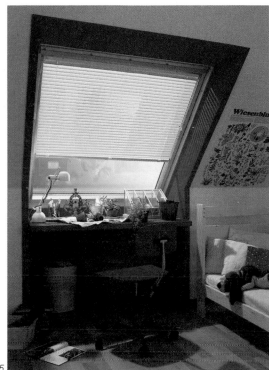

5

6

7

8

Windows often enable a desk to take advantage of natural daylight and window treatments should take note of this.

5 A skylight in an attic bedroom painted scarlet has a smart red worktop built underneath. Venetian blinds screen it.

6 More scarlet frames, this time at a modern window where the printed fabric is stiffened with a roller blind kit, set simply at the window. With such a bold children's print, it is worth keeping the window treatment simple.

7 Trompe-l'oeil wall paintings in a children's room can look marvellous. But often the child wearies of the scene, or outgrows the parents' enthusiasm for Mickey Mouse or space-age fantasies. A simpler way to inject individualism into a room, as well as mask a tiresome inner-city view of buildings, is to paint a roller blind. Or, as here, use metallic paint in high gloss upon Venetian blinds.

8 A novel idea is to dress the window with muslin drapes pleated at the heading and attached by painted pegs to a flattened batten. The desk on crayon legs, designed by Frenchman Pierre Sala, has a lift-up laminated top attached by spiral ring-binder clips, with a drawing pad as its base.

# BATHROOMS

More than any other room, the bathroom is the place to pamper yourself, even though warm, pleasurable bathrooms often must be planned in tiny spaces. It is the skimpiest room in the modern house; the average bathroom built today measures just 1.5m × 2m (5ft × 7ft). A standard 1.5m (5ft) bath fits snugly along one wall and is usually 76cm (2½ft) wide, effectively squeezing the basin and toilet into the remaining 1.37m (4½ft) of the abutting wall. Planning a bathroom in a space the size of a closet is a real challenge.

There is limited scope for individuality in bathroom design since the room contains the least flexible of all household items – the bath, basin and toilet, rigid objects which conform to a basic shape. Interior designers and architects relieve this uniformity in many ways, often by introducing different surface finishes, such as plain or patterned ceramic tiles, various paint finishes, tongue-and-groove wood panelling, laminates, mirrors, marble, plastics and many more.

If you are planning a completely new bathroom you have far more opportunity than if you are redecorating an existing one. A visit to bathroom dealers' showrooms, where baths, basins, toilets and other fittings are displayed in room sets, will help you envisage the impact of the various styles available. Consider them in relation to your bathroom: will a boldly coloured suite make your space look smaller? Will ultra-modern fittings blend well in an older building?

With the measurements and specifications of the fittings you like, work out how you can place them in your bathroom. The lay-out must follow basic plumbing and electrical wiring considerations, so seek expert advice as soon as possible. Allow for safety and comfort when placing the fittings, and check that the floor will support the weight of heavy fittings, such as old-fashioned cast-iron bath tubs.

Just because the bathroom is the smallest room in the house there is no need for it to be the dullest. Patterned and coloured surfaces will bring the room to life. Adding a co-ordinated range of bathroom accessories – soap dish, toothbrush holder, cupholder, shelf, medicine cabinet, toilet-roll holder, framed mirror, towel rail, wastepaper basket, laundry basket – can brighten and unify an existing bathroom. Remember too that bathroom linens – towels, face cloths and shower curtains – can be used to great effect.

## PLANNING CHECKLIST

- How many people use the bathroom?
- Are any users young or elderly?
  *Provide non-slip surfaces, easy access to lights and mirrors, hand-grip baths.*
- Do you have room for a full bath?
  *If not, consider a corner bath, deep-soak tub or shower.*
- Will the shower head be at least 1m (3¼ft) below the water tank base?
  *If not, install a pump.*
- Is it necessary to move the toilet?
  *Re-site it as close as possible to existing soil pipes to save money.*
- Do you want to install a bidet?
  *It is cheaper to install an over-rim bidet than a rim supply model.*
- Are shaver sockets out of reach from the bath?
- Is there good general, as well as directional, light?
- Are light fixtures operated by either a pullcord switch or a remote switch next to the door?
- Is the bathroom overcrowded?
  *Relieve the pressure by adding:*
  - separate toilet
  - bedroom
  - alcove shower
  - wash basin

*Bold bathrooms need not be expensively fitted. This dramatic chequerboard pattern is easy to reproduce with cheap tiles. Use graph paper to pace out the measurements and changes in pattern, and work from the centre outwards.*

*1  A porcelain roll-top bath left
free-standing, like an old-
fashioned hot tub, next to an
elegant basin. These traditional
fittings, reproduced today, do
not attempt to conceal the
plumbing, so the pipes that
lead to the taps are often left
on view. In this plain white
bathroom, central wall-
mounted taps with concealed
plumbing give an uncluttered
effect. Elegant chromed legs
support a wall-mounted basin
with fine chromed towel rails
at each side. The clean lines of
the contemporary fittings –
wall mirror above the basin,
shaving mirror clamped to the
bath and small table with
perspex surround – distinguish
the background. The narrow
blue edge bordering the large
wall tiles and bonsai tree
provide splashes of colour and
points of interest in an
otherwise bare background
which offsets the strong
shapes of the basin and bath.*

1

## FITTING A BATH PANEL

Traditional baths made from enamelled cast iron are
undoubtedly durable and handsome, but the high cost and
weight of cast iron make it an impractical choice for most
bathrooms. Modern baths made from a variety of materials,
usually either moulded acrylic sheet or cast perspex sheeting
reinforced with glass fibre with a vitreous enamel finish, are
lightweight, chip-proof and, because they retain heat, energy-
saving. The matching side panels supplied with many baths
are intended to fit the maximum installed size, but these can
easily be cut to fit the height of the bath as installed.

**1** Fix a 12mm (½in) plinth
within a line drawn on the
floor below the bath rim.

**2** Fit edge of panel under lip
of bath, noting where it
contacts the plinth.

2

2 *A more luxurious treatment for the same small bathroom is to have it entirely panelled with a practical spatter-effect laminate. It creates a blue haze attractive for contrasting contemporary fittings: a very plain white rectangular bath and elaborate burnished chrome basin both boxed in the same laminate. A heated tubular steel towel rail and a small glass-topped table look good with the 1930s-style metal fittings for taps, soap, splashbacks and basin. The laminate is used to make a recessed panel behind the bath and a fitted unit which provides useful shelving for storage of towels and bottles under the basin.*

**3** If the panel is too long, trim a section from the wall end.

**4** Push panel edge firmly under bath lip and screw bottom edge to plinth.

**5** Place end panels in position before front panels using same method.

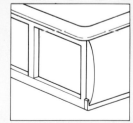

**6** Fit panels to baths with timber frames by fixing plinth to bottom batten.

*Space planning in bathrooms needs careful consideration: they are statistically the smallest room in the house, yet contain certain bulky fittings which, when plumbed in, become fixtures. There are certain essentials which cannot be altered and must be taken into consideration before planning starts: the bulky shapes of the ceramic ware and a water source with adequate inlet pressure and outlet drainage. The bath is the first consideration since it is so bulky. Corner baths free floor space, as do rectangular baths set flush against a wall. A free-standing bath, on the other hand, can be used to partition space. In a tiny bathroom, the easiest solution is to line up the sanitary ware against the outside wall. Various combinations are offered here. By the time a full-size bath tub shower, basin, toilet and bidet have been installed, even the best-planned bathroom can begin to seem cluttered. Choose one of the lighter shades of sanitary ware if the room is small, to create an illusion of space, and consider matching wall and floor tiles.*

## THE COMPACT BATHROOM

This compact bathroom is designed to be built into a walk-in cupboard, although the plan would do as well for an impossibly tiny bathroom. Within a meagre 1830mm × 1830mm (6ft × 6ft) space, all the basic products are plumbed in, and an allowance is made for the opening of the bathroom door, which cuts a 915mm (3ft) swathe through the room.

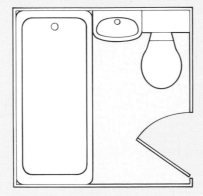

This space-saving bathroom contains everything required in a 2285mm × 2285mm (7½ft × 7½ft) room. A shower over the bath cuts hot water consumption – an important consideration in these days of energy conservation – and the bidet is sited in the best possible place, next to the toilet, for ease of use.

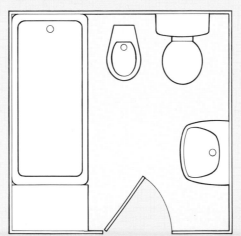

## ROOM FOR IMPROVEMENT

**BEFORE**
A large bathroom is wasted when everyone squabbles over who is to use it first.

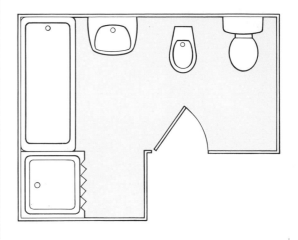

**BEFORE**
It can make good sense to combine separate facilities in one room.

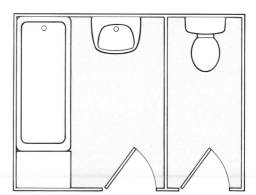

**AFTER**

A bathroom which contains the sole household toilet is far from ideal. If there is no space or budget allowance to add a second bathroom, dividing a large bathroom with a partition wall into two separate areas can be the best solution. In this conversion, one room is reserved for bathing and the other self-contained room houses a toilet, bidet and small hand basin. The original room had two windows, but when dividing a room with one window, remember to allow for adequate ventilation.

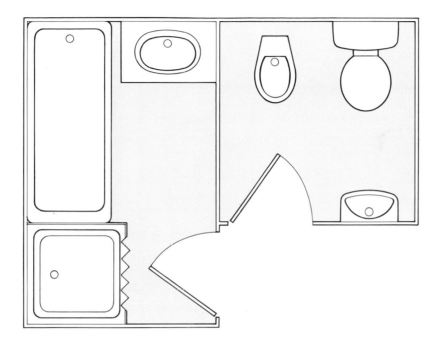

*When you have managed to squeeze the essentials into your existing bathroom, whether large or small, it is not uncommon to find that no additional amenities can get around the perennial problem of morning-time congestion when there is only one bathroom to serve a large family. Take a good look round the house, remembering that a toilet or a shower occupies very little space. If a cupboard under the stairs serves as a refuge for outdoor clothing or cleaning equipment, perhaps the space could be put to better use as a mini-shower room complete with toilet and small wash basin, as illustrated below. Such a conversion would require special plumbing, but the expense and trouble could be well worth it. A windowless bathroom created underneath a staircase or in a closet should be ventilated by a fan which comes on automatically.*

**AFTER**

Removing a wall and a door has opened out this bathroom. Without moving the toilet there is now room for a double 'his and hers' wash basin to cope with the morning rush, and space for the bidet. This solution is not recommended for the large, one-toilet household. For a small family, however, or in a home with a second toilet, combining the spartan toilet and the separate bathroom creates a large, luxurious room. Now there is room for another product, whether a bidet or a shower, or even a comfortable easy chair.

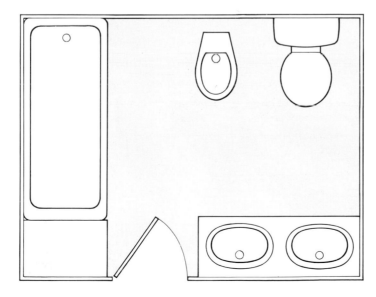

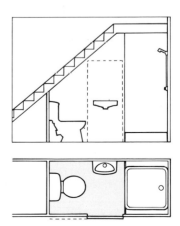

Your choice of bath needs careful consideration to fit the space since it is the bulkiest fixture. If the bathroom already installed is not to your taste, either in colour or shape, consider decorative treatments around the bath.

1  Corner baths can wedge neatly into a room. Here, an awkwardly shaped semi-circular bay has a corner bath — and a modern, sculptural slim-line basin. The triptych mirror with arched tops is similarly geometric in its angles and curves, centrally placed for display. Slabs of white marble — reproduced in look-alike Corian — give this elegant bathroom its luxurious finish.

2  Whatever it is called — 'Champagne', 'Savannah' or 'Pampas' — the beige bath is anonymous. It is more difficult to use since it lacks individuality. Plain white goods are easier; so, too, are the more emphatic colours. Here the bath is given distinction by the white glossy surface surrounds and Art Deco styling, always outlined in black, with the mirror and palms and sandalwood boxes.

3  A free-standing roll-top cast-iron tub, placed centrally in a room, makes a feature of the plumbing. The pipes are brass and the six graphic paintings are all framed in brass.

1

2

3

## BASIC BATHS

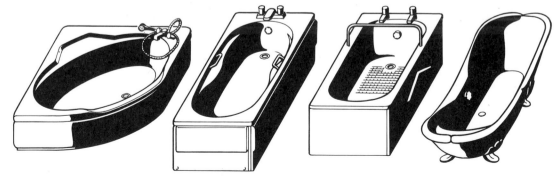

Corner bath

Contoured bath with hand grips

Bath with support rail and grip base

Traditional claw foot bath

4

5

6

## FITTING A SHOWER SCREEN

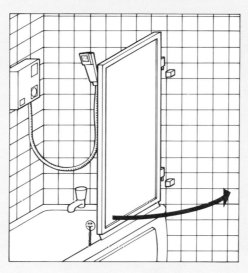

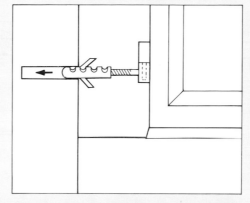

**1** Position the screen on the top rim of the bath. Ensure that it is held vertically and that the bottom flipper makes an adequate seal on the bath edge. **2** Mark the position of the hinges on the wall, drill holes with a 7mm (¼in) bit, making the hole deeper than the plug. **3** Fit the plug into the wall and screw the cup into the plug. **4** Drop the screen into position. **5** To align the bottom flipper with the bath rim, simply adjust the cups.

4 *Here, a centrally placed bath in a large room acts as a partition between bedroom and dressing room. Curtains on rods suspended from the ceiling close off the area, providing privacy for this unusual lay-out and creating an impromptu bathroom.*

5 *Striped lavender wallpaper visually extends the height of this small bathroom, while the horizontal stripes of louvred shutters appear to widen what is, in fact, the narrowest wall. The bath is similarly deceptive, creating more space than a block of solid colour would, though the basin is grey. Even the space in the corner is used with a wicker storage unit housing mementoes of seaside holidays.*

6 *This panelled bath disguises the workings of a whirlpool bath with controls that vary the intensity of the water jets. Sloping walls of the attic bathroom are useful in the bath area where the occupant need never stand up, while the shower section moves forward into the room for greater height. The boxed-in partition wall at the back creates a small step-in shower behind glass doors.*

*Planners recommend installing a built-in pump to boost water pressure. With the right rose and a booster pump aerating the water, it can feel as luxurious as if you were showering with champagne.*

1 *Here, a round deep tub is reached by a tiered platform, tiled in white. The basin has the same lines. At the foot of the hot tub, a shower cubicle is glassed in behind doors. In this confined area, the use of tiles, mirrors and glass creates an impression of spaciousness.*

2 *The central triangular pillar houses the water pipes and booster pump for this shower. Variations in floor level height are minimized by the use of narrow tiles, varying in scale from the wall tiles. Both the round mirror and the bulkhead light give a ship-shape finish to the bathroom.*

3 *This tailor-made shower cubicle is added to the base of a panelled bath which is set on a long wall. Tongue-and-groove panelling with a matt varnish finish increases the sauna feeling, as does the step up into the shower above the skirting. You can build your own cubicle around a shower tray or buy pre-fabricated cubicles complete with tray, back panel, sides and doors.*

1

## SHOWER TRAYS AND HEADS

Shower trays

Sliding and pivoting shower heads

Edwardian bath mixer

4 A cast-iron roll-top bath becomes a walk-in hot tub, evoking a Japanese interior with its wooden platform leading simply to the central tub. Pipes and taps set in the wooden panelling like a screen against the wall add to this illusion. At the window is a tatami grass reed woven blind, much wider than the window.

5 An alternative shower fitted above a bath has been created by boxing in an area in the awkwardly shaped bay with low partition walls, which house the taps and inlet water pipes. This type of shower uses water directly from the mains, which is heated by a small instant heater fitted close to the shower behind the tiled panel. As the water temperature increases, the shower water pressure may decrease.

2

3

4

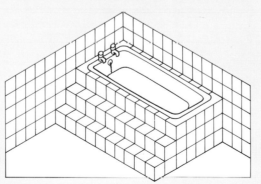

5

## MAKING A SUNKEN BATH

Steps leading to a raised and tiled area around the tub create the impression of a simple sunken bath. A bath filled with water and a person is very heavy, so place boards beneath levelling feet to spread the load over the floorboards.

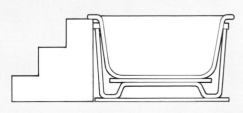

Toilets need to be set against the outer wall for access to soil waste. Modern toilets are usually made with one of two sorts of flushing mechanisms: wash-down or syphonic systems, both found in many styles. This cistern may fit to the back of the bowl without any visible connection, or may be hidden, along with the pipes in ducted units, behind removable panels or wall-hung systems.

1  This wall-hung toilet has a steel cistern set above like a wall safe of burnished steel. Concealed ducts are hidden in the tiled wall. This syphonic model is quieter than the flushing mechanism of the wash-down toilet.

2  Neater, more stylish, this close-coupled toilet is a favourite for modern apartments. It features a cistern that fits directly to the back of the bowl without any connecting pipe. Here, the room achieves an Oriental simplicity with parchment blinds outlined in charcoal.

1

2

3

## TOILETS AND BIDETS

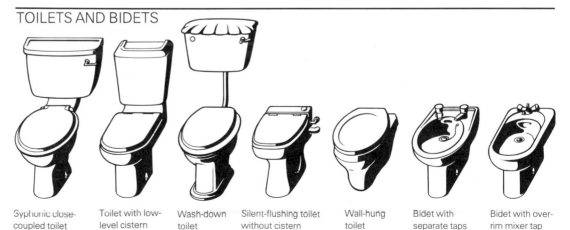

Syphonic close-coupled toilet

Toilet with low-level cistern

Wash-down toilet

Silent-flushing toilet without cistern

Wall-hung toilet

Bidet with separate taps

Bidet with over-rim mixer tap

4

3 *The least expensive, wash-down, plain white sanitary ware is elevated by more expensive fittings – the platform floor that raises this section of the bathroom and the low-level shelving. It acts as a storage system as well as shielding this area.*

4 *This back-to-the-wall toilet cistern with matching bidet is separated by a low-level wall structured to screen only at sitting height. On most bidet models you sit facing the wall, so there should be enough room for knees. Some bidets are fitted with an ascending spray in their base: bidet mixer taps may also incorporate a spray. This model has wall-mounted taps, surely an encouragement to face the right way. Water comes into a bidet either through over-rim supply from basin-like taps, or heated rim mixer taps which control the temperature of the water coming into the filling from the rim.*

## INSTALLING A BIDET

Over-rim bidets are plumbed in exactly the same way as wash basins. In most cases, this means branching off pipes which supply other bathroom equipment. Always ensure that the position of the bidet allows plenty of room at the back for properly connecting the waste pipe. If possible, site it next to a toilet. Before fixing the bidet, do as much plumbing as possible. Connect the waste pipe to a hopper or soil stack. Fix the taps, which can be two single taps or a 100mm (4in) basin mixer tap. Finally, secure the bidet to the floor using carefully tightened brass screws.

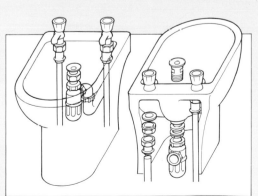

Basins come in many shapes and sizes. The two standard sizes are 455mm × 635mm (18in × 28in) and 405mm × 560mm (16in × 22in), while the shapes are oval, rectangular, square or circular. There are three main types of basin: pedestal, wall-hung and built-in. The base for a basin built into a countertop, which can be a standard self-assembly or custom-built unit, always provides storage. Variations on these three main types are illustrated here.

1   Wall-hung basins are usually set at a height of 815mm (32in) from floor to rim, though this height can vary. The basin is usually provided with an additional means of support, as here. A cross bar between supports provides a useful towel rail.

2   The pedestal basin has a central support stem which partly conceals plumbing. Here, the ceramic detailing suggests an earlier age, as does the shaped ceramic splashback that is a part of the basin top. Accessories are in mahogany and brass with cross-head taps to keep to the turn-of-the-century theme.

## BASIC WASH BASINS

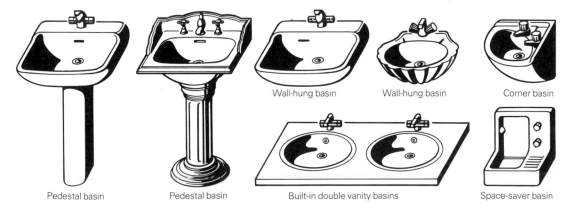

Pedestal basin

Pedestal basin

Wall-hung basin

Wall-hung basin

Corner basin

Built-in double vanity basins

Space-saver basin

3 *A slimline hand basin, too small for hair-washing, is ideal for this tiny bathroom planned in a cupboard. Shower mixer heads added to the bath bring a shower as well to this area.*

4 *In a long, narrow bathroom a double basin housed in a custom-built worktop breaks up the corridor-like space. The basin backdrop is the narrow line-up of vertical panes of glass. A tangle of creepers provides privacy without any window cover.*

5 *An oval hand basin set into a black tiled worktop has its shape emphasized dramatically. Fine striped muslin curtains cut short to worktop height frame the window which is painted lavender. Attention to detail is important with this sophisticated colour mix of lavender, black and white: even the irises match.*

6 *An oval basin with its own white splashtop area is set into a purpose built worktop tiled in terracotta ceramic tiles and with storage shelves below. The arrangement of mirrors and storage shelves has been designed to make the most of the asymmetrical placement of the basin on the worktop.*

## TAPS AND ACCESSORIES

Basin mixer tap

Basin pillar taps

Basin mixer tap with fixed spout

Basin mixer tap with swivel spout

Accessory set in plastic-coated wire

Cup and toothbrush holder

Towel-hanging ring and rails

Mirrors are essential in any bathroom since the very nature of the room involves shaving, washing, putting on make-up. Most often placed above the basin, mirrors can be found in less likely places as well – beside the bath or lining an entire wall to give the illusion of more space. For large areas of mirror, you need a solid wall, rather than a flimsy partition. Mirrors need to be well lit. Good lighting makes your bathroom more attractive, pleasant and safe to use. Options include wall-mounted surface fittings, the popular bulkhead light, recessed downlighters and diffused fluorescent lighting usually found in battens installed above the mirror or bathroom medicine chest. Whilst it is not the most flattering light, it lasts the longest. Remember, extra light is needed on the front and sides of the mirrors.

1  In practical rooms like bathrooms there is rarely space for any idiosyncrasies to be highlighted. Yet the owner of this bathroom has fixed a mirror to the wall at the right height for shaving while seated in the bath. Centrally placed taps make this feasible. Some other highly individual possessions are housed in this unconventional little bathroom.

3

4

2 *A more conventional treatment is a long mirror edged with a specially designed light fitting above it, like an actor's dressing room mirror. Light is important in this small space – even the windows are not covered but left bare with frosted glass.*

3 *Mirrored panels across the cupboard doors double the images of this tiny bathroom with its white panelled bath, pedestal basin, and special fitment for the bathroom mirror. Yellow striped wallpaper creates an illusory height in the room, and the bold blue and white striped director's chair fits neatly beside the bath for the bathtime supervision of the rubber dinghy launch.*

4 *Navy tiles form a nautical line-up above the red louvred doors of this wash basin unit. Above it the pin board has clips to hold toothmugs and other items. The mirrored panel is lit with a red bulkhead light. Trolleys provide useful trundle-around storage and this scarlet, epoxy-coated wire trolley suits the red, white and blue theme of the bathroom.*

## FITTING MIRROR TILES

**1** Wall surface must be clean, dry and free from flaking paint. Divide wall into quarters by drawing a vertical and a horizontal line across centre. **2** Remove protective wax paper from one side of four pieces of mounting tape and stick them on each corner of the back of a mirror tile about 12mm (½in) from the edge. Press firmly. Remove remaining wax paper and mount the first tile at centre of area where two lines intersect. **3** Work outwards in a horizontal row, filling each quarter section until only tiles which need to be cut remain. **4** Measure distance to be filled and mark measurement on mirror side of a tile. Place on a firm surface and score with a glass cutter. Break in two, then mount as before.

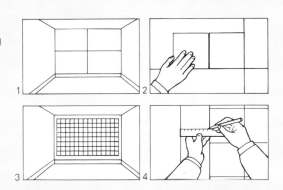

Just because bathroom surfaces have to be tough, waterproof and easy to clean, there is no need to keep them workmanlike. Theatrical backgrounds can be created with tiles, mirrors, paints and borders, as you can discover in the bathrooms illustrated here.

Certainly, in the steamy atmosphere of the bathroom, moisture-proof wall coverings are essential. Coated washable papers or sheeny water-resistant paints are best. Glossy paint shows marks upon its shiny glazed surface, which is fine for small surface detailing, but not so good over large areas.

The new marble look-alike, Corian, is light, durable, easy to batten to the wall and more fashionable than the tongue-and-groove panel boards reminiscent of Scandinavian saunas. Hardwood panels, boarding and marble slabs all share a great advantage, despite their discrepancies in cost and application – they hide the pipes. So do wall units in the fitted bathroom.

Shower walls should be tiled, with a grooved, non-slip floor area. Perspex, shatter-proof glass, tiles or plastic laminate boards can be used to panel the shower.

Ceramic tiles are always popular. Colourful patterned tiles now available can re-create any backdrop, such as an Islamic carpet, a seaside scene or a flowery glade. Floor tiles can be cold in winter, so only use them, with accessible walkways, in a warm bathroom. Water-resistant flooring, like cushioned vinyl, is not slippery. Continuous sheet flooring is more difficult to lay than vinyl tiles in an awkward or irregular space, but the joints between tiles can admit moisture and tiles lift more easily over a duration of time. Cork and duckboard are popular surface finishes for tiles – untreated cork is better than polyurethane-sealed cork. Plastic laminate boards one metre square have become a fashion flooring, despite their cost, since they can reproduce on a smaller scale the dazzling patterns of grand Italian terrazzos, copied from the squares and churches in Rome and Venice. To unify a small space, employ these patterns boldly and use the same surface pattern to cover the bath panels.

If you want to tackle a painted duckboard floor, paint sanded sheets of duckboard with yachting shipdeck paints, seeking inspiration for your design from earlier examples, such as the floor at the Victoria and Albert Museum in London, or the stencilled floorboards of the American Museum in Bath. Begin at the borders to anchor your pattern and set you on the right scale.

Windows can be screened with etched, opaque or stained glass. Stick on your own coloured cellophane paper for mock stained glass – there are kits that reproduce some dazzling patterns from baroque houses and Gothic churches. Consider removing the window panes and replacing them with mirror tiles, which will provide twenty-four-hour privacy and the illusion of space.

The longtime favourites for bathroom surfaces, ceramic tiles, are durable, scrubbable and good-looking. Cushioned vinyl sheeting or tiles now imitate some of the specialized surfaces that once only ceramics could produce. Other options include marble, marble look-alikes such as Corian, and wood, with choice limited to materials resistant to damp and moisture. Today, marble, terracotta or glazed surfaces may look like the real thing, but are cushioned for softness and warmth. Here, plain white tiles in two sizes are teamed with black tiles to create a stylish interior. The chequerboard effect is echoed by the towels. Plan your own scheme in two-tone tiles, plotting out the effect first on graph paper. The tiles may be set on points in a diamond pattern, or used in border patterns round the mirrors, as shown on the following pages.

Spectacular effects can be created with a mosaic of tiles, mixing patterns and colours. Or you can finish off plain tiles with a coloured grout to outline each one in a finely detailed colour that matches or contrasts. Expensive patterned tiles can be used as small details, either as a splashback or as a border edging an area of white tiles.

1 Post-modern pastels in pink, peppermint and citrus yellow are lined up for bold contrasting candy stripes that emphasize various angles in this bathroom. Even the accessories like soap dishes and nail brushes are chosen to match and great attention is given to lighting. A large mirror set above the basin and a gloss paint on the ceiling bounces back light from myriad small starlight downlighters.

2 At the turn of the century, elaborately patterned tiles that evoked Islamic designs were reproduced by the Victorians. Collectors' items today, they can enliven a small base wall at the foot of a plain white bath or be used to form a splashback, as here. The bath is panelled with stained plywood decorated with mouldings and a simple lace curtain screens the area. The colours of cream and ivory with sepia are used round the room.

1

## FIXING CERAMIC TILES

Ceramic tiles are a good choice for bathrooms, where their tough, easy-to-clean and long-lasting surface is both practical and decorative. As with mirror tiles, it is best to begin by measuring the area to be tiled and calculating the number of tiles needed. Successful tiling requires careful planning. Ceramic tiles can be used for almost any bathroom surface – walls, shower compartments, countertops, ceilings and floors – but special considerations apply to using them on bathroom floors. Extra work, and thus extra expense, is likely to be necessary when laying ceramic tiles on a suspended wooden floor. Glazed ceramic tiles are slippery when wet, although unglazed tiles would be suitable for a country-style interior.

**1** Fix a horizontal batten at the height of one tile above the lowest point.

**2** Use a strip of wood marked off in tile lengths to mark the batten.

3 *Tiles need not be laid in regular blocks, square upon square, but may be used in a variety of ways. Here, they are tilted up in diamond-shaped patterns, creating a vigorous trellis of pale blue until the plain white border introduces a frame to the scheme. Art Nouveau detailing forms a painted border to the mirror. Fine blinds at the window keep to the same simplicity, as does the globe light above the vanity mirror.*

4 *Here a dramatic use of Victorian tiles encloses a bath which is divided from the bathroom by a partition. This enables the end of the bath to double as a shower, with the showerhead (not shown) fitted into the wall.*

5 *In the all-white bathroom, or any monochrome room, surface interest is created with texture. Here, the bevelled edge of white tiles inset along bath panels and on walls above the plain white area creates visual interest. Eau-de-Nil painted window frames and glossy cream paint create a period effect, as do the pictures engraved like old etchings and the plain wooden towel rails.*

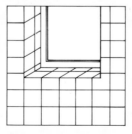

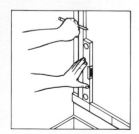
**3** Fix an upright batten, using a spirit level to get a true vertical.

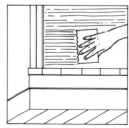
**4** Apply 0.8 sq m (1 sq ft) of adhesive, ridging it with a notched spreader.

**5** Lay tiles in horizontal lines starting from the intersection of battens.

**6** Cut tiles should fill odd spaces at the end of walls and ledges.

Bathroom surfaces must be waterproof, especially the floor. Linoleum is the cheapest practical flooring, with ever-popular cork tiles a close contender. Cushioned vinyl tiles, rubber-stud industrial flooring and ceramic tiles are more expensive alternatives.

1 Tiles with fine graph-paper patterns permit accurate placement of every product and accessory in this bathroom, as well as giving a neatly squared-off precision to the finish. The floor is tiled in dappled vinyl. Mirrored walls, the clear glass-domed shower screen and opaque glass squares panelled in the partition all visually extend the actual space.

2 Cork tiles on the floor and the sides of the panelled bath give a warm glow to this bathroom. The coated spongeable vinyl paper has a small repeat pattern of birds on the wing.

3 Thatch is an unusual choice for a wall surface, yet outside a thatched wall of climbing plants, green in summer and densely vined in winter, provides an impenetrable screen to the shower. White tiles grouted in grey mix with the modern shapes and pale grey ceramics of the basin and shower tray. They bring distinctive elegance to this restrained, unusual bathroom.

1

3

2

## TILES

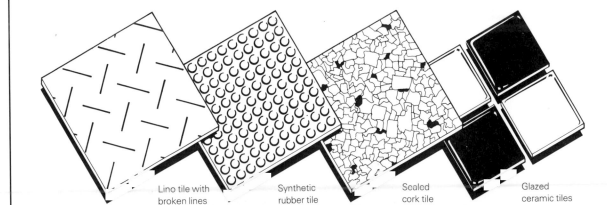

Lino tile with broken lines

Synthetic rubber tile

Sealed cork tile

Glazed ceramic tiles

4

5

6

## SHEET VINYL

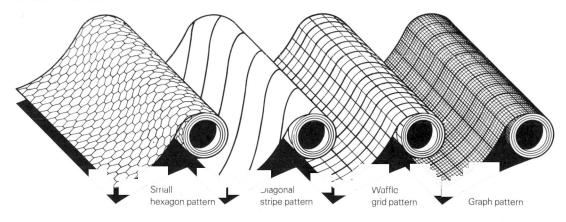

Small
hexagon pattern

Diagonal
stripe pattern

Waffle
grid pattern

Graph pattern

4 Honeycomb-patterned flooring in white appears to push out the boundaries of this small bathroom. With such an emphatic textured floor, changing the wall surface would distance it, so the same surface finish is taken up on the walls in reverse colours of charcoal outlined with white.

5 This linoleum flooring imitates square tiles laid in a diamond pattern. In a bathroom where you have to cut round basin and toilet bases, it is often easiest to use vinyl sheet flooring. Here the blue and white pattern visually extends the eye to the bath panelled in glossy white ceramic tiles and the matt-finish painted wall.

6 This bathroom is designed to show that pattern can work effectively to extend small spaces in appearance: an elegant duo-tone reduces the impact of too many colours, while the use of small-scale patterns reduces the dramatic effect of a grand overall pattern which would visually box in the bathroom. This mosaic of tiny tiles is in reality vinyl sheeting. The walls are tiled in wheaten yellow and the entrance left a silken grey without any distracting detailing outlined in separate colour.

*Warmth is essential in the bathroom, but since electricity and water do not mix, portable electric heaters cannot be considered. Built-in electric heaters placed out of reach and operated by a pull cord are often used, and another effective solution is to have radiators or other systems linked to the heating circuit for the whole house or apartment.*

1 *A heated chrome towel rail which is part of the central heating system looks extremely attractive in this bathroom. The room has a strong style and Victorian atmosphere – double basins set in marble with simple, modern mixer taps; an ornate Victorian mirror; and bare floorboards echoed by the natural wood in the cupboard doors and the stripped window frame with its floral-patterned fabric blind. Since the heated towel rail takes up space where a normal radiator could have been placed, a clever solution for heating has been found in using a slimline skirting board radiator beneath the pine vanity unit. It is effective but discreet.*

1

## BATHROOM SAFETY

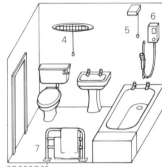

**1** Cord-operated light switch **2** Enclosed lampholder **3** Mirror light with built-in isolated shaver socket **4** Cord-operated, wall-mounted heater **5** Cord-operated, shower heater switch **6** Shower unit connected to separate fuse **7** Heated towel rail wired to fused connection unit outside bathroom

## VENTILATION

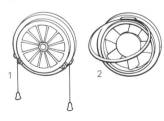

**1** Window ventilator **2** Window ventilator and fan

*2  In this elegant white bathroom each element has been carefully chosen to stand out against the plainest of backgrounds. The basin is a beautiful pedestal; there is lovely old free-standing furniture and two decorative figures stand between the sophisticated brass and glass lights. An old-fashioned, solid, curvy radiator fits into the room perfectly. It also offers plenty of warmth.*

*3  One advantage of leaving the pipes on show in a bathroom is that hot pipes can assist with heating the room. To look attractive, they must be part of the decorative scheme. Otherwise it appears that the pipes are merely badly installed. In this bathroom they are made part of the scheme because of the free-standing traditional claw-footed bath and the old-style basin hung on the wall with its pipes on view. This basin is not only highly attractive to look at, but also practical to use because its built-in back and winged sides prevent water splashing. Hot pipes do not provide sufficient heat for the whole room and are supplemented here by a low-level modern radiator which tucks in neatly below the window.*

# GARDEN DESIGN

The problem with most books on design, and garden design in particular, is that they over-complicate what is essentially a simple subject. What is worse, they attribute to the designer some sort of magic whereby any successful composition is a spontaneous creation. Any designer worth his salt, and gardening is one area where there are many gifted amateurs, knows that a satisfactory result is usually achieved by following a well-tried formula that relies almost entirely on common sense.

For the first-time gardener, this problem can be compounded by keen botanists, horticulturalists and, to a lesser extent, by the media, who tend to be most enthusiastic about the newest blooms, vegetables and plants. The Latin terminology used to name plants can seem at times no more than a confusing way to explain how to grow bigger and duller varieties of plants on which ever more virulent pests survive.

This is not gardening at all, but rather an attitude likely to turn you off the subject for life.

Any small garden is really an extension of the home. The smaller that space the more important intelligent organization becomes. Gardening should not be hard work and you need never be a slave to what is essentially an oasis, particularly if it is set in the heart of a city.

As soon as you stop thinking of your backyard as an alien environment you will quickly be able to realize its full potential. What that potential is really depends on you. The danger in studying gardening books, and glossy magazines is the temptation simply to copy ideas.

Gardens are primarily concerned with personality – your personality – which is precisely why three identical plots will all turn out quite differently. If you approach planning your garden in the same way as any of the rooms inside the house you will not go far wrong. By doing this you will be able to plot circulation patterns, designate sitting areas, screen bad views or enhance good ones. Changes of level will be important, as will the demands of children, toys and pets. Remember the garden has to accept both the ugly and charming so bins, bikes, compost and rubbish will all need somewhere to go.

Take the time to make a careful list of all your requirements, beginning with the items listed at the end of the checklist opposite.

## PLANNING CHECKLIST

- Have you carried out a survey of your garden (see page 243)?
- Are there any features you want to keep? Trees, shrubs, pools, paths, steps, fences, patio, barbecue?
- What sort of boundaries are there, if any? Fence, hedge, wall?
- Are there good or bad views to be emphasized or screened?
- Is there a change of level?
- Do prevailing winds or annoying draughts affect your site?
- How much sun do you get, and for how long, in different areas?
- Have you made a scale plan incorporating all the survey information (see page 244)?
- What is your budget?
- Are you competent at DIY construction?
- How much maintenance are you prepared to undertake?
- Have you listed your requirements? Do you need?
  - water supply
  - outdoor lighting
  - garden furniture
  - power points
  - containers
  - greenhouse
  - patio or deck
  - barbecue
  - shed
  - play areas
  - pool
  - garage

*A garden often has to cater for everything and everybody – paving, paths, plants, pots, pool, lawn, children, pets, storage. This attractive little composition is simple and straightforward and works well for those who use it. The juxtaposition of planting frames the view from the window.*

1 *This cheerful front garden has been designed as much for the pleasure of passers-by as for the private satisfaction of its owners. Many garden owners forget how much others genuinely appreciate their work. Here, maintenance has been kept to a minimum by installing simple brick paving instead of a lawn, which also provides a visual link with the adjoining building. This is matched by the sensible, slanted coping on top of the garden wall. Unfortunately, coping bricks such as these are not always available today.*
*Colour is provided largely by annual plants, petunias and pelargoniums, which spill out of the troughs and beds. Climbing plants soften the house while the two tall conifers on either side of the window add an air of formality.*

2 *Urban backyards can have an undeniable charm and this is the perfect outdoor room. The main garden is entered via a simple wrought-iron stair, which creates a particularly attractive split-level effect. Apart from the central sitting area, not a single square foot is devoid of plants. Pots and containers are used particularly well, even on the parapet wall. Crazy paving, although not always suitable for a small garden, is effective here, providing a low-key backdrop for the simple chairs and bamboo table.*

1

2

3

3 *Scale is important in a small garden and so too is an overall theme. This 'busy' design combines a number of elements with varying characteristics in a tiny area. The planting, however, acts as a soft green mantle that draws the composition together, provides continuity and screens the fence and protective netting of the local football ground which backs on to the yard.*

*The simple green seat, which blends perfectly into the surrounding foliage and whose thin slats act as a foil to the bold pot opposite, is particularly effective. The arching palm frames the golden-leafed robinia in the background. Stepping stones reinforce the feeling of uniformity and here the random slabs are sensibly separated by washed gravel. An alternative treatment might have been to use grass, but maintenance would be difficult. Colour is perhaps the most important factor in a garden. Here, green is the dominant hue, with just a splash of red to lift the border beside the seat. Without this accent, the garden would be altogether too bland, mundane rather than pretty. Finally, this illustrates the effectiveness of an easily maintained utility lawn, as opposed to a lush bowling green. Zealous gardeners can waste countless hours on the lawn, and often the end result just is not worth it.*

1 *A wooden deck by its very nature provides an ideal link with the surrounding landscape. Here, the naturally weathered timber platform seems to float against a gentle backdrop of trees. The awkward change in level has been handled by constructing a series of platforms. Furnishings are always desperately important and gardens should be made as comfortable as possible. Here, white is the overall theme, with a couple of pots of bright red geraniums and a paler yellow parasol in the background supplying an uplifting accent.*

2 *A view out of a garden is often indispensable, drawing the wider landscape into a more intimate setting. In this view, the landscape is framed by the simple loggia and sitting area beneath. The straightforward, unfussy furniture and floor do not detract from the setting. The variegated ivy wrapped around the massive pier complements the house.*

3 *This patio is very crisp, very modern and a real invitation outside. The grey carpet indoors and grey tiles of the terrace form an obvious link, while the vivid red furniture is even more striking against the dark paving. The background is low key, underlining the point that 'hot' colours most certainly draw the eye.*

1

2

3

4

4 *This simple, sheltered patio underlines one of the prime requirements of the backyard. The point is, of course, that such areas must be multi-purpose, serving a wide range of requirements. It does not really matter whether this is a front, back or side door: the space outside has been planned both to permit access and to provide a subsidiary sitting area. The table and built-in seating tuck neatly into a backwater alongside the main pedestrian flow into and out of the house.*

*The feeling of enclosure is reinforced by the neatly detailed overhead canopy, which is softened by climbing plants. Such a canopy is ideal in this sort of situation, but be careful to roof it well. Although it might be tempting to use an inexpensive translucent material which would admit as much light as possible, corrugated plastic or fibreglass sheeting not only looks cheap, but also produces a noise like thunder in anything but the lightest shower. Better, as here, to paint all surfaces a bright white to reflect light. Potted pelargoniums and petunias introduce colour and can be moved about at random. The use of both statues and small pictures hanging on the walls outside makes this area seem even more like an indoor room and emphasizes the link between inside and out.*

1 *The bare bones of this backyard could have been not
only dull, but downright ugly.
The designer had to cope with
a slightly ramshackle garage
and an utterly nondescript space.
The first step towards
improvement was to paint the
garage all one colour, thus
minimizing the contrast
between the different
materials used in its
construction and providing
cohesion. White does the job
best of all, not only because it
reflects light into the small
open area, but also because its
brightness glosses over the
awkward details between
timber and brick.
The choice of simple, neutral
grey paving is particularly
appropriate, and laying the
slabs in a 'staggered' pattern
helps to lead the eye down the
space, giving an impression of
movement and greater area.
The furniture reinforces the
bright, white theme, while a
superb climbing white rose
sprawls its way across the face
of the spruced-up garage. The
planting otherwise forms a soft
envelope. Although this is a
small space, there is still plenty
of room for flowers and foliage.
One great bonus of town
gardens is the view into them
from upstairs windows. Not
only do you see them laid out
as if on a drawing board, but
you also see the surrounding
landscape with the garden as
your own sheltered oasis.*

1

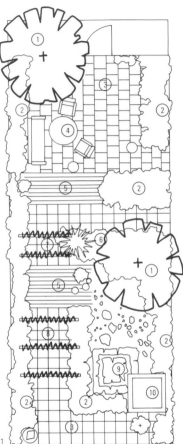

1

The plan of the backyard shown at left
reveals how the owners have created
an informal, secluded seating area in a
sunny spot at the bottom. The long
narrow shape of the plot has been
broken up by a screen and planting.

**1** Tree
**2** Plants
**3** Paving
**4** Seating area
**5** Brick paving
**6** Screen
**7** Arch
**8** Pergola
**9** Herb garden
**10** Raised bed (for annuals)

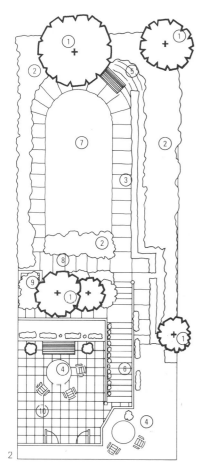

In the garden shown at right, change of level and hard landscaping, rather than planting, are used to create a shaded seating area near the house and a secluded retreat at the bottom of a long town garden in a warm climate.

**1** Tree
**2** Plants
**3** Paving
**4** Seating area
**5** Brick paving
**6** Change of level (stairs, railings)
**7** Lawn
**8** Path
**9** Raised bed
**10** Patio

2

2 *From an upstairs, bird's-eye perspective, the architecture of the surrounding townscape is very much drawn into the overall composition of this urban backyard. Although the lower patio, with its chequerboard paving, black table and white furniture, might seem too formal or clinical at first, it produces what is obviously a very personal space.*
*There is a refreshing strength of purpose which is reinforced by the formal placement of all the components within the patio area. The long white seat takes pride of place and is flanked by a pair of white Versailles tubs planted with matching standard bays. Lighting is symmetrically but sensibly placed to illuminate the sitting area. Pink walls help to soften and warm the otherwise stark lower level. Steps climb to an upper terrace and here the mood is altogether different, with a mass of soft green foliage sweeping off into the more distant parts of the garden. Bright red geraniums introduce colour, and are placed so as to create a visual link between the lower patio and the upper terrace, which are otherwise quite different in style.*
*Visual continuity between the two levels is more subtly reinforced by central placement of the long seat in the formal, lower patio, which is echoed by the traditional bronze sculpture.*

One of the most important rules of design is not to crystallize your ideas too soon. Take the time to complete the checklist on page 229, which will help you rationalize your planning sequence by quantifying your needs and analysing the physical characteristics of the plot. It will form the basis of a design that is right for you and could save endless frustration later on.

Before you put pencil to paper you will also have needed to carry out an accurate survey, measuring the lengths of the boundaries, the dimensions of the house, positions of doors and windows as well as any features within the garden. Don't be tempted to rush out and remove anything that is immediately unsightly. While this may bring short-term satisfaction, it could be a costly mistake in design terms.

Other survey information will include the direction of any cold prevailing wind that will need screening, those good or bad views that we mentioned before, the type and condition of existing boundaries, neighbours, soil type and even the colour schemes of rooms adjoining the garden. A final vital factor and one that is all too often forgotten is the 'North Point', or the position of the sun in relation to your garden.

Once you have gathered all this information, simply transfer it to a scale drawing, either on graph paper, where a square can represent a given distance, or on tracing paper laid over a similarly scaled grid.

The next stage is to rough in where the main features ought to go. Keep things of a kind together, such as dustbins, oil tank and log store; sheds, greenhouse and general maintenance gear; terrace, barbecue and built-in seating. Site these in relation to the general topography, so that sitting areas and vegetables are in sun, sheds and tanks are least obtrusive, sandpits and play space are in easy view of the house.

Link areas with paths that follow obvious 'desire lines' rather than with under-utilized serpentine meanders. Intervening areas will be taken up with paving, planting or lawn: the smaller the garden or yard, the simpler these shapes need to be.

As a general rule, areas close to the house should be 'architectural' to link with the building. Further away and around the perimeters they can be planned as a soft embracing backdrop that gives an impression of greater space.

Many of the thoughts painstakingly gathered during the survey and planning process may have to be rejected at some point. The usual problem is to find that not everything on a long list of requirements can possibly be accommodated. It is better to be realistic and cross the least important items from your list than it is to make an overly complicated plan.

Lastly, remember that designing is pattern-making and the simpler the pattern the more effective the end result.

So often modern gardens lack any real purpose and, while architects and interior designers produce schemes of real merit within a building, their ideas are far from practical when they move outside.
This garden is quite different, and sets out to provide an environment not just for plants but for people too. The materials used are straightforward and underline the point that simplicity is paramount to any design. As a boundary, solid concrete block walls have been colour washed and capped with a neat brick coping. The line of the wall has been extended by crisp overhead beams that will, after a few years, be smothered in fragrant climbers and also provide light shade.
Planting is of course vital in what is an inherently architectural garden and the use of bold foliage and contrasting textures far outweighs brash colour. It is also interesting that many of these plants will provide a pattern throughout the year, rather than for a few months.

1   *City backyards can form a mosaic of often interlocking patterns which is invisible from the street. In many ways such gardens are not individual entities at all, but borrow trees and plants from one another until the whole centre of an urban block becomes a green and pleasant oasis.*

*This tiny backyard illustrates the point perfectly, with ivy, roses and clematis smothering the boundaries and cascading into adjoining properties. Trees, too, are important, as they break the line of surrounding walls and often provide privacy from neighbouring windows. The combination of shade-casting trees and high walls in a limited space can make grass impractical. In this case, the problem is resolved by paving the garden in random rectangular slabs of York stone, which will last a lifetime.*

*A number of design factors can create interest, the most important being the change of level and the distribution of space. Here, the two go together, as the garden has been subdivided by planting with a simple step joining the two halves.*

*In design terms, this makes the whole composition far more interesting, particularly at ground level: one is directed through the space and not all is revealed at a single glance (see page 25). Garden furniture is agreeably simple and effective.*

**Before**

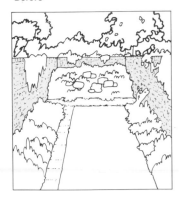

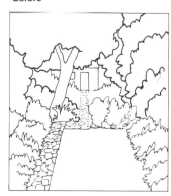

**Before**

2

2 *In this much larger garden, a lawn comes into its own. Don Drake, the designer, is an excellent plantsman. and what is more, he actually builds the gardens he designs himself, unlike most designers and landscape architects. Here, the soft green lawn flows like a river, sweeping away from the house in a series of delightfully fluid curves and providing continuity.*

*In many gardens this underlying design would lack strength of purpose, but the planting has been imaginatively planned and bold drifts tie the whole pattern together. The plants closest to the house, shown here in the foreground, are small and intimate, and the more distant areas are planted with larger species chosen for their handsome leaves and striking foliage.*

*'Tension points' are important design tools which guide both feet and eyes in a particular direction. The first of these is close to the house, between the pool and the planting; the second lies halfway up the garden and is dramatically highlighted by the brilliant drift of yellow alyssum.*

*The stepping stones in the strip of grass at the narrowest point of the garden reflect both practical and aesthetic considerations. Not only do they save wear on the turf, particularly in wet weather, but they arc an added punctuation mark in the overall design.*

1  *The simple fact of the matter is that not all garden design is good and, while this particular composition is acceptable, it could be much improved. When a garden is long and narrow the prime consideration, in all but a few specialized instances, is to subdivide that space into more manageable sections. All too often one sees a path down the middle, flanked by a washing line and planting in monotonous rectangular beds which only serve to emphasize the boundaries. This treatment exacerbates the problem.*

*In this long, narrow garden, the path has at least been laid out off-centre, but the rigid ranks of vegetables in the patch to its left and the rectangular lawn to its right do little to soften or enliven the overall picture. A pool has been placed at the bottom of the garden in an obvious attempt to create a focal point – and it certainly does draw the eye. However, this is largely due to the soaring, spiky-leaved yucca in full flower behind it and the tall, cone-shaped conifers that act as punctuation marks.*

*The small stones that flank the lawn at the pool edge must be a continual nuisance when mowing the lawn.*

*By comparing this and the illustrations on the two previous pages you can see how different designs can radically alter the perspective of a garden.*

1

2

3

2   There is an unspoken rule in landscape design that 'less is more' and this garden illustrates the point perfectly. It is a simple setting in a contemporary mood with a timber-decked terrace adjoining the house. A change of level in this situation can often be awkward. Here a dry stream bed perfectly in harmony with the casual, naturalistic style of the house and deck has been created with boulders, washed gravel and planting.
This garden also explodes the myth that gardens must be full of colour. The shades of green, the variegated leaves and the use of purple and black foliage add up to a controlled understatement.

3   This delightful, unashamedly rural garden is in direct contrast to the distinctly urban gardens depicted elsewhere in this volume. Springtime gardens have a charm of their own. Here the pure white blossom of a flowering cherry tree underplanted with colourful tulips and hyacinths makes a perfect sitting area.
The old stone wall provides stability, while the white deck chairs bring a feeling of freshness down to ground level. Spring grass is always greener and it is refreshing to see it left slightly longer. A closely mown lawn would look distinctly out of place.

1    Whatever anyone says, first
impressions count and this
makes the treatment of a front
garden particularly important.
That first horticultural divide on
entry to any domestic garden
gives a very good idea of the
owner's personality.
The owner's personality is,
however, only one facet and a
front garden should take into
account the character or style
of the house, the possible
inclusion of parking space and,
of course, pedestrian access to
the front or side doors. In other
words, what is often a small
space has to cater for a wide
range of activities and
requirements. Woven into and
around fulfilment of the
owner's requirements will be
the distribution of plants and
consideration of the inevitable
impact on neighbours and the
street scene as a whole.
Whether it is formal or
asymmetric, traditional or
modern, the composition
should above all be practical.
This garden is one of ample
size that has been developed
as a little formal courtyard.
The features are arranged
symmetrically to balance the
front elevation of the house,
which has itself been softened
by clematis and honeysuckle.

1

2  Timber cladding and bright walls frame a collection of herbs that carry around the corner of the house to the steps. The sensibly broad path is edged in brick, which always forms an ideal backdrop for warm terracotta pots, and the theme is echoed by the course of brickwork on top of the wall.

3  Gravel is a no-nonsense, low-maintenance ground cover, ideal for an urban situation. Its 'fluid' nature enables it to conform to any awkward shape, in this case the pattern set up by the bay window. Planting can also be allowed to grow through gravel, so there is no real need for a formal bed. The troughs on the window sills add colour.

4  With a small space, and particularly when an immediate impression is important, it can be vital for a design to turn in upon itself. This symmetrical pattern centres on an octagonal bed planted with spring-flowering daffodils. Later this could be changed to summer bedding plants or a permanent display of shrubs.

5  A well-planted garden path is always inviting. The charm of this green entryway embraces even the gateposts at the entrance, which are in need of attention. Broad-leaved hosta, bergenia and euonymus all spill out to soften the line.

The drawings on this page and those following illustrate, step by step, the stages involved in coming to grips with a design for any garden, from surveying the existing garden, to making a conceptual sketch plan for the new one, to working out a detailed plan for hard landscaping and planting. Before starting your survey, make a list of everything you might want from your garden. If you have moved house, take a full year to see what plants appear from season to season and to learn which parts of the garden receive sun and shade at different times of the year. Then go out into the garden with a long measuring tape, paper and pencil and make a rough survey of the existing garden. Draw a plan of the site, indicating the house (with windows and doors marked). Be sure to note down all relevant items: changes of level, the north point, bad views to be screened, good views to be enhanced and the location of existing features, such as plants, trees, other buildings, fences and so forth. Take running measurements of important distances.

The survey drawing of this sample garden reveals a large central lawn bisected by a clothesline with features clustered along two boundaries. There are some features worth retaining, such as the trees, shed and roses.

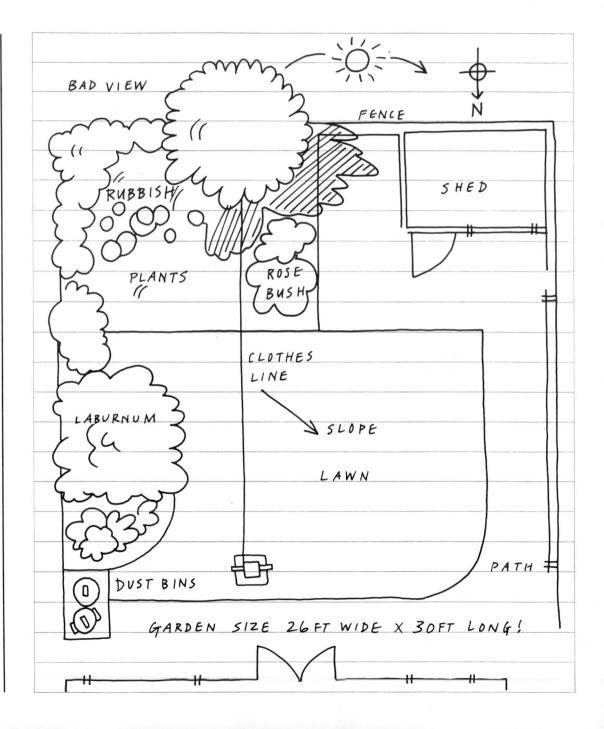

BAD VIEW

N

FENCE

SHED

RUBBISH

PLANTS

ROSE BUSH

CLOTHES LINE

SLOPE

LABURNUM

LAWN

DUST BINS

PATH

GARDEN SIZE 26 FT WIDE X 30 FT LONG!

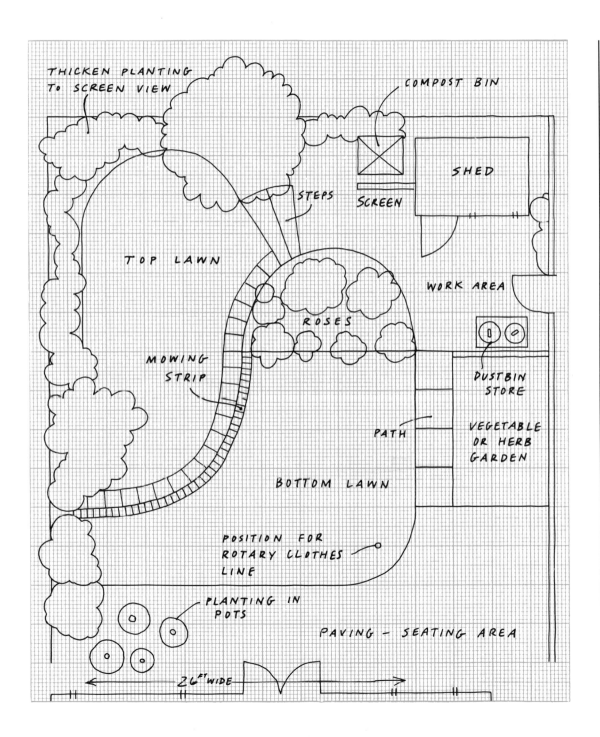

THICKEN PLANTING
TO SCREEN VIEW

COMPOST BIN

SHED

STEPS

SCREEN

TOP LAWN

WORK AREA

ROSES

MOWING
STRIP

DUSTBIN
STORE

PATH

VEGETABLE
OR HERB
GARDEN

BOTTOM LAWN

POSITION FOR
ROTARY CLOTHES
LINE

PLANTING IN
POTS

PAVING - SEATING AREA

26 FT WIDE

Once you have measured and mapped existing features on a rough survey drawing, transfer the information you have gathered to a scale drawing, using the running measurements to plot accurately those existing features you wish to keep or change. Some prefer to do this using gridded paper, where each square represents a unit of measurement (1m or 1ft). With your list of garden requirements and survey drawing you are ready to start designing the new one. Begin with your list of requirements, numbering each item in order of priority. Work through the list, marking the area to be allocated to each function on a copy of the scale drawing, giving the most space to those features which you consider most important. It will be handy at this stage to have several copies of your scale drawings, since even experienced garden designers make several conceptual sketch plans as their ideas develop. Especially in a small garden or backyard, it is important to think carefully about the location of each feature and to try and draw related elements together. The challenge posed by the small backyard illustrated here is to give the eventual design a real feeling of space and movement which is lacking in the original.

*The finished plan of the sample garden reveals ample room for a sitting/dining area, and for a small food garden with espalier fruit trees. Dustbins, which previously were an inconveniently located eyesore, occupy the space beyond near the gate and are concealed by a screen smothered in evergreen ivy. There is space for a work area near the original shed, with a compost heap next to it also screened by a climbing plant. The sloping lawn has been rationalized by creating two lawns on different levels divided by a path and a neat 'mowing strip'. The main lawn and border shapes are built up from strong, flowing curves, giving a sense of continuity. When the basic framework of the garden has been established, it can be useful to make sketches of the elevation of those areas where planting is required in order to help visualize the final effect (see opposite). Here, maximum use has been made of walls and fences for climbing plants. Fast-growing bamboo (Arundinaria nitida) screens the bad view from the far corner, and other planting has been chosen to provide colour and foliage year round. Even in winter, the red stems of the dogwood (Cornus alba) at the bottom add interest. There is plenty of room for adding spring-flowering bulbs and summer-flowering annuals.*

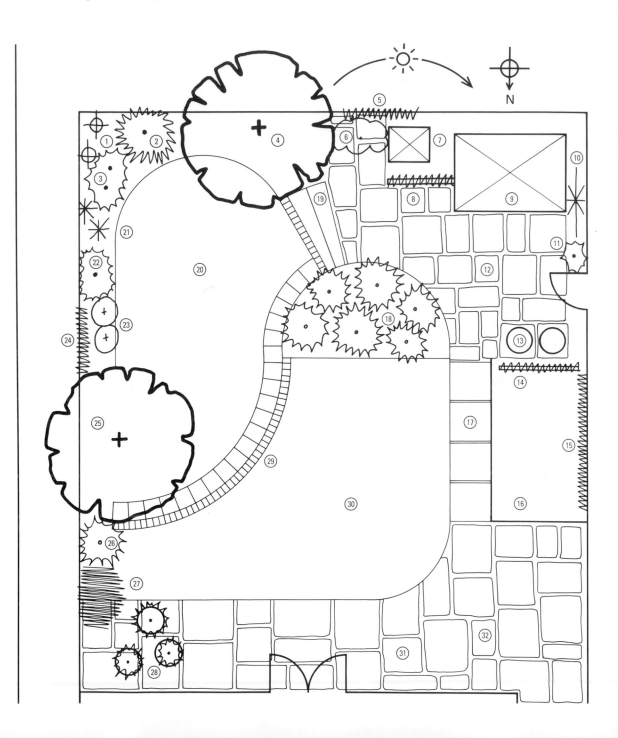

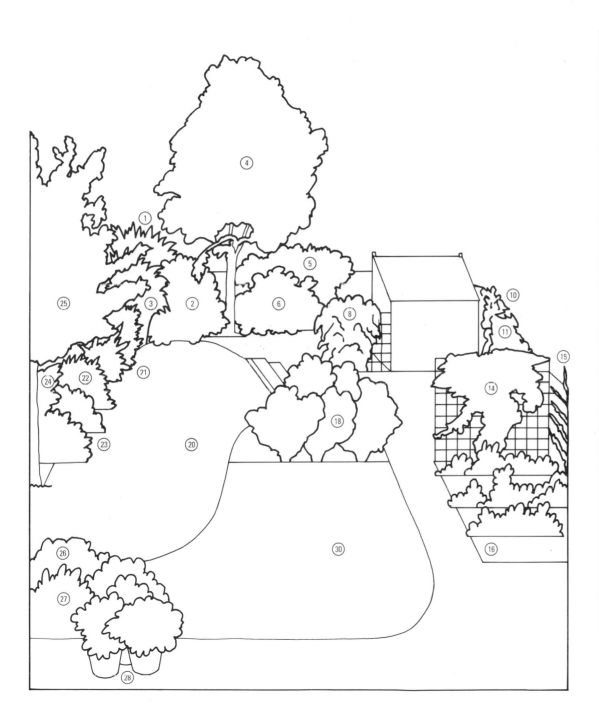

1 *Two* Arundinaria nitida
2 Cornus alba *'Elegantissima'*
3 *Two* Weigela *'Bristol Ruby'*
4 *Existing birch tree*
5 Clematis montana *growing on fence*
6 Hydrangea *'New Wave'*
7 *Compost heap*
8 *Screen for compost heap with* Jasminum nudiflorum *growing on it*
9 *Existing shed*
10 Hydrangea petiolaris *growing on fence*
11 Kerria japonica
12 *Random paving*
13 *Dustbins*
14 *Screen for dustbins with ivy growing on it*
15 *Espalier fruit trees growing on wall*
16 *Vegetable and herb garden*
17 *Steps*
18 *Floribunda roses*
19 *Curved steps*
20 *Upper lawn*
21 *Two* Mahonia japonica
22 Buddleia *'Black Knight'*
23 *Two* Spiraea *'Anthony Waterer'*
24 Lonicera periclymenum *'Belgica'* and *'Serotina'* growing on wall
25 Existing laburnum tree
26 Cytisus kewiensis
27 Potentilla *'Katherine Dykes'*
28 *Flowering annuals in pots*
29 *Brick mowing edge*
30 *Lower lawn*
31 *Random paving*
32 *Seating/dining area*

1　*Brick building, brick walls, brick floor — all in harmony and small enough in scale not to become oppressive. Simple steps lead up from a basement flat with plants growing on every possible square inch, including the walls. Terracotta containers of different shapes and sizes associate well with the brickwork. The flimsy plastic trellis, however, breaks the line of the wall. A discreet horizontal wire, fixed unobtrusively with nails or vine-eyes, would have been a better choice of support for the climbing plant.*

2　*This tiny backyard is completely surrounded by walls, and the feeling of enclosure is heightened by the use of overhead beams to support light-loving climbing plants. Surfaces have been painted white to reflect maximum light. Even so, only shade-tolerant plants will thrive in such a sheltered spot. Statuary adds personality and year-round interest.*

3　*This splendid little garden gets away with breaking the rule of simplicity. There is so much going on that it really should not work well at all. However, rules are there to be broken. Most designers would have kept to a single paving material, but the central panel of slabs is strong enough to be positive and it acts as a host to the fine range of pots.*

4

5

6

4  *Roof gardens are quite literally in a world of their own. More often than not they are created despite the hostile roof environment with its unique microclimate of high winds and lack of shelter. But roofs are often the only space available to urban gardeners and this makes the effort they require worthwhile.*
*The load-bearing potential of a roof and the question of shelter are so important that professional advice is vital. In this garden, both factors have been catered for with an opaque glass screen and lightweight asbestos tiles. The lush planting is entirely in containers and provides a successful alternative to the surrounding roofscape.*

5  Trompe-l'oeil *painting employs perspective and delicate shading to deceive the eye and create an illusion of space. The* trompe-l'oeil *wall of this enclosed garden, much like more common indoor* trompe-l'oeil *painting, is used to create an architectural interest which is lacking. This is not to everyone's taste: a more horticultural approach to such a wall would be to smother it with plants.*

6  *This is the tiny backyard garden shown on page 238 as it looks at ground level. It illustrates just how much a different viewpoint can alter one's perception of a well-designed garden.*

1 Much of garden design is about surprise. In a small area this often means creating discreet areas with dividers so that the observer is drawn by curiosity from one space to another. In this garden a clematis-covered screen and arch act as wall and doorway framing a view of the raised pool which is set as a focal point within the composition as a whole. The planting is cool, casual and undemonstrative, the fountain simple yet effective, with the pool surround doubling as an occasional seat.

2 Two materials infrequently used in Britain are exposed aggregate concrete and timber decking, which is a pity as both have attractive characteristics. Here concrete cylinders of different heights set in a staggered pattern form steps up to the deck, an imaginative solution to a common problem in garden design. Small-scale ground-level circular paving continues the theme and plants act as a foil to the architectural composition.

3 This English garden has a distinctly informal Mediterranean feel. The architect owner designed the sensitive grouping of plants and the use of the marvellous pot as sculpture. It often makes sense to resist the temptation to cram every container full of foliage.

4

5

6

7

4   *Slate may be expensive, but in gardening, possibly more than anywhere else, you get what you pay for. This superb slate surface acts as a perfect foil for planting and sets up the most fascinating reflections, even when dry. The loose cobbles are an attractive contrast, leading the eye away to the timber-decked terrace.*

5   *A formal and elegant simplicity is achieved by setting a sculptural glazed pot against a background of natural stone paving. At poolside, the paving slabs overhang the water and create a clean, sharp, dark line of shadow. The important balance between 'hard' and 'soft' landscape is handled sensitively in this garden, preventing either element from becoming dominant.*

6   *Here, two outdoor rooms are divided by a fine old brick wall clothed in rampant rambling roses. The archway highlights the transition from one to the other, as does the band of shade it casts between the sunlit areas.*

7   *It is difficult to create an authentic Japanese garden outside Japan, but a suggestion is always possible. Here, chippings, stepping stones, a lantern and the bold-leaved lungwort combine to form an attractive little Japanese-style composition.*

1  This extraordinarily attractive frontyard is an excellent example of how to extend living space outside. The long roof frames a wall of sliding glass doors which open on to and reflect the bold, simple and imaginative planting. Otherwise, paving and soft landscaping have been kept to a minimum. The result is a perfectly understated setting for an outdoor meal.

2  This impeccably handled front approach sets the building off beautifully. The grading and juxtaposition of the plants, from the overhanging robinia right down to the ground-hugging species, is particularly effective. The use of warm, terracotta tiles provides intimacy and overall continuity.

3  Built-in seating is both attractive and practical. In a small garden it also saves space. Here, a change of level has been particularly well handled, with plants softening the line of the retaining walls. Raised beds make it easier to observe small plants.

4  Here the thin slats of built-in timber seating draw the eye and then turn across the garden to form a step. In this clever design the steps themselves are well detailed; both they and the retaining walls are softened by planting.

5

5 Paving and planting are truly vital, basic garden ingredients and they are combined here to form a superb arrangement. This seemingly haphazard arrangement did not just 'happen', but was very, very carefully planned, with great attention to detail and the placement of plants and furniture. This spot serves both as a sitting area and as a pathway out into the garden beyond. The designer has used his limited space imaginatively, creating a soft and intimate alcove for the assortment of seats, table and chairs.

In direct contrast to the small-scale brick paving, the planting relies heavily on the sculptural use of foliage rather than brash flower colour. The giant leaves of Gunnera manicata associate particularly well with the adjoining hosta and the nearby bronze-leaved Japanese maple. Even after these latter two deciduous plants have lost their summer foliage, there is sufficient evergreen material here to provide winter interest as well.

Many people find it difficult to place statues, sculpture or other objects of intrinsic interest in a garden. They should have a positive position and should not be dumped down anywhere. As focal points in and of themselves, they often look well with handsome foliage, as the bust does here.

The paving, walling and hard surfacing of a garden really provide the basic structure of any composition. They also account for roughly seventy-five per cent of the total garden budget.

In design terms, the problem with hard surfaces is largely one of choice as the market is flooded with a wealth of materials, natural and artificial, all with widely differing properties, design characteristics, availability and prices.

The best way out of this particular maze is once again to think of paving in terms of flooring. Very few people would think of mixing their internal floor coverings, but how many times do you see elaborate, hideous amalgamations of paving that are as hard on the eye as they are on the pocketbook?

In fact paving, whether it be in the form of terraces, paths, drives or hardstanding areas, should have a unifying influence, providing a sensible, low-key background for the wealth of activities proper to a small garden, from barbecuing to babysitting.

To a large extent this applies to walling as well, where there is in addition a greater responsibility to respect local traditions and the surrounding environment. The practicality of extending a brick wall from a brick building should be obvious in both visual and financial terms. Not only are the materials compatible but they will almost certainly be available locally. It would be foolish to import natural stone over vast distances in such a case. Planning in terms of the existing built environment can leave you with a more manageable shortlist of acceptable options.

For those lucky enough to have a stone, brick or slate floor indoors, the treatment of an adjoining paved area is ready-made. When reinforced by planting, continuity of paving will form the ultimate link between inside and out.

Simplicity is once again the key to these areas, so only a few materials should be used within a design. If a single surface, perhaps of brick or slabs, could become visually heavy, it can make sense to mix materials. In a traditional setting, random rectangular stone flags could be interspersed with panels of brick. In a contemporary design, crisp brick courses could run out from a building to form a grid which is then filled in with neatly pointed precast slabs.

Some materials, such as gravel, concrete and tarmac, are 'fluid' and can be cast or laid to a free-flowing pattern, which is ideal for a drive or broad winding path where larger individual modules would need cutting to shape. This also applies to small-scale materials such as cobbles or granite paving stones.

Finally, choose and use your hard landscape materials sensibly: they are expensive, and they will last a lifetime. They form the basic framework of your garden, to be decorated to your taste with plants and furnishings, but changed only with difficulty.

There are a number of unusual things about this composition, not the least of which is that it works so well. Drama is an essential design tool, but only effective if used sparingly. Sculpture can take many forms and need not necessarily be a single subject. This small corner of what is undoubtedly a far grander lay-out forms a unified sculptural group. The dramatic herringbone brick path gives a focus to the equally bold stone seat. The latter is probably eighteenth century and there is no doubt that age, which is obvious here, has a charisma of its own. The gryphon armrests are a sort of latter-day 'gnomery', amusing in their own right and simply hinting at the grander architectural style used elsewhere in the garden. The hedge is of pleached lime trees, a device that can be used to good effect in both large and small gardens. It is all the more telling here for being left slightly ragged, as it heightens the drama below. The real point is that this is 'landscape architecture' in the fullest sense.

1   *Garden structure can be classified into two broad categories: hard and soft landscape. The proportion of one or the other is largely determined by the pattern of use – pedestrian traffic or seating mean hard landscaping, plants and lawns mean soft. In reality there is usually a pretty even split. Whereas plants may look satisfactory with only a modicum of care, provided that their soil and situation are suitable, paving can look a total disaster if incorrectly or poorly laid. Attention spent on hard landscape work is therefore essential, not only because of its high cost but also because it can last a lifetime.*

*This particular composition is strongly architectural; the line of steps and paving link positively with the strong lines of the house. Indeed, the very materials of the hard landscaping complement and echo those of the building with its prominent roof. Steps radiate from pivot points established by the raised beds. Each riser of the steps is formed by sawn-down sleepers, and plants soften the natural flight.*

*It is a common myth that trees planted close to a building are naturally destructive. Some species, such as willow and poplar, should certainly be avoided, but less rampant varieties are acceptable.*

1

2

3

## HOW TO LAY PAVING

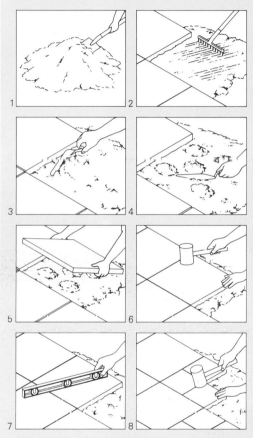

1    2

3    4

5    6

7    8

Where paving slabs meet up with buildings, paving surfaces must be at least 155mm (6in) below any damp course.
**1** Mix sand and cement with a shovel until the colour of the mixture is even throughout. **2** Lay a thin bed of sand for each paving slab and rake it smooth. **3** Use a trowel to scrape any excess sand to ensure that there is a clean edge between paving slabs. **4** Make five small mounds of sand for each slab. **5** Ease each paving slab carefully and gently into position. **6** Gently firm the slabs in place using a mallet. **7** Check with a spirit level to ensure that paving slabs slope away from the house. **8** Small paving slabs may be laid directly on to a bed of sand unmixed with cement.

2   *Not all paving is tasteful and the pink stepping stones across this pool are distinctly dubious. Coloured slabs are visually dangerous: they fade to pallid tints and tend to clash with furniture, plants and virtually everything else. In this case, it would have been better to continue the line of paving in the neutral buff colour. Colour control is also less than perfect with the planting. The variegated hosta vies uncomfortably with the fiercely pink azalea blossom. The terracotta pot contains a diversity of material lacking cohesion, and its position is arbitrary. It is far too easy to slap a pot down anywhere: rather use them like sculpture, either singly or in well-positioned groups.*

3   *This immensely effective design demonstrates what a versatile material timber can be in the hands of an imaginative designer. Sleepers have been used to form steps, while solid balks of wood act as a retainer to the raised bed flanking the flight on the left. By varying the height of these uprights the designer has set up a rhythm that echoes the flight itself. The planting is refreshingly simple and naturalistic. Over-zealous weeding between the slabs would destroy the charm of the design.*

1   In this crisp Mediterranean setting, tiles form an ideal link between inside and out. In colder climates, care must be taken to ensure that such tiles are frost-proof, as many will not stand a severe winter. Porches or verandahs are ideal in hot weather, allowing a cool circulation of air and a gentle transition from the house into the garden.

2   This patio is a scaled-up version of a far-from-restful Victorian tiled floor. Bright colours are appropriate here and the cheerful tulips are particularly effective.

3   For many years clay bricks were one of the few small-scale paving materials available. Although attractive, they could be damaged relatively easily, particularly by frost. Recently a number of manufacturers have started producing concrete paving slabs that can be quickly and easily laid on a bed of sand. They have chamfered edges and can be butt-jointed, eliminating pointing.

4   Lightweight tiles are often essential for a roof garden and these asbestos squares are commonly used. They provide a neat, straightforward, no-nonsense background for furniture and planting.

5   Hard bricks are still an excellent choice and are laid here in a traditional 'basketweave' pattern. The pattern, or bond as it is more correctly called, has considerable visual impetus. If a path or terrace is laid in bricks positioned end to end, this will lead the eye on. Herringbone laid across the line is more static.

6   These are very hard pavers, completely frost-proof and capable of withstanding a life-time's wear. They have been laid in a random pattern in this tiny backyard, forming a practical path to the back door and an attractive foil to the white-painted house. As they run into the planting, the edge of the path need not be cut to form a rigid line.

7   This timber deck visually echoes the broad boards of the fence and the section in the foreground of the picture is carefully varied with uneven widths. The planting is restrained and the furniture simple. How pleasant to step out from those sliding doors!

8   Log slices can make very attractive informal stepping stones through a lawn, planting or, as in this case, gravel. The type of timber is important and any of the hardwoods is ideal. If this treatment is used across a lawn, be sure to set the slices below the turf to prevent difficulty when mowing.

9   Cobbles are a traditional paving and have been used for many thousands of years. While they have been superseded for most roads and footways owing to their irregular nature, they still form an attractive small-scale surface. The municipal habit of laying them like currants in a bun should be avoided at all costs. They should be packed tightly together like eggs in a crate.

10  Granite paving stones, or setts, are another traditional material originally used for street paving. In Britain, they can still be obtained from demolition contractors or council yards and are extremely hard. Their slightly uneven nature makes them unsuitable under tables and chairs, but for drives and paths they provide an ideal non-slip surface.

11  Brick paving, another traditional material, is here laid in soldier courses which lead the eye towards the sundial. Shallow steps, however, can be a little awkward. An ideal height for a garden step is 15cm (6in), or two bricks deep.

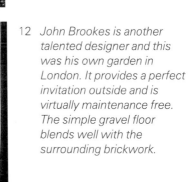

12  John Brookes is another talented designer and this was his own garden in London. It provides a perfect invitation outside and is virtually maintenance free. The simple gravel floor blends well with the surrounding brickwork.

1   *Fencing is one of the most expensive jobs in the garden, and often one of the most poorly designed features. The problem is, of course, that there is a lack of really attractive fencing available and most people think solely in terms of closeboard or interwoven panels. In reality, the choice is far wider than this. Any fencing should be selected with respect for its surroundings, including both the owner's home and garden and the neighbours' scheme. Although timber is the natural choice, fences are also made in wire and plastic. Wire fencing is generally chosen when security is important, both to keep pets in and unwelcome visitors out. It is not practical for screening a view or acting as a wind-break, but could have its uses where a glimpse of landscape would be pleasant.*

*Plastic fencing can be appalling. If used properly, taking account of its inherent versatility, it can also look superb.*

*The fence illustrated here is made from simple vertical timber slats, spaced with a slight gap between each. It is handsome, relatively inexpensive and an ideal foil for planting. It is also worth remembering that a 'permeable' screen, such as this, tends to filter the wind, causing far less turbulence than a solid barrier.*

1

## TYPES OF FENCING

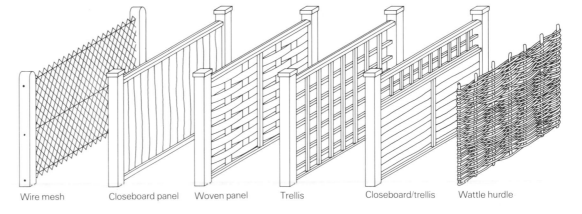

Wire mesh          Closeboard panel          Woven panel          Trellis          Closeboard/trellis          Wattle hurdle

2

2 *Beehive, roses and salad greens are here mixed together in a traditional setting. The fine osier hurdles in the background are woven from willow stems and were originally designed for penning sheep. They are a little more expensive than conventional fence panels, but are easy to erect as they are simply wired to round posts driven into the ground. Their life expectancy of eight to ten years is quite respectable, often ideal while a developing border or hedge takes hold. They are a wonderful foil for planting and in such a position form an elegant backdrop. Here, they provide a contrast to the striking white beehive. Other woven fences include wattle hurdles, which are made from strips of hazel, and also reed fences which use bundles of reeds bound in panels. The path in this garden is equally attractive, the herringbone brick being well laid and retained by neat soldier courses on either side. Maintenance of fences is important too and a coat of non-toxic (never creosote) preservative should be applied every two years. In order to prevent rotting at the bottom, fit a gravel board nailed or screwed to the posts. This can be replaced when necessary without renewing the panels. Finally, support climbing plants on wires stretched between the posts.*

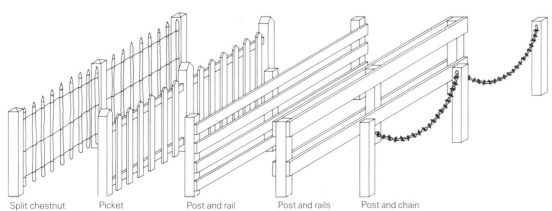

Split chestnut    Picket    Post and rail    Post and rails    Post and chain

1   *This is an altogether charming garden, somewhat unkempt and almost entirely natural. This belies careful planning and reinforces one of the basic rules that a garden should remain architectural close to a building, but merge into a softer, looser composition further away. By doing this one can create a far greater feeling of space.*

*One of the secrets of informal steps is that the ends of the treads can merge into the planting on either side. There is no need for a rigid flight – in fact, the pattern can be staggered from side to side so that one step offsets the next. In many ways the materials are unimportant. Whether the steps are composed from timber, slabs or brick, it is the character of this garden that really matters.*

*These are in fact railway sleepers, ideal for the purpose and virtually indestructible. They can be simply bedded in position on a minimal foundation of well-compacted soil, although two wedges, one on either side, will ensure there is no movement, especially after wet or frosty weather. As far as the planting is concerned, poppies and wild flowers are here far more effective than 'architectural' shrubs. It underlines the point that species have unique and individual characters.*

1

2

3

2   *Landscape architecture, a multidisciplinary blend of building and horticultural design, can be practised on an infinite number of scales. It presupposes that architecture and landscape are complementary. Although small in scale, these steps perfectly illustrate the art. Here, brick steps run directly off a building. The junction between them and the white wall is enlivened by a sprawling mat of Mexican wall daisies (Erigeron mucronatus). Bricks turned on edge are almost the ideal height for the riser of a step, but it is particularly important to use a hard, well-fired variety of brick that will be frost resistant. Engineering bricks, although very durable, are often glazed and can become slippery when wet, so they are best avoided.*

3   *The concept behind this garden is clever, but the construction of the steps is not. The levels are slightly wrong and the treads run at awkward angles. In theory, L-shaped steps can be very attractive and the more space there is available for them the better. There should be ample room for pots and plants, as here. In this case, the positioning of the flight to one side of the garden is more effective than it would have been right in the middle. The planting is pretty and the overall setting attractive, but the steps could be better.*

1  *In this gentle garden with muted colours, the low hedge allows one's view to run out to the more distant parts of the composition, creating a feeling of space and an element of surprise. The arch framing the pathway does more than just support climbing plants: it invites the visitor in positive terms to walk under or through to the next area. Space division is one of the garden designer's most useful tools. It creates a feeling of mystery, adds depth to a composition and provides endless scope for surprise. Such internal separations can be achieved by a variety of means — from walling, through fences and screens, down to hedges — and the height of all of these can be varied.*

2  *This is another arch in a quite different situation. This really is full of promise. A curved path always gives a hint of the unexpected, and this one is most evocative. The series of arches establishes a rhythm that carries the eye onward. Wire or iron arches cause minimal visual disruption and allow any climbing plants visual success. These arches are perfectly built and their shape echoes that of the old brick path. Pale yellow climbing roses link with the lady's mantle* (Alchemilla mollis) *at ground level, while trees form a canopy at a higher level.*

3 *Where the two gardens on the opposite page are distinctly informal, these rigid, neatly clipped hedges take on a more controlled presence. While one can see over them when standing, the sight-line is broken when sitting down. This is another fundamental consideration in garden design and opens up a number of interesting possibilities.*
*The brick paving and low walls mimic the line of the hedge and are precisely positioned to match the end of the run in the middle distance. The steps provide a transition between two levels, and this garden provides the perfect vehicle for developing separate themes or colours in different sections.*
*A number of famous English gardens do just this: Hidcote Manor in Gloucestershire and Sissinghurst in Kent are perhaps the most famous. Such subdivision not only allows diversity within an overall garden concept but also increases the feeling of space. Sissinghurst is surprisingly small when seen from the tower, but has an enormous amount of rich detail when seen at ground level. Continuity, however, is important and this can be achieved in a number of ways. The dividing walls or hedges can be of a type and so too can the paving. These will act as a framework against which more complicated themes can be allowed free rein.*

If we continue to think of the backyard as simply another room adjoining the home, then furnishing that space is vitally important. The size of the garden poses certain limitations, but surprising results can be achieved in a very limited space, especially using pots, containers, hanging baskets and window boxes. One very famous balcony garden set in the heart of London is suspended many hundreds of feet above the city. In this tiny and unlikely area the gifted owner has created a paradise of plants fitted into every conceivable corner. Many of the containers have been recycled from other uses, but once smothered in foliage no one knows the difference.

Conversely, the most unexpected and successful compositions can often be achieved by featuring unlikely objects as plant containers. For example, a delightful Alpine garden can be created in a bath tub filled with rubble and topped with sharp-draining soil. The plug hole allows excess water to escape and the whole composition can be most effective, almost a self-contained miniature landscape.

Water has a charm all its own and in a small urban garden it can make all the difference on an overpoweringly hot summer day by transforming a stuffy courtyard into a refreshing oasis. Scale is of course vital – there is little point in building a vast pool to house a large fountain in a tiny courtyard. It is perhaps the sound of water that is most important, the splashing of a bubble jet or a simple slide that sends a cascade into a pool below.

In many situations a pool of standing water is not necessary at all and a millstone or boulder can be drilled to accept a pipe. The whole arrangement can then be positioned over a water tank, let into the ground or a raised bed, and a submersible pump installed to recirculate water continuously around the system.

Furniture is another area where people's ideas tend to dry up when they move outside, although careful shopping for garden furniture and other features is worth the effort. The range of items from which to choose is enormous: tables, chairs, trolleys, lounge chairs, parasols, garden benches, swings and more are made in a wide variety of styles. Remember that painted finishes will soon become shabby with exposure to the elements and that you must be prepared for frequent repainting if you opt for painted metal or timber furniture.

In a small space it makes sense to build in seating, and in so doing it is often possible to produce a continuity that pulls the design together. Raised beds and broad walls at the right height are always inviting, while overhead beams or arbours can define a sitting area, casting welcome shade.

As with hard and soft landscape, keep furnishings to a theme. The odd, well-chosen piece or feature can certainly act as a contrast, but let it work against a sensible rather than discordant background.

A conservatory is a hybrid, halfway between house and garden. Its original function in historical terms was as a glorified greenhouse, in which plants were grown specifically for use in the adjoining house. In the nineteenth century all this changed and, with the greater facility for the production of glass and wrought iron, a superb range of buildings arrived.

Some of these remain today and there are also a number of excellent reproductions that are worthy of the name. The function of such a building is to form a transition. A conservatory can be enormously attractive. As a sitting room it is delightful, particularly on those winter or spring days that look inviting enough to sit outside but are really just too cold. They also extend the range of plant material that can be grown. The setting in this garden room is softened by a sensitive planting scheme and paved with old York stone, reinforcing the traditional setting.

1   *People always confuse pergolas, arbours, gazebos and pavilions. The last two are buildings; the first, a series of arches framing a path; while an arbour is a place in which to sit. All these structures are subject to a form of gardening snobbery which considers it advantageous to boast some sort of feature, no matter how far removed it may be from the original concept.*

*The arbour illustrated here is of the very best kind. It is a pretty little structure, with fine old cast-iron columns and a soaring, peaked lattice-work roof that is smothered in climbing plants. White paintwork is traditional for a structure of this sort, although painted finishes are not always practical, as they can become drab in a short period.*

*Potted plants are arranged on a series of white wire racks, an unusual but attractive idea. The curved seat continues the theme of white metalwork, but the blue tablecloth and patterned cushions introduce a welcome colour break, preventing the composition from becoming bland. Fragrance is an essential ingredient of such an idyllic setting: honeysuckle (Lonicera) is always a favourite climbing plant, though summer-flowering jasmine (Jasminum officinale) or roses would be equally good.*

1

2   *Good design is timeless and is to do with proportion, form and balance. This garden illustrates all these qualities and features built-in furniture as an integral part of the design. It is composed of a number of elements, but notice how the simple fence has been lined up exactly with the concrete-block wall. The raised pool is attractive, while the timber seat cleverly runs around the right angles, drawing the whole composition together.*

3   *In this pretty little garden an old hand pump has been used to create an unusual feature. Water is recirculated from the pool below using a submersible electric pump. The sound of playing water gives this garden its greatest inherent charm. The planting is both delicate and successful, using a combination of waterside species, climbing plants and herbs. The background fence is constructed from osier hurdles.*

4   *Running water can feature even in a garden lacking a pool. Here an old millstone has been drilled to accept a pipe. The whole arrangement has been positioned over a water tank and water is pumped through the stone to fall back into the tank on a recirculating basis. The arrangement of loose cobbles, planting, gravel and brick is unusual, but effective.*

1   *Humour can be an integral part of any garden which reflects its owner's personality and individual taste. Sculpture, and the use of interesting objects in sculptural ways, is a time-tested way of adding unique interest, whether it be a garden gnome, perhaps a little red-capped fellow leaning on a rake — an example of much-maligned but classic English garden kitsch — or a sculpture by Henry Moore. Here, planting plays second fiddle to this quite delightful group of pots.*

2   *This sophisticated garden underlines the point that it is often the planting rather than the container that is important. The pot could be any container — a bucket or a priceless vase — it simply does not matter. The colour combination of pink pelargonium, blue lobelia and grey helichrysum is charming and works well against the architectural garage doors behind. The cobbles are also superbly laid.*

3   *The strong primary colours of these gay pots are reminiscent of the signwriting and painting so often found on English canal narrowboats and barges. Far from being irrelevant to the overall effect, these pots fight for attention with their bright colours, and it is right to plant them with something undemonstrative — bright flowers in this case would ruin the effect.*

1

2

3

4    *Seats and pots are two vital garden furnishings and are often sited with little regard to their own intrinsic character or the overall garden pattern. Here, the siting is quite superb: the old iron seat nestles comfortably below the wisteria. The half-barrel is host to sprawling agapanthus and helps to bring the eye down to a lower level. In this case, the choice of simple hard landscape materials and design is a happy one.*

5    *Water gardens in containers are not always easy to maintain, as plants can often quickly outstrip their allotted space. There is also a problem with the oxygen balance – perhaps we should say imbalance – and such small areas can turn green very quickly. However, if tended regularly they can be both attractive and practical, as this old half-barrel shows. The timber edging for the raised beds is made from sawn logs set in concrete. To be really successful, the planting should be more generous, spilling over and softening the outline.*

6    *The colour and planting of these bowls is excellent, while the setting is eminently suitable. Such groups are sculpture in their own right and it would be quite wrong to straighten up the right-hand pot, as some over-zealous gardeners might do.*

# PLANTING

Once the structure of the hard landscape is in position we can move into the third dimension with planting.

To many people this is really what gardening is all about and there is no doubt that plants, trees and shrubs bring a carefully planned design to life. But where there were a few pitfalls to avoid and sound rules to obey when planning the lay-out, there are even more when considering planting design.

Any oak woodland, one of Britain's richest natural habitats, has a definite vertical stratum of vegetation. The trees themselves form the highest canopy, under which occurs a shrub layer that in turn overshadows a layer of low ground-covering plants. This pattern should be echoed in the garden with a progression of elements from the highest tree that provides vertical emphasis, right down to carpeting species that reduce maintenance to a sensible minimum.

The way in which such a composition is built up can follow a planned sequence. Trees come first and should be sited with regard to screening, the creation of shade and their general large-scale impact on the design as a whole.

Shrubs come next, and here a framework of taller, often evergreen plants provides shelter and protection. Faster-growing species which can be removed once surrounding plants have reached maturity are often useful at first.

With this framework in place, fill in with lighter, more colourful plants, such as smaller shrubs, herbaceous perennials, bulbs and areas for annuals and containers.

Over-complicated planting schemes are the curse of many gardens. As a general rule use drifts of material, allowing these to lead the eye through the curve or around a corner.

Colour, too, is vital but here again there are sensible rules that engender harmony. Hot, vibrant colours such as orange, red and yellow draw the eye and foreshorten a space, so keep them close to the house or viewpoint for maximum effect. This will allow the cooler range of blue, purple, pink and white to run on to the boundaries, creating a feeling of greater space. Grey, possibly the designer's most useful colour, is a harmonizer, useful as a softening influence and a vital link between more demonstrative colours.

## PLANTING CHECKLIST

- Have you carried out an accurate survey and prepared a scale plan? (See Garden Planning Checklist, page 5.)
- What existing plants, trees or shrubs do you wish to keep?
- Are you bringing plants from elsewhere – if so, what?
- Do you have any favourite plants or particular dislikes?
- What type of soil do you have? Sandy, clay, loam, acid or chalky?
- How much sunshine do different areas get; and for how long?
- What are the prevailing weather conditions? Rainfall? Temperature?
- How long will you stay at this house? Short-term, medium-term or long-term?
- What is your budget for plants?
- Do you wish to exclude all poisonous plants?
- What are the colour schemes of the rooms adjoining or overlooking the garden?
- Do you have any colour preferences?
- Do you want year-round interest, or seasonal emphasis at a particular time of year?

*In most respects plants are a garden. It is their form, colour, texture and size that breathe life into a composition. To be successful there should be a balance of species. Because of its predominance of summer-flowering herbaceous plants, this garden is at its best from June to August.*

1 Plants can conjure up any mood, from crisp and architectural to flagrantly rural, as here. This classic English cottage garden mixes an assortment of shrubs, perennials and annuals. The daisied lawn and slightly ragged bushes express the owner's respect for natural-looking forms and plants.

2 Conifers, if properly used, can provide enormous interest at times of year when other species are not at their best. This arrangement emphasizes the point that they are most impressive in a group, where differences in colour and texture can be appreciated. Be careful to learn what the ultimate size of any conifer will be.

3 Pink, purple and grey is a classic colour combination in almost any design situation, especially in a garden. Clematis is a climbing plant which blossoms abundantly. Helichrysum angustifolium and Lamium maculatum complete the colour scheme close to the ground.

4 Good design often looks uncontrived, as here, where a simple seat echoes the solid line of the railway sleepers that edge the lawn. It also 'ties' together the two wings of planting, with lady's mantle (Alchemilla mollis) acting as a carpet.

1

2

3

4

5

5 *This garden has all the hallmarks of a successful composition. Hostas are another essential plant for any garden; their broad leaves and distinctive colouring act as a foil in any situation. Their foliage ranges from the bold glaucous leaves of* Hosta sieboldiana, *illustrated here, through the variegated types, of which the green and white striped variety 'Thomas Hogg' is perhaps the best, to those with undulating and even yellow foliage. Hostas tolerate both sun and shade and are a 'must' for flower arranging. Here, delphinium makes an unusual but effective partner and the tall spike of dark blue does much to 'lift' this corner. Perhaps the most intriguing component of this design is the old wall with its open door, which affords a tantalizing glimpse of an altogether wider, sunlit landscape, illustrating once again the vital role played by surprise in garden design. Here, the drama is heightened by the transition between shadow and light. This is a technique used most often in hot climates, but it can be used to good effect in more temperate zones as well, where shadows cast by walls and trees can add interest and depth to a situation.
The brick path serves the practical function of simplifying maintenance and protecting flower and foliage from the blades of a lawnmower.*

1  *The area at the side of a house, generally little more than a long, narrow thoroughfare with little room to spare, is often a problem. More often than not it gets forgotten or becomes a storage area for hiding away all those unsightly odds and ends that accumulate in any garden. Here the approach has been altogether different and a sensitive planting plan has been carried out to provide a great deal of interest in a very small space.*
*Arched gateways tend to be rather suburban but that most useful variety of ivy, 'Goldheart', has been trained to cover the fence and archway, blending the whole structure into the adjoining border. Another attractive idea that would work well here would be to extend overhead beams out from the house. These would form a series of archways which could support climbers.*

2  *Brash flower colour can often be the antithesis of good planting design. It would be difficult to fault this group of plants in any situation and it works particularly well against the clean lines of the adjoining house. Euphorbias are essentially 'architectural' plants, with their flower-like bracts. They associate well with a vast range of species, certainly adding emphasis to this particular composition of unusual plants.*

1

2

3

3 This is essentially a plantsman's garden, with heavy emphasis on foliage rather than flower. Hostas again make their mark, while rodgersia, ferns, mahonia and rheum add breadth to the picture. Most of the plants shown are herbaceous perennials or deciduous shrubs, so in this particular garden the planting would provide little interest during winter. Fortunately, such species are fast growing and recover quickly each spring. They are invaluable in a young garden for adding instant maturity during the summer months. The yellow lilies are another herbaceous plant which provide spectacular summertime colour.

Many broad-leaved plants look their best close to water, and in fact a high proportion of them enjoy moisture at their roots. Rheum and its giant cousin gunnera set up dramatic reflections. This too is the place for weeping willows – not in small front gardens where they quickly dominate everything. The timber deck forms an attractive path, but should preferably be constructed from a timber which is naturally resistant to damp conditions, or one which has been specially treated to resist dampness. It follows a gentle curve and the boards have been shaped accordingly. The gravel path provides simple access for maintenance.

1   *In this unquestionably Mediterranean garden, a high, walled courtyard is smothered in climbing plants. In this warm climate, pelargoniums are permanently planted outdoors where they can grow very large. How much better than having to bring them indoors each winter.*

*The distribution of colour not only affects the way in which we look at a garden, but also tells us a good deal about personality. Hot colours – reds, oranges and vivid pinks – are dominant and produce spectacular restless compositions, so use them carefully and in tonal ranges. Bright light does much to temper a hot colour scheme, which is why municipal bedding displays look out of place when they use masses of tropical or sub-tropical plants in a temperate climate.*

*Bright annuals are often used to provide 'instant' colour. Try to plant them in drifts rather than in rigid ranks. If necessary, scatter seeds straight from the packet on to a prepared bed and thin out the plants as they come through.*

*Remember, too, that any garden can have a succession of year-round colour, from the earliest spring bulbs through to late-flowering Japanese anemones and asters. Colour schemes can therefore be planned in sequence, but do not forget to have a stable background of foliage.*

1

2  *This garden uses a more limited range of colour, with two shades of pink in contrast to pure white. Astilbe, which forms the middle planting, is indispensable in any collection, its foliage being almost more attractive than its plumes of flower. It enjoys a cool root run and looks particularly good close to water.*

3  *Lavender* (Lavandula angustifolia) *and pale pink roses make up this typically English planting. Apart from the colour, this plant group will also be fragrant, adding another dimension to the garden designer's palette. Most fragrant plants are attractive to bees and butterflies as well. In this age of agricultural chemicals, many gardens provide a haven for insect life. The old yew hedge and brick steps are traditional features and the latter have been carefully built in a curving pattern. The shape is pleasing, but slightly impractical, as it is difficult to sweep.*

4  *Although it makes sense to work in either a hot or a cool colour range, the odd highlight can always prove attractive. The delicacy of this border is enhanced and highlighted by the splash of red roses. One of the jobs that can extend flowering times considerably is the removal of spent blooms, known as 'dead-heading'.*

1 *Monotone gardens with plants of one colour can either be bland or stunning. More often than not it is the former. There are, of course, exceptions. The famous White Garden at Sissinghurst in Kent is a superb case in point, where the monotone planting theme is one of several in a large garden whose success depends in part on the transition between one area and the next.*
*Far more successful in a domestic situation is the provision of a corner or area which can be given over to planting along a single colour theme. This is precisely what has been done here and there is no doubt that white can be extraordinarily restful and elegant. Philadelphus acts as the background, its long arching branches laden with fragrant blossom. There are single and double forms of flower available; both are deliciously fragrant. White delphiniums can be more striking than the usual blue and here they lead the eye down to the old terracotta urn and simple paving of rectangular York stone. White-flowered* Hosta elegans *spreads its broad leaves in the middle of the group, in direct contrast to the sword-like leaves of the yucca, another plant with white flowers.*
*Although this example relies on flowers to carry the monotone theme, it is possible to work coloured foliage in as well.*

1

2 *By using plants that grow close to the ground it is possible to reduce maintenance, especially weeding, to a minimal level. Such treatment over large areas is usually called 'ground cover' and can prove very effective. When choosing a species for ground cover, check its rate of growth. This planting is a combination of cotton lavender, stonecrop and violet.*

3 *Steps, raised beds and most hard landscaping benefit from the softening influence of plants. In fact, the one is not really complete without the other. Potentilla is a valuable species and most varieties grow in a carpeting pattern. One of the best known is Potentilla fruticosa 'Tangerine', shown here in full flower.*

4 *Ground cover need not necessarily take the form of shrubs or hardy perennials. Annuals can smother the ground very quickly. Here, white Marguerite daisies are teamed with pretty yellow African marigolds.*

5 *This soft and loose composition uses a wealth of different species to make up the overall concept. The density of the planting, rather than any one carpeting species, provides ground cover.*

1   *Trees are the biggest living things in the world and, apart from houses, they are usually the most dominant element in a garden. They take many years to develop and should be carefully chosen if they are not to grow out of proportion. This Robinia pseudoacacia 'Frisia', the golden-leaved robinia, is an ideal tree for the smaller garden with its stunning foliage. It does need shelter from high wind, as the branches are a little brittle.*

2   *Rhus typhina 'Laciniata', the stag's-horn sumach, is really a large shrub, but is big enough to act as a tree in many gardens. It has architectural line and the branches take on a sculptural air in winter. Its rich autumn colour is glorious, but this sumach does have an annoying tendency to send suckers to adjoining lawns.*

3   *This grouping of shade-tolerant plants is appropriate for its location on a wall that only catches very little sun in the late afternoon. The variegated philadelphus in the centre is plenty large enough in most borders, reaching 4.5m (15ft) in quick time.*

4   *This interesting combination of purple-leaved berberis (Berberis thunbergii 'Atropurpurea') and conifers is unusual but most effective, with minimal maintenance once established.*

## PLANTING A TREE

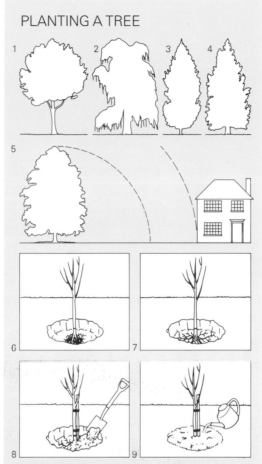

Trees have different growing habits, both in terms of shape and height. You can choose between trees of four types: **1** spreading, **2** weeping, **3** fastigiate and **4** conical. **5** In addition to selecting a tree which will not become too large, plant elm, oak, willow, poplar and cypress no closer to the house than one and a half times their mature height. **6** Dig a hole deep enough to plant the tree to the depth of the nursery mark on the stem and large enough to take the roots without cramping. Add leaf mould and peat before planting. **7** Trim off any damaged roots and spread the roots out. **8** Knock in a support, then fill in soil between the roots, firming as you go, up to the nursery mark on the stem. **9** After planting, water it well to settle the soil around the roots and speed growth.

5 *This attractive form of the common sycamore (Acer pseudoplatanus 'Brilliantissimum') has fine spring foliage, and this photograph shows it at its best, in May. Like most broad-leaved trees, it does cast heavy shade and this is always a point to be borne in mind when making a selection.*
*Another consideration, if choosing a deciduous tree, is leaf fall, which in a well-treed garden can generate a great deal of work each autumn.*

6 *This spring photograph shows the weeping whitebeam (Sorbus aria 'Pendula'), a tree tolerant of pollution and winds. Weeping trees are generally difficult to site in a garden as they are very obvious focal points. Most are too large for the small garden, but there are some good small-scale weeping trees available, including the willow-leaf pear, Pyrus salicifolia 'Pendula', and the weeping pussy willow, Salix caprea 'Kilmarnock'.*
*The care of trees is no less important than the care of any other plant. The problem is that most people tend to forget about them. Regular feeding can certainly be beneficial, while the removal of dead or diseased timber is necessary to prevent the ingress of disease. The removal of a large tree is a job best left to expert professionals.*

1 *Climbing plants are essential in any garden or backyard for a number of reasons. Perhaps most importantly, they can soften the line of overpowering boundaries. The smaller the garden, the more important this is. Plants may be grown against walls in small gardens where there is lack of space on the ground; they may enhance a building in some way. Climbing plants are also used to cover unsightly features. Climbing plants fall into two categories, those that cling to a wall (known as self-clingers) and those that need support. There is a third type that needs a wall to lean against, such as pyracantha or ceanothus, but these are really shrubs, not true climbing plants.*
*There is a myth put about, largely by architects and engineers, that climbing plants harm a building. Generally this is not the case at all, but a thick mass of foliage could just hold a degree of moisture and cause dampness on a wall. Most climbers should never be allowed to form such dense growth and they usually benefit from selective thinning. They should also be kept clear from eaves and gutters, which can quickly become clogged with leaves. Hops, generally grown on a commercial basis for beer-making, are attractive as a garden twiner. Here, the golden form (Humulus lupulus 'Aureus') makes an attractive foil to brickwork.*

2  *Ivies are self-clingers and one of the few climbing plants to thrive in really shady conditions. There are many types, from the broad-leaved* Hedera colchica *down to the smaller* Hedera helix *varieties. Here* Hedera helix *'Goldheart', whose variegated ever-gold foliage cheers up the coldest winter's day, has been trained to frame windows.*

3  Clematis montana *is one of the most valuable of the spring-flowering climbing plants. It is both vigorous and pretty, covering a wall or scrambling through a tree within two or three years after planting. The variety shown here is* Clematis montana *'Rubens', but there is a white-flowering form, 'Alba', which is equally attractive.*

4  *Virginia creeper* (Parthenocissus quinquefolia), *best known for its brilliant autumn foliage, is a self-clinging plant and one that can be grown in full shade. Chinese Virginia creeper* (Parthenocissus henryana) *has rich dark velvety-green or bronze leaves with veins picked out in pink and purple.*

5  *Honeysuckle* (Lonicera) *is the traditional sweet-smelling climber of country gardens. It flowers from June onwards and has a vigorous twining growth that is ideal for the face of a building or a pergola.*

1   *Vegetable gardening is above all a practical activity, but this is not to say that vegetable plants cannot contribute as much to a garden as strictly ornamental plants. On the Continent you can find them mixed up in the borders, contributing with their handsome foliage and often splendid flowers to the overall charisma of a garden. What could be more spectacular than a globe artichoke or a row of brilliant runner beans at the height of their flowering display? Even cabbages and in particular rhubarb can be interesting.*

*All too often we relegate vegetables to a miserable patch tucked away in an obscure and out-of-the-way corner. Not only do we miss the joy of seeing them, but it is highly impractical to have to tramp long distances in the pouring rain to pull carrots. If vegetables are grown together in their own patch then access for maintenance is important, although stepping stones can be a nuisance. Far better to use paths, as shown here, and if these can be made attractive at the same time with a pattern of bricks or slabs, so much the better. Such paths can also form useful divisions for crop rotation or fruit. The latter is another essential ingredient and in a small garden fruit trees or shrubs can often be grown on wires or against a wall to save space.*

1

2 *This close-up view of the garden shown on the opposite page illustrates just how decorative vegetables can be. Runner beans and cabbages are at two ends of the vertical scale. There are a vast number of original ways to support beans, from fixing old bicycle wheels on to the top of poles to leaning old bedsteads together tent-fashion, and the results are superb.*

3 *This vegetable garden is of course pure pattern-making, and very successful it is too. In many ways it is reminiscent of a knot garden, but here the divisions are created with neat paths rather than hedges.*

4 *The old argument that herbs have no place in the vegetable garden is of little merit, especially when considering extremely small gardens with limited space. Herbs are certainly excellent in pots and a large strawberry pot, like the one shown here, is ideal. Tomatoes are another pot-loving plant. Indeed, it is quite feasible to grow most vegetables in containers.*

5 *In this very cosmopolitan garden, tomatoes, African marigolds and begonias all form a strictly regimented but colourful collection. This does in fact make excellent use of limited space and the wall could be neatly wired to support the tomatoes.*

1   *Whether grown in a patch dedicated to vegetables or nurtured in patio containers, food plants can be as decorative as strictly ornamental plants – an important consideration in a small garden. Look for varieties which will be as versatile as possible. For example, Swiss chard is immensely practical in a small garden. The wine-red leaves and crimson stem of rhubarb chard, the variety shown here, are decorative enough to feature in the border or a patio tub. New leaves, which taste like spinach, grow from the centre as the outer leaves are harvested for a good three months.*

2   *The ferny leaves of Florence fennel (also known as finocchio or anise) make an attractive backdrop to any planting – a double bonus for lovers of its faintly liquorice-flavoured bulb.*

3   *Fruit-bearing trees and vines, such as the handsome Chinese gooseberry (Actinidia chinensis) shown here, can be squeezed into a small garden by training them, like climbing plants, to cover a warm wall.*

4   *Globe artichokes, prized for the delicious 'heart' of their flower buds and for their superb silver-grey foliage, reward negligent gardeners with this spectacular thistle-like flower when they go to seed.*

5

6

7

5　There are many good reasons for growing food, even though fruits and vegetables are available year-round. Freshly picked fruits, herbs and vegetables are undoubtedly more flavourful, and there is a certain thrill to growing your own food, no matter how small the scale of production. Many cooks supplement store-bought produce by growing varieties which are not commercially cultivated. The long, thin Japanese aubergines shown here have thinner skins and milder, more delicate flavour than the globe-shaped ones.

6　For salad-lovers, cloches, like portable greenhouses, can extend the growing season, making it possible to pick a fresh salad throughout the winter. In a small garden, grow salad vegetables which are difficult to buy, such as the elegant Red Verona chicory (radicchio) shown here, corn salad (lamb's lettuce), endive and Chinese cabbages.

7　The custard marrows shown here (also called scallop or patty pan squashes) and golden courgettes, with their yellow flowers and fruit, look bold and gay. Both are delicious raw if harvested when extremely young, with the flowers still attached, although only more mature fruits are usually sold in stores.

1   Herbs have played a vital role in both the development of gardens and man's social history. From the very earliest times the culinary and medicinal powers of herbs have been well known, and in Europe this knowledge has been systematically refined and developed for centuries, first in medieval monastic gardens and later in scientific 'physic gardens'. Many have healing powers that are still valued today. Although herbs are now mainly cultivated for cooking, they are also grown in contemporary gardens largely for their inherent beauty. They are on the whole a striking group of plants, often with superb foliage and an architectural line. The fact that they are also aromatic adds to their charm and it therefore makes sense to grow them close to a house where they can be enjoyed to the full and easily picked. Because many varieties are rampant, such as mint, it is sensible to grow these in pots where a vigorous root run can be held in check. Traditionally herbs have been grown in elaborate knot gardens, with individual species each allotted to a defined segment of the overall pattern. This delightful composition has been set out along similar lines in the shape of a wheel, the spokes of which separate the beds. Gravel paths provide access and a simple backdrop.

2   *This type of pot is ideal for the less rampant varieties of herbs. Here a collection of basil, lemon balm, parsley and thyme is positioned close to a kitchen door for easy picking. The terracotta pot provides a cooler root run than plastic or metal. Regular watering is essential for any pot and particularly one that is set on a dry, hot, paved area. For this reason, large containers which retain more moisture are the best bet, particularly when you go away on holiday.*

3   *This pretty collection in a small domestic garden underlines the point that herbs can provide an enormous diversity of leaf and colour. Mint, marjoram, rosemary and parsley are all jumbled up together to give summer-long interest. This is the sort of collection where ruthless thinning is essential every couple of years.*

4   *Containers often start life as something else: this one was an old cattle manger. The fact that it is raised makes it easier to gather herbs and also gives a far better view from the adjoining windows. Old favourites and less common, though traditional, herbs are planted here, including sage, borage and thyme. All are handsome, and sage is particularly useful as it can have plain, variegated or multicoloured leaves.*

The naming and placing of plants within a garden is perhaps the most daunting task facing the amateur. Common plant names, although often easy to remember, are quite unreliable, and it is important to learn specialist nomenclature. The local name used for a plant in one part of the country could be totally different in another. It is important to know the whole name. *Viburnum davidii*, for example, is a ground-hugger, while *Viburnum rhytidophyllum* is a giant.

The guide to the top 100 plants for small gardens and backyards presented on the following pages can form the initial basis of a planting design. It lists a range of plants to provide an exciting and colourful array for all seasons, height ranges, formal and informal uses, floral effects, foliage effects and fragrance. Remember, though, that it is by no means comprehensive. One of the great joys of gardening is the discovery of new and unexpected delights that extend your knowledge of plants.

For ease of use, selected plants have been listed by type: trees; shrubs; perennials (long-lived plants which usually flower each year); annuals and biennials (plants which die or are discarded after flowering in their first or second year); and bulbs, corms and tubers. Some plants which are in fact perennial are often treated as annuals for practical purposes, and these have been listed along with the annuals and biennials. In addition, there are lists of perennial plants for water gardens and rock gardens. On page 295, there are index boxes to help you quickly find plants for any purpose.

The key features of each plant are described in abbreviated form: growing habit and type, size (height x spread, or height only), flowers and foliage, and a summary of growing requirements (hardiness and sun requirements). For trees and shrubs, the description will let you know whether the plant is deciduous (losing its leaves each winter) or evergreen.

## KEY TO ABBREVIATIONS

| | | | | | |
|---|---|---|---|---|---|
| ann. | annual | FR | fruits | S1 | sun |
| bien. | biennial | LV | leaves | S2 | sun/semi-shade |
| decid. | deciduous | per. | perennial | S3 | semi-shade |
| evg. | evergreen | v. | very | S4 | shade |
| FL | flowers | vars | varieties | S5 | sun/shade |

Hardiness (minimum temperatures)
H1    Extremely hardy −29°C (−20°F).
H2    Very hardy −18°C (0°F).
H3    Fairly hardy −6°C (21°F) to −15°C (5°F).
H4    Slightly hardy −6°C (21°F).
H5    Tender −1°C (30°F).

## TREES

*Acer pseudoplatanus* 'Brilliantissimum' (sycamore var): slow-growing to 4.5×3.5m(15×12ft); LV decid., pinkish to yellow-green; H2; S1.

*Betula pendula* (silver birch): elegant and airy, to 9×4.5m(30×15ft); LV decid.; catkins, spring; white bark; H2; S1.

*Crataegus monogyna* 'Paul's Scarlet': to 6×6m(20×20ft); LV decid.; FL scarlet, late spring; FR red; H2; S1.

*Chamaecyparis lawsoniana* vars (Lawson's cypress): conifer, variable to 9m(30ft); LV evg., green, yellowish or grey/blue; H2; S1.

*Eucalyptus gunnii* (cider gum): to 15m(50ft) or more; LV grey, aromatic, whitish bark; FL cream, late spring; H2; S1.

*Juniperus chinensis* vars (Chinese junipers): to 4.5×1.2m(15×4ft); LV evg., greyish-green; H1; S1.

*Laburnum × watereri* 'Vossii' (golden rain tree): to 6×4.5m(20×15ft); LV decid.; FL yellow, spring; H2; S1.

*Malus* hybrids (crab apples): to 4.5-6×3-5.5m(15-20×10-18ft); LV decid., autumn colour; FL white/pink, spring; FR red/yellow; H2; S1.

*Prunus* hybrids (Japanese cherry): to 4.5×4.5m(15×15ft); LV decid., reddish when young, aut. colour; FL pink/white, spring; H2; S1.

*Pyrus salicifolia* 'Pendula' (willow-leaved pear): weeping, to 4.5×3.5m(15×12ft); LV decid., silver; FL cream, spring; H2; S1.

*Robinia pseudoacacia* 'Frisia' (black locust var): to 12×6-9m(40×20-30ft); LV golden; dark bark; H1; S1.

*Salix matsudana* 'Tortuosa' (corkscrew willow): to 9×4.5m(30×15ft); LV decid.; catkins, spring; H2; S1.

*Sorbus* 'Joseph Rock': to 6×3.5m(20×12ft): LV decid., autumn colour; FL white, late spring; FR yellow; H2; S1.

*Taxus baccata* vars (yew): bushy, to 3.5×1.8m(12ft×6ft); LV, green/yellow; FR red/orange; H3; S5.

## CLIMBING PLANTS

*Chaenomeles × superba* vars (flowering quince): 1.2×2.5m (4×8ft); LV decid.; FL red/pink/white, spring; FR yellow: H2; S1.

*Clematis* hybrids: 2.5-4.5m(8-15ft); LV decid.; FL large, purple/mauve/pink/white, spring/summer; H2; S5.

*Hedera helix* vars (ivy): to 9m(30ft); LV evg., green or cream/yellow; H2; S5.

*Jasminum officinale* (summer jasmine): to 9m(30ft); LV decid.; FL white, fragrant, summer; H3; S2.

*Lonicera periclymenum* (honeysuckle): to 6m(20ft); LV decid.; FL cream/purple, summer; FR red; H2; S3.

*Pyracantha coccinea* vars (firethorn): 2.5×2.5m(8×8ft); LV evg.; FL white, summer; FR orange/red; H2; S1.

*Rosa* hybrids (climbing rose): to 6m(20ft); LV decid.; FL red/pink/yellow/white, fragrant; H3; S1.

*Vitis coignetiae* (crimson glory vine): to 9m(30ft); LV decid., large, fine autumn colour; FR black; H2; S1.

## SHRUBS

*Aucuba japonica* 'Variegata' (spotted laurel): to 3×3m(10×10ft); LV evg., yellow-spotted; FR red; H3; S4.

*Berberis darwinii* (barberry): to 3×3m(10×10ft); LV evg.; FL golden, spring; FR purple; H3; S3.

*Berberis thunbergii* vars: neat, 0.6-1.5×0.6-1.8m(2-5×2-6ft); LV decid., red-purple; FR red; H1; S1.

*Buddleia davidii* (butterfly bush): to 3×3m(7×7ft); LV decid.; FL lilac to purple, summer/autumn; H2; S7.

*Camellia* vars to 2×1.5m(7×5ft); LV glossy; FL large, pink/red/white, winter/spring; H3; S3; acid soil.

*Choisya ternata* (Mexican orange): 2×2m(7×7ft); LV glossy, evg; FL white, fragrant, spring; H3; S1.

*Cotoneaster* hybrids: to 1.8m(6ft); LV evg./decid.; FL cream, spring; FR red: H2/H3; S1.

*Cytisus* hybrids (broom): to 1.5×1.5m(5ft×5ft); LV decid.; FL cream/yellow/pink/red, spring/ summer; H2; S1.

*Euonymus fortunei* vars: bushy/ spreading, to 1×1.5m(3×5ft); LV evg.; often variegated; H2; S2.

*Fatsia japonica* (false castor-oil plant): bold, to 2×2m(7×7ft); LV evg., large; FL cream, autumn; H3; S3.

*Fuchsia* hybrids: bushy, to 1.2×1.2m(4×4ft); LV decid.; FL nodding bells, red/pink/purple, summer; H3; S1.

*Hydrangea macrophylla*: bushy, to 1.5×1.8m(5×6ft); LV decid.; FL pink/blue/white, summer; H2; S4.

*Hypericum* 'Hidcote' (St John's wort): bushy, to 1.5m×1.8m(5×6ft); LV decid.; FL golden, summer; H2; S1.

*Lavandula spica* (lavender): low/bushy, to 60cm(2ft); LV evg., grey; FL mauve/purple, summer; H2; S1.

*Magnolia stellata* (star magnolia): bushy, slow-growing to 2.5m(8ft); FL large, white, spring, H2; S1.

*Mahonia japonica*: upright, to 1.8×2.5m(6×8ft); LV evg.; FL yellow, fragrant, winter; FR bluish; H3; S4.

*Philadelphus* hybrids (mock orange): to 1.8m×1.8m(6×6ft); LV decid.; FL white, fragrant, summer; H2; S2.

*Potentilla fruticosa* hybrids: bushy, to 0.75-1.2×1-1.2m(2½-4×3-4ft); LV small, decid., greyish; FL cream/ yellow/peach/red, summer/ autumn; H1; S5.

*Rhododendron* hybrids (inc. Azaleas): size variable; LV evg./decid.; FL wide colour range, spring/ summer; H1/H2/H3; S5; acid soil.

*Rosa* species & hybrids (rose): bushy, to 1.8×1.5m(6×5ft); LV decid.; FL red/pink/yellow/white, often fragrant, all summer; H2/H3; S1.

*Skimmia japonica*: bushy, to 1×1.5m(3×5ft); LV evg.; FL white, fragrant, spring; FR red, persistent; H3; S5; need cross-pollination.

*Spiraea* × *bumalda* 'Goldflame': to 60×90cm(2×3ft); LV decid., red to yellow; FL reddish, summer; H2; S1.

*Syringa vulgaris* (lilac): upright, to 3×2.5m(10×8ft); LV decid.; FL lilac/rosy-mauve/purple/white, fragrant, late spring; H1; S5.

*Viburnum opulus* (guelder rose): 2.5× 1.8m(8×6ft); 'Compactum' dwarf; LV decid., autumn colour; FL white, spring; FR red/yellow; H1; S1.

## PERENNIALS

*Achillea* 'Moonshine' (yarrow): to 60×45cm(2×1½ft); FL canary-yellow, early summer; H2; S1.

*Anemone* × *hybrida* vars (Japanese anemone): to 1-1.5×0.6m(3-5×2ft); FL pink/white, late summer to mid-autumn; H2; S1.

*Aster novi-belgii* vars (Michaelmas daisy): 0.3-1.2×0.3-0.45m(1-4×1-1½ft); mauve/purple/pink/red/ white, autumn; H1; S1.

*Astilbe* × *arendsii* vars: 60-90×60cm(2-3×2ft); FL pink/red/ white, summer; H2; S2; moist soil.

*Bergenia* hybrids: 30-45×30cm(1-1½ ×1ft); LV evg., winter colour; FL pink/white, spring; H1; S5; easy.

*Chrysanthemum maximum* (Shasta daisy): to 90×45cm(3×1½ft); FL showy, white, summer; H2; S1.

*Cortaderia selloana* 'Pumila' (dwarf pampas grass): 1.2m(4ft): FL cream, autumn; H3; sun.

*Dryopteris filix-mas* vars (male ferns): to 1.2×1m(4×3ft); H1; S5.

*Epimedium pinnatum colchicum* (bishop's hat): to 30×40cm(12× 16in); FL, yellow; H2; S3; moist.

*Eryngium* × *oliverianum* (sea holly): to 1.5×0.6m(5×2ft); LV blue-green; FL mauve-blue, summer; H2; S1.

*Euphorbia griffithii* 'Fireglow' (spurge): to 75×60cm(2½×2ft); FL yellow/ red bracts, spring/summer; H3; S1.

*Geranium grandiflorum* (cranesbill): to 30×60cm (1×2ft); LV autumn colour; FL mauve, summer; H2; S1.

*Helleborus orientalis* (Lenten rose): 45-60×45cm(1½-2×1½ft); LV evg.; FL cream to plum, winter; H1; S3.

*Hosta* hybrids (plantain lily): to 60-90×60cm(2-3×2ft); LV showy; FL white/violet, summer; H1; S5.

*Lamium maculatum* (spotted dead nettle): to 30×60cm(1×2ft); LV evg., marked silver; FL purplish, spring/summer; H1; S4.

*Sedum spectabile* (ice plant): to 45×45cm(1½×1½ft); LV grey-green; FL pink, autumn; H1; S1.

## WATER PLANTS

*Acorus calamus* (sweet flag): 60-90cm (2-3ft); LV iris-like; H1.

*Aponogeton distachyus* (water haw-thorn): 45cm(1½ft); LV green; FL white, spring-autumn; H4.

*Caltha palustris* (kingcup): to 30-40cm (12-16in); FL golden, spring; H1.

*Eichhornia crassipes* (water hyacinth): FL lavender-blue, summer; H5.

*Iris laevigata* (water iris): 45-75cm(1½-2½ft); FL blue-purple, summer; H2.

*Nymphaea* hybrids (water lily): spread to 1-1.5m(3-5ft); FL red/pink/ yellow/white/, summer; H2.

*Orontium aquaticum* (golden club): to 45cm(1½ft), FL yellow; H2.

*Pontederia cordata* (pickerel weed): 60-90cm(2-3ft); FL blue; summer; H1.

*Sagittaria sagittifolia* (arrowhead): to 60cm(2ft), FL white, summer; H2.

*Scirpus tabernaemontani* 'Zebrinus': to 1m(3ft); LV banded white; H3.

## BULBS, CORMS AND TUBERS

*Agapanthus orientalis:* to
1.2×0.6m(4×2ft); LV evg.; FL
blue/white, summer; H4; S1.

*Allium giganteum* (giant onion):
1-1.5×0.3m(3-5×1ft); FL pink,
summer; H2; S1.

*Begonia x tuberhybrida:* to
30×40cm(12×16in); FL vivid,
summer; H5; S1.

*Crocosmia × crocosmiiflora* (mont-
bretia): to 75×25cm (30×10in);
LV semi-evg.; FL orange/red/
yellow, summer; H3; S1.

*Crocus vernus* vars (Dutch crocuses): to
12cm(5in); FL purple/lilac/yellow/
white, spring; H2; S1; easy.

*Endymion hispanicus* (Spanish
bluebell): 30-45cm(1-1½ft); FL
violet-blue, spring; H2; S5.

*Galanthus nivalis* (snowdrop): to 20cm
(8in); FL white, winter; H1; S3.

*Gladiolus × hortulanus:* 1-1.2m(3-4ft);
FL wide range, summer; H4/5; S1.

*Hyacinthus orientalis* (hyacinth): to 25-
30cm(10-12in); LV strap-shaped; FL
pink/blue/white/yellow, v. fragrant,
spring; H2; S1.

*Iris* bearded hybrids: 40-120cm(16-
48in); LV greyish, semi-evg.; FL
wide range, summer; H2; S1.

*Lilium regale* (regal/royal lily): 1.2-
1.8m(4-6ft); FL white, v. fragrant,
summer; H1; S1.

*Narcissus* hybrids (daffodil): 35-45cm
(14-18in); FL yellow, spring; H1; S5.

*Tulipa* hybrids (tulip): 25-60cm(10-24in);
LV often greyish; FL vivid colour
range, spring; H2; S1; easy.

## ALPINE (ROCK GARDEN) PLANTS

*Ajuga reptans* (bugle): 10-30×45cm (4-
12×18in); FL blue, summer; H1;
S3.

*Alyssum saxatile* (gold dust): to
30×45cm(1×1½ft); FL golden,
spring; H1; S1.

*Aubrieta deltoides:* to 15×60cm(6×
24in); FL purple, spring; H2; S1.

*Calluna vulgaris* (heather): to 10-
60×10-75cm(4-24×4-30in); LV
coloured; FL pink/mauve/white,
summer/autumn; H2; S1.

*Campanula portenschlagiana*
(bellflower): to 15×60cm(6×24in);
FL mauve-blue, summer; H2; S5.

*Dianthus deltoides* (pinks): 15-
25×40cm(6-10×16in); LV evg.; FL
red/pink/white, summer; H1; S1.

*Gaultheria procumbens* (creeping
wintergreen): to
15×60cm(6×24in); LV evg.; FL
white, summer; FR red; H1; S4.

*Helianthemum nummularium* vars (sun/
rock rose): 15-30×60-90cm (6-
12×24-36in); FL golden/pink/
white, summer; H2; S1.

*Phlox subulata* (moss phlox): 10-15×45
cm(4-6×18in); FL pink, spring; H1; S1.

*Saxifraga,* mossy: 8-15×30-45cm (3-
6×12-18in); FL pink, spring; H2; S3.

*Sedum acre* (stonecrop): 5×25cm
(2×10in); LV evg.; FL yellow,
summer; H2; S1.

*Thymus serpyllum* (thyme):
8×60cm(3×24in); LV evg.; FL
crimson, summer; H1; S1.

## ANNUALS AND BIENNIALS

*Ageratum houstonianum* (floss flower):
bushy ann., 10-45×15-30cm(4-
18×6-12in); LV hairy; FL blue/pink/
white trusses, summer; H4; S1.

*Alyssum maritimum* (sweet alyssum):
compact, bushy ann., 8-15×20-
30cm(3-6×8-12in); FL profuse,
white/lilac/purple, fragrant, all
summer; H3; S1.

*Antirrhinum majus maximum* vars
(snapdragon): shrubby per., grown
as ann., to 75×45cm(2½×1½ft);
FL in colours, summer; H4; S1.

*Bellis perennis* (English daisy): rosette
per., grown as bien., to 10-
15×15cm(4-6×6in); FL white/pink,
mainly semi-double, spring/
summer; H2; S1; easy.

*Callistephus chinensis* (China aster):
bushy ann., to 20-75×30-60cm (8-
30×12-24in); FL in wide colour
range, summer; H3/H4; S1.

*Dianthus barbatus* (sweet William):
upright bien., 15-60×15-25cm (6-
24×6-10in); FL red/pink/white,
often bicolours, summer; H2; S1.

*Eschscholzia californica* (California
poppy): ann., 30-40×15cm(12-
16×6in); LV greyish; FL orange/
yellow/pink/red/white, summer;
H2; S1.

*Felicia bergerana* (kingfisher daisy):
mat-forming ann., to
20×15cm(8×6in); LV grey; FL
steely-blue, yellow eye, summer;
H4; S1.

*Impatiens walleräna* (busy Lizzie,
patient Lucy): per., grown as ann.,
15-60×25-45cm(6-24×10-18in);
LV pale green/bronzed; FL white/
pink/red/orange, summer; H4; S1.

*Lavatera trimestris* (annual mallow):
bushy ann., to
1.2×0.45m(4×1½ft); FL pink/
white, summer; H3/H4; S1.

*Lobelia erinus* vars (trailing lobelia):
cascading ann., to 60cm(2ft); FL
tiny, profuse, blue/purple/carmine/
white, summer; H4; S1.

*Lunaria annua* (honesty): upright bien.,
to 75×30cm(2½×1ft); FL purplish,
late spring; seed pods flat, silvery
discs; H3; S1.

*Myosotis sylvatica* (forget-me-not):
clump-forming bien., 15-40×15cm
(6-16×6in); FL sky-blue/pink,
spring; H3; S3.

*Nemesia strumosa:* ann., 20-
30×15cm(8-12×6in); FL wide
colour range, summer; H4; S1.

*Pelargonium* vars (regal, ivy & zonal
geraniums): bed. per., to
45×40cm(18×16in); FL mauve/
pink/white/red/orange, summer;
H5; S1.

*Petunia × hybrida:* bushy ann., to 20-
40×25cm(8-16×10in); FL in wide
colour range, summer; H4; S1.

*Tagetes patula* (French marigold): bushy
ann., to 20-30×30cm(8-12×12in);
FL orange/bronze/yellow, summer;
H4; S1; easy.

*Verbena × hybrida* (vervain): lax per.,
grown as ann., to 15-45×30cm (6-
18×12in); FL vivid purple/red/pink,
summer; H4; S1.

*Viola × wittrockiana* vars (pansies):
compact ann./bien., 15-25×20-
30cm(6-10×8-12in); FL flat, showy,
wide colour range, often with
'faces', late spring/summer/winter;
H3/H4; S3.

## PLANTS WITH OUTSTANDING FOLIAGE

| | | | |
|---|---|---|---|
| Acer tree | Calluna alpine | Hedera climber | Robinia tree |
| Ajuga alpine | Chamaecyparis tree | Hosta per. | Spiraea shrub |
| Aucuba shrub | Epimedium per. | Juniperus tree | Taxus tree |
| Berberis th. shrub | Eucalyptus tree | Lamium per. | Viburnum shrub |
| Bergenia per. | Euonymus shrub | Pyrus tree | Vitis climber |

## PLANTS FOR WINTER COLOUR

| | | | |
|---|---|---|---|
| Aucuba shrub | Euonymus shrub | Helleborus per. | Skimmia shrub |
| Bergenia per. | Galanthus bulbs | Juniperus tree | Taxus tree |
| Chamaecyparis tree | Gaultheria alpine | Mahonia shrub | Viola ann./bien. |

## PLANTS FOR SPRING COLOUR

| | | | |
|---|---|---|---|
| Acer tree | Camellia shrub | Galanthus bulbs | Narcissus bulbs |
| Alyssum sax. alp. | Chaenomeles climb. | Hyacinthus bulbs | Phlox sub. alp. |
| Aubrieta alpine | Choisya shrub | Laburnum tree | Prunus tree |
| Bellis ann./bien. | Crataegus tree | Lunaria bien. | Rhododendron |
| Berberis dar. shrub | Crocus bulbs | Magnolia shrub | Syringa shrub |
| Bergenia per. | Endymion bulbs | Myosotis bien. | Tulipa shrub |

## PLANTS FOR SUMMER COLOUR

| | | | |
|---|---|---|---|
| Agapanthus bulbs | Dianthus alpine | Jasminum climb. | Spiraea shrub |
| Allium bulbs | Fuchsia shrub | Lavandula shrub | Thymus alpine |
| Begonia bulbs | Gladiolus bulbs | Lilium bulbs | See also: |
| Buddleia shrub | Helianthemum alp. | Lonicera climber | Annuals/bien. |
| Campanula alp. | Hydrangea shrub | Philadelphus shrub | Perennials |
| Clematis climber | Hypericum shrub | Potentilla shrub | Water plants |
| Crocosmia bulbs | Iris bulbs | Rosa shrub/climb. | |

## PLANTS FOR AUTUMN COLOUR

| | | | |
|---|---|---|---|
| Acer tree | Chaenomeles climb. | Epimedium per. | Sedum spect. per. |
| Anemone per. | Cortaderia per. | Malus tree | Sorbus tree |
| Aster per. | Cotoneaster shrub | Prunus tree | Viburnum shrub |
| Berberis shrub | Crataegus tree | Pyracantha climb. | Vitis climber |

## PLANTS FOR CONTAINERS

| | | | |
|---|---|---|---|
| Agapanthus bulbs | Felicia ann./bien. | Lobelia ann./bien. | Tulipa bulbs |
| Aucuba shrub | Fuchsia shrub | Narcissus bulbs | Verbena ann./ |
| Begonia bulbs | Hedera climber | Nemesia ann./bien. | bien. |
| Camellia shrub | Hyacinthus bulbs | Pelargonium annual | Viola ann./bien. |
| Crocus bulbs | Hydrangea shrub | Petunia annual | |
| Euonymus shrub | Impatiens annual | Rhododendron | |
| Fatsia shrub | Lilium bulbs | shrub | |

## PLANTS FOR HANGING BASKETS

| | | | |
|---|---|---|---|
| Begonia bulbs | Hedera climber | Nemesia annual | Petunia annual |
| Fuchsia shrub | Lobelia annual | Pelargonium ann. | Verbena annual |

## PLANTS FOR GROUND COVER

| | | | |
|---|---|---|---|
| Ajuga alpine | Epimedium per. | Hedera climber | Potentilla shrub |
| Aubrieta alpine | Euonymus shrub | Hosta per. | Saxifraga alpine |
| Bergenia per. | Gaultheria alpine | Lamium per. | Sedum acre alp. |
| Campanula alp. | Geranium per. | Phlox alpine | Thymus alpine |

## SHADE-TOLERANT PLANTS

| | | | |
|---|---|---|---|
| Ajuga alpine | Endymion bulbs | Hydrangea shrub | Rhododendron |
| Aucuba shrub | Epimedium per. | Impatiens annual | shrub |
| Bergenia per. | Euonymus shrub | Lamium per. | Skimmia shrub |
| Campanula alpine | Fatsia shrub | Lunaria ann./ | Taxus tree |
| Clematis climber | Gaultheria alpine | bien. | |
| Dryopteris per. | Hosta per. | Mahonia shrub | |

## SCREENING & HEDGING PLANTS

| | | | |
|---|---|---|---|
| Aucuba shrub | Chamaecyparis tree | Crataegus tree | Rosa shrub, |
| Berberis dar. shrub | Cotoneaster shrub | Mahonia shrub | climber |
| | | | Taxus tree |

# PRACTICALITIES

It is fair to say that any garden, however well designed, will need a degree of on-going maintenance. Wear and tear is bound to be a factor in hard landscape areas, while plants will need encouragement and pruning from time to time.

Tools and equipment are increasingly easy to care for, but always ensure that power equipment is regularly serviced, particularly electrical appliances. Hand tools work much more efficiently if kept sharp and lightly oiled, while timber fences and buildings need treating with non-toxic preservative every two years.

Good-quality, well-laid paving needs little attention, apart from sweeping down and keeping free from slime in pedestrian areas. For this, use a proprietary pool additive that discourages algae, watered down and swept over with a stiff broom. Occasionally, paving slabs get broken or bricks deteriorate owing to frost damage. They can be carefully chopped out using a hammer and bolster, then replacements laid in mortar to match the surrounding levels.

Walls, too, can show the effect of age, particularly in mature town gardens. Renovation will involve raking out the old joints, sweeping down and repointing. Provided it is otherwise sound, this will extend the life of a wall almost indefinitely.

Climbing plants, contrary to common belief, do little harm to a wall in good condition, but they may damage roofs and eaves. It is best to support climbers by horizontal wires spaced up the wall at 61cm (2ft) intervals. A trellis can often destroy the visual unity of a building and usually needs far more maintenance.

Pruning seems confusing to many people, but the rules are on the whole very straightforward.

Trees need thinning if they get too dense and any damaged or diseased branches should be carefully removed. Shrubs which flower in spring and early summer can be pruned after flowering, which means removing dead or weak growths and clipping over the more 'leggy' species. Later-flowering shrubs such as buddleia and hydrangea should be cut back in the spring so that young flowering stems can develop. Species such as the dogwoods (*Cornus*), which are planted for the winter interest of their stems, depend on new growth, and can be cut back hard in early spring during March.

## HAND TOOLS CHECKLIST

- Spade(s) – choose between full-size digging spade and border spade. Stainless steel blades are more expensive than carbon steel.
- Fork(s) – choose between digging fork and border fork.
- Rake(s) – a lightweight head with about a dozen teeth will do for most soils. Fan-shaped rakes are good for lawn care.
- Hoe(s) – choose between long-handled Dutch-type hoe with a flat blade and draw hoe intended to be pulled backwards rather than pushed.
- Trowel – essential for planting.
- Shears – choose between long-handled edging and lawn shears and hedging shears.
- Secateurs – choose between curved- and straight-blade types.
- Hose.
- Hand sprayer.
- Watering can.
- Stiff broom.
- Wire and vine-eyes for supporting climbing plants.

*This charming corner has it all: a barbecue area, log store and dining space set under the trees. This is simply good garden design: nothing contrived here, just sound common sense, which is precisely why it works so well.*

Why should potting benches be both ugly and boring? This is a practical yet well-detailed corner which has been constructed from simple horizontal boards. It cleverly conceals an ugly concrete-block wall to the left while the roof is made of clear sheeting to admit maximum light.

Gardens have to contain the ugly as well as the beautiful and dustbins should always have a place to go. This store has been cleverly fitted into a bank and climbers soften its outline. It is close to the back door, so the timber has been stained to match that of the house.

Garden tools will give years of use, if you follow a few rules: never leave them outdoors when you have finished working; always clean and dry them after use; keep blades and fork tines lightly oiled; sharpen spades with an oil stone or a file occasionally and oil any wooden handles; always store in a dry place; only use tools on jobs for which they were intended.

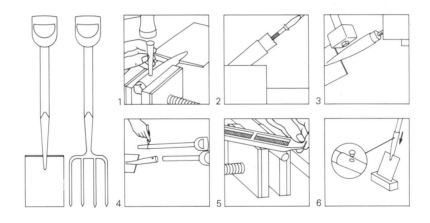

To replace a broken handle: 1 Punch out the rivet holding handle, working against the head. 2 Clamp spade in a vice, then drive a 152mm (6in) screw into broken end. 3 Holding the screw in a vice, tap the spade to release it. 4 Cut new handle to size. 5 Using a surform, taper the end to fit the spade socket. 6 Tap the handle home, then fit a screw to hold it in place.

Fence posts need to be really stable. To secure them you can set them into concrete 1, or you can add extra support with fence spikes 2 or concrete spurs 3 – both also excellent for repairing rotten or rickety posts. If you have many posts to sink, consider hiring or buying a post-hole borer 4 – but be warned, you need to be strong to use it!

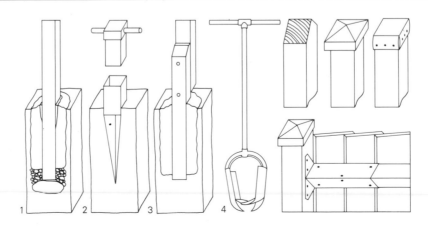

The tops of fence posts should be protected against rain penetration and eventual rotting. Do this by cutting the top with angled sides or by fitting special caps. The timber must have been treated against damp with a non-toxic preservative. To secure arris rails to fence posts, use angled arris rail brackets which have splayed ends for attaching to the post.

Make the most of walls in the garden by growing climbing plants over them, creating a living background for your garden. You will need to give the plants something to cling to, like a trellis, and most versatile is a trellis attached to a frame that is hinged at the base. This means you can swing it down to give access to the wall if you need to paint or repoint it at a later date.

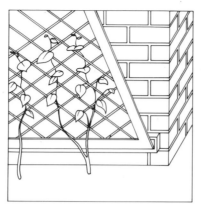

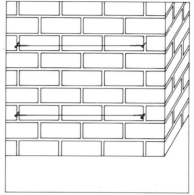

Another successful and less obtrusive way of growing climbers up a wall is to position horizontal wires at 305mm – 457mm (12in – 18 in) intervals for the plants to grow around. Wires should be about 76mm (3in) from the wall and attached by masonry nails or metal vine-eyes inserted into drilled and plugged holes to ensure that the full weight of the climber can be supported.

A glass or plastic tunnel cloche is ideal for protecting young plants against bad weather, helps speed growth and extends the growing season. Offering less protection but excellent for keeping off birds is a net cloche. Net can also be used with canes to form a 'tent' for sweet peas and runner beans to grow over, giving the plants maximum light and you easy access.

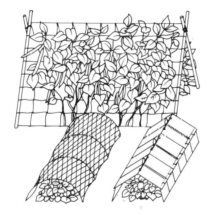

Perfect for patios, verandahs and greenhouses are grow-bags. Filled with a soil-less compost, these bags can support most flowers and vegetables, but are particularly good for tomatoes, beans and marrows. Always keep them well watered and fed though, as the compost can dry out very quickly in hot weather. Position them in a sunny place.

Supports come in all shapes and sizes, from crisp planed lengths of timber to the rustic poles shown here, and in all moods, from architectural to distinctly rural. The only problem with these poles is that they can rot quickly, particularly if the bark is left on.

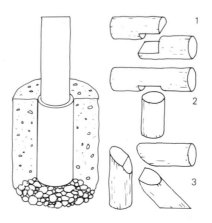

Construct an arbour using either squared timber or rustic larch poles. Secure in the ground by sinking in a section of plastic pipe positioned over hardcore, then embed in concrete. You can join lengths of larch pole with a halving joint 1; join verticals to horizontals by means of a notch in the cross beam 2; and use a birdsmouth notch 3 to fix a diagonal to a vertical post.

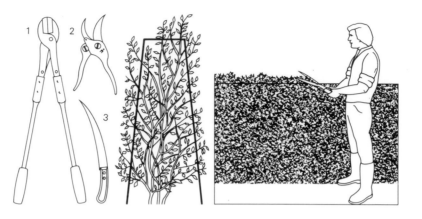

Using the right tools makes pruning easy. Long-handled pruners **1** give extra leverage for cutting through tough stems and are perfect for branches that are just out of arm's reach. For general work a pair of pruning shears or secateurs **2** are essential, but when you need greater control of the cut, use a pruning knife **3**. A selection of saws is necessary for trees.

Clip hedges two or three times during the summer months using sharp, well-oiled shears. Shape so that the hedge is narrower at the top — this allows light to the base and helps to shed winter snow. To keep the top straight, stretch garden line between posts at the desired height, checking with a spirit level. Use this as a guide to work to but be careful not to cut through it.

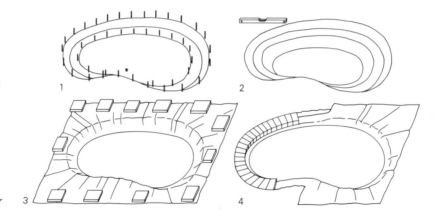

Making a garden pool with a pond liner could be done in a weekend. **1** Mark out the required shape, including any marginal shelves, with a series of pegs and string. Dig out to this shape and firm down. **2** Use long battens and a spirit level to check the edges are level. Be sure to remove any sharp stones that could penetrate the liner, then cover the hollow with newspapers or

sand for extra protection. **3** Fit the liner into the hollow and secure at the perimeter with paving slabs or stones. Fill with water, the weight of which will fit the liner to the hollow. **4** Trim off any surplus liner, then bed decorative paving on to sand and cement to complete the pool edges. Plant out as desired, then leave the pool to settle and the water to clear, which may take a few weeks.

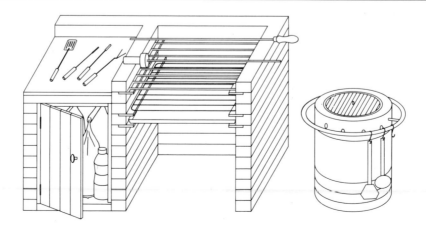

A permanent barbecue makes an interesting garden feature, plus it means the end of the storage problems caused by portables. If you're stuck for ideas, look out for DIY kits or copy this one with its variable grill heights, work space and storage area. Build against a wall, add a chimney and a small roof to protect against bad weather and you can use it throughout the year.

Oil drums have their uses and this has been made into a particularly sophisticated barbecue with vents and a circular hanging rail for utensils. Barrels and metal dustbins can likewise be converted into barbecues.

The lawnmower you opt for depends on the type and size of your lawn and the finished effect you want. For the classic striped effect a cylinder mower **1** is best – the more blades it has, the finer the cut, and this is important if you have a high-quality lawn. If you have an uneven lawn composed of rougher grass, a rotary mower **2** would be a better choice. If you have slopes to deal with a

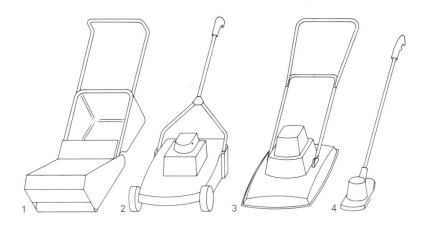

hover mower **3** is worth considering and these are ideal for those who lack the strength to deal with a heavier mower. A grass box can be an important addition if your lawn is large, as raking lawn clippings can take longer than mowing! Finally, for cutting edges and up to trees and fences there's a nylon thread trimmer **4** – easier and quicker than using edging shears.

Mow your lawn from March to October, judging frequency by growth. Never cut the grass too closely – to about 12mm (1/2in) minimum, but longer in dry spells to conserve moisture. Avoid mowing when the grass is wet – the end of the day is best – and don't leave cuttings on the lawn except in dry weather. Raking is necessary in spring and autumn to remove debris from the lawn.

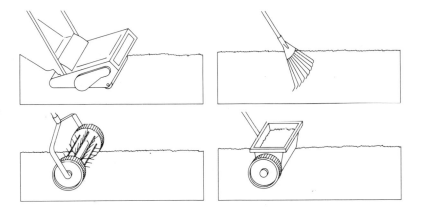

Aerating the lawn with a mechanical spiker or, on a smaller lawn, a fork, helps promote root growth and is essential for heavy or badly drained soils. Apply a light top dressing after aerating. For healthy lawn growth apply fertilizer in early April and later in the year, including an autumn feed, as necessary. A mechanical spreader distributes the fertilizer evenly.

Practicality is one of the keys to garden design and there is nothing more awkward or frustrating than having to mow close to a wall. By laying a course of bricks flat at the base of the wall you overcome this problem and create an attractive detail at the same time, as demonstrated by the graceful curved mowing strip illustrated here.

Removing a large bump or filling a hollow in a lawn is a relatively simple job but is best done between October and March. Using a knife, cut across the offending area, then gently ease back the turf. Remove excess or fill with top soil, then replace the turf and firm down. Fill in the cuts with sieved top soil. If the area is large, first cut turves from the centre, then fill or reduce as above.

## A

arbours, 268, 299
attics: bathrooms, 211
  bedrooms, 158, 177, 182,
  193, 198, 203
  living rooms, 35
  sitting rooms, 51

## B

barbecues, 297, 300
bathrooms, 204-27
  accessories, 204, 217
  basins, 216-17
  baths, 206-7, 210-11, 213
  in bedrooms, 211
  bidets, 214-15
  electricity, 227
  fittings, 210, 218
  flooring, 220, 224-5
  heating, 226-7
  lighting, 218
  planning, 205, 208-9
  size, 204
  space, 208, 211
  surfaces, 220, 221-5
  taps, 217
  tiles, 219, 220, 221-5
  toilets, 214-15
  wall coverings, 220, 221-5
  windows, 220
bed-linen, 162, 163-9, 172, 202
bed-sitting rooms, 170, 171-5
bedrooms, 154-203
  bath areas, 211
  children's, 192, 193-203
  country style, 166
  dual purpose, 170, 171-5
  open plan, 155
  sleeping platforms, 156, 159,
  195, 200
  storage, 176, 177-83
  work areas in, 156
beds, 160-11, 196-7
bidets, 214-5
blinds, 40, 43, 67
  bathrooms, 212, 222
  bedrooms, 186, 188, 189, 190
  Holland, 41
  kitchens, 82, 128
  Roman, 189, 222
  Venetian, 10, 44, 56, 57, 186
bookshelves, 12, 17, 46, 47, 48,
  141, 148

## C

carpets, 68, 71
  halls, 9, 14, 18
  kitchens, 132
  living rooms, 28, 31
ceilings, 68, 98, 139
children's rooms, 192, 193-203
  beds, 192
  curtains, 203
  electronic equipment, 192
  flooring, 192
  lighting, 200-3
  nurseries, 194-5
  space, 192, 193, 194
  storage, 192, 194, 197
  teenagers', 198-9
  trompe-l'oeil, 203
  wall coverings, 192
  windows, 203
conservatories, 267
curtains: bedroom windows,
  188, 189
  beds, 162, 168-9
  children's rooms, 203
  four-poster beds, 159

## D

desks, 16, 30, 31, 33
  in bedrooms, 156, 174
  in children's rooms, 199, 201
dhurries, 28, 42, 54
dining areas, 85, 88
  in kitchens, 140-5
  lighting, 140, 145
  open plan, 142-3
  room dividers, 140, 144-5
dining rooms, 146-53
  chairs, 146, 148-9
  dressers, 150, 151
  furniture, 146, 148-51
  lighting, 146, 152-3
  sideboards, 146, 150-1
  tables, 146, 148-9, 151
  windows, 146
drapes, 42, 77
  bed, 162, 168-9, 188
  bedroom windows 188
  children's rooms, 203
dual-purpose bedrooms, 30, 49,
  156, 170, 171-5, 192, 193-203

## E

equipment, kitchen, 100-1
  electronic, 46, 52-3, 192
extractors, 92, 98-9
  ducting, 98, 99
  hoods, 81, 93, 94, 98-9

## F

fabrics, 36-7
  upholstery, 38-9
  wall coverings, 72
fences, 260-1, 269, 298
fireplaces, 42, 44, 51, 58, 141
  as focal points, 54, 55, 60-3
flooring: bathrooms, 220, 224-5
  carpets, 9, 18, 28, 31, 68, 71
  ceramic tiles, 87, 136
  children's rooms, 192, 194, 195
  cork, 132, 136, 137, 153
  flagstones, 132
  halls, 8, 9, 12, 18-19
  kitchens, 132-7
  linoleum, 8, 19, 132, 133
  living rooms, 68, 70-1
  marble, 132
  nurseries, 194, 195
  parquet, 18, 66
  plywood squares, 71
  quarry tiles, 132, 137
  slate, 132
  synthetic rubber, 135, 137
  terracotta tiles, 67
  terrazzo, 132
  vinyl, 8, 12, 56, 83, 132, 133,
  136, 145
  wooden floorboards, 18, 40,
  42, 50, 60, 68, 70, 73, 125,
  128, 132, 134
food storage, 106
  freezers, 97, 112-13
  larder units, 111
  larders, 114-15
  refrigerators, 112-113
  storage times, 112-13
front gardens, 242

## G

galleries, bedrooms, 226-7
galley kitchens, 86
garages, 234, 270
garden design: effective
  planting, 240-1

focal points, 253
furniture, 252-3, 266, 271, 274
planning, 236, 237-51
tension points, 239
garden tools, 296, 298, 300
garden walls, 254, 275
  brick, 230
  climbing plants, 284, 299
  concrete blocks, 237
  enclosed areas, 248-9
  maintenance, 296
  trompe-l'oeil, 249
ground cover plants, 280-1

## H

halls, 6-23
  entrances, 8-9
  flooring, 18-19
  houseplants in, 67
  lighting, 6, 10, 12, 22-3, 40
  storage, 6, 10-11, 12-13
  walls, 20-1
hedges, 255, 264, 265, 300
herbaceous plants, 277
herbs, 83, 243, 287, 291
houseplants, 14, 16, 17, 33, 41,
  49, 54, 64-7, 74, 75

## K

kelims, 40, 42, 71, 156
kitchen units, 82-3, 106-17
  carousels, 110, 111
  corner units, 110
  handles and knobs, 130, 131
  island units, 89, 90, 93, 96
  larder, 111
  modular, 84
  plinths, 83, 84
  pull-out shelves, 110
  replacing doors, 130
  wood, 124-5

## L

landings, 16-17
  lighting, 16, 23
  walls, 21
larders, 111, 114-15
laundry facilities, 116-17
lawns, 231, 239, 259, 274, 301
  mowing, 241, 301
lighting, 74, 75-9, 235
  bathrooms, 218

bedrooms, 184, 185-91
children's rooms, 200-3
dining areas, 140, 142, 145
dining rooms, 146, 152-3
downlighters, 12, 23, 40, 74, 77
dual-purpose rooms, 170,
171, 173
fluorescent, 138, 140
halls, 6, 10, 22-3, 40
houseplants, 67, 74, 75
kitchens, 83, 86, 138-9
landings, 16, 23
mirrors, 191
reflections, 23, 79
stairways, 23
task lighting, 10, 33, 74, 78-9,
138-9, 191
uplighters, 22, 74, 75-7
living rooms, 24-79
arrangement of furniture, 28-9
colour schemes, 24
as dual-purpose rooms, 30-1, 49
focal points, 28, 54, 55-67
lighting, 74, 75-9
storage, 45, 46, 47-53

**M**

mattresses, 154, 158, 160
children's, 192
futons, 154, 157, 160-1, 162
types, 160

**N**

nurseries, 194-5

**O**

one-room apartments, 170,
171-5

**P**

paint finishes, 68, 72-3, 126-7,
130-1
paths, 236, 240, 243, 254,
255, 264, 275, 277, 286
patios, 232, 233, 235, 258
paving, 234, 248, 250, 253,
254, 256-7
pictures, 54, 58, 74
plants, 17, 33, 41, 49, 54, 64-7
guide to, 292-5
play areas, in the garden, 236

pools, 240, 250, 251, 266, 269, 300
porches, 258

**Q**

quarry tiles, 132, 137

**R**

roof gardens, 249
room dividers: 100, 140, 144-5
rugs, 42, 44, 54, 65, 68, 69, 70,
71, 156

**S**

sculpture, in the garden, 253,
255, 270
seating, 32, 33-4
buying, 32
garden, 252-3, 266, 271, 274
loose covers, 38
platforms for, 32, 34-5, 78
reproduction, 42-3
twentieth-century classics,
44-6
upholstery, 38-9
wicker, 33, 56, 65
sheds, 236
shelves, 46, 48, 50, 55, 175,
181, 199
adjustable, 181
bedrooms, 178
for books, 12, 17, 46, 48
children's rooms, 197
dining rooms, 151
folding, 175
in halls, 12-13
kitchens, 84, 85, 93, 107, 109
pull out, 110
showers, 211, 212-13, 220
tiling, 220
shrubs, 280-1, 296
sideboards, 59, 69, 146, 150-1
sinks, 102-3, 109
ceramic, 103
double, 87, 102, 105, 120
enamelled, 104
heights, 89
stainless steel, 103
storage below, 105, 117
skylights, 6, 17, 35, 87, 145,
152, 203
sofas, 28, 29, 35, 39, 40, 41, 42,
44, 47, 50, 57, 64, 70

cane, 10, 45
convertible, 156, 157, 162
stairways, 14-15, 18
carpeting, 19
landings, 16-17
lighting, 23
storage under, 10, 12, 13, 47
storage: bathrooms, 207
bedrooms, 176, 177-83
below sinks, 105, 117
carousels, 110, 111
children's rooms, 192, 194,
195, 197, 199
china, 111
corner space, 110
cube, 25
cupboards, 10-11
custom-built, 183
dining rooms, 146, 150-1
dual-purpose bedrooms, 170
electronic equipment, 46, 52-3
equipment, 100-1
fitted, 176, 180-1
free-standing, 176, 178, 179
halls, 6, 10-11, 12-13
kitchens, 82-3, 106-17
larder units, 111
larders, 114-15
laundry equipment, 116-17
living rooms, 45, 46, 47-53
modular, 51
nurseries, 194, 195
pull-out shelves, 110
shoes, 13
small spaces, 11-12
under staircases, 10, 12, 13,
47
utility cupboards, 116-17
work areas in bedrooms, 31,
174, 175
studios, 170, 171-5
surfaces finishes, 68, 69-73
bathrooms, 220
details, 130-1
kitchens, 118-31
laminates, 84, 118, 119, 125,
128-9
painted, 126-7
splashbacks, 122-3
wood, 120, 124-5
worktops, 118, 120-1

**T**

tables, 233
coffee, 33, 35, 40, 41, 50, 56,
57, 58
dining, 29, 140, 141, 142,
143, 144, 146, 148-9, 151
garden, 233
halls, 9, 13
as kitchen work surfaces, 90, 91
occasional, 39, 57-8
trestle, 28
work areas, 30
task lighting, 10, 33, 74, 78,
138, 191
teenagers' rooms, 198-9
terraces, 232, 241, 250, 251, 259
tiles, 87
bathrooms, 219, 220, 221-5,
222-3
cork, 220, 224
flooring, 132, 136
in the garden, 258
mirror, 219
showers, 220
splashbacks, 83, 87, 91, 122-3,
139
windowsills, 123
worktops, 87, 121
toilets, 214-15
town gardens, 234-5
trees, 238, 256, 282-3, 296
trompe-l'oeil, 19, 203, 249

**U**

upholstery, 32, 38-9
utensils, storage, 93, 98
utility cupboards, 116-17

**W**

wall finishes, 68, 72-3
bathrooms, 220
children's rooms, 192
hallways, 8, 9, 20-21
living rooms, 34
wallpaper, 68, 123
white gardens, 280
wicker seating, 33, 56, 65
work areas: in bedrooms, 156,
170, 171-5
in children's rooms, 199, 201
on landings, 16
in living rooms, 30-1, 35

The publisher thanks the following photographers and organizations for their kind permission to reproduce the photographs in this book:

Abitare (Ornella Sancassani) **10** 2, **58** 1, **61** 4, **174** 1, (Gabriele Basilico) **42** 1; Heather Angel **250** 1, **251** 6, **254-5**, **263** 2, **274** 3, **276** 2, **276-7** 3, **284** 1; ARCAID (Richard Bryant) **250** 3, **252** 2, (John Croce) **230-231** 3; Behr Furniture **173** 3; Berrymagicoal **97** 4; Vivian Boje **181** 3; Bosch **84** 1, **85** 2, **95** 3, **110** 3, **111** 5, **130** 4; Guy Bouchet **151** 3; Michael Boys **232** 3, **248** 2, **268** 1; Bulthaup **97** 3, **101** 5, **105** 6 and 7, **111** 7, **114** 4, **121** 2, **123** 2, **129** 3, **130** 1, 3 and 5, **143** 1; Linda Burgess **249** 5, **258** 2, **270** 3; Camera Press **12** 2, **13** 6, **30** 1, **30-31** 3, **34** 2, **35** 4, **38** 1, 2 and 3, **48** 2, **49** 5 and 6, **51** 3, **59** 2, **64** 3, **65** 4, **67** 2, **78** 3, **79** 4, **91** 2, **98** 3, **100** 1, **101** 4, **110** 4, **122** 1, **126-7** 3, **168** 2, **169** 6, **170-171**, **173** 2, **174** 2, **182** 1, **186** 1, **194** 1, **196** 2, **198** 3, **200** 1, **201** 3 and 4, **202** 1, 2 and 3, **203** 5 and 8, **210** 1, **211** 6, **214** 1 and 3, **219** 4, **220-221**, **222** 1, **225** 4 and 6, **233** 4, **235** 2, **251** 4, **259** 10; Collier Campbell **64** 2, **72** 2; courtesy Conran's USA **156** 1, **180** 1; Gilles de Chabaneix **14** 2, **92-93**, **152**, **158** 1, **213** 5, **217** 6; Floor by Sheppard Day Designs **19** 6 and 7, **126** 2; Council of British Sanitaryware Manufacturers (Allia, Armitage Shanks, Ideal-Standard, Johnson Brothers, Shires Bathrooms and Twyford Bathrooms) **208-209**; Divertimenti **105** 5; Dorma **159** 6, **172-3** 1; Dux Interiors Ltd **158** 2; DD Flicker Ltd **45** 3, **164-5** 1; Elon Tiles **104** 1, **137** 4; Inge Epsen Hansen **287** 4, **291** 4; Robert Estall **240-1** 1; Gautier **196** 3; John Glover **251** 7; Goldreif Kitchens **114** 1, 2 and 3; Good House-keeping (Jan Baldwin) **40-1** 1, **97** 2, **148-9** 1, **150-1** 1, **178** 2, **184-5**, **266-7** 1, (David Brittain) **9** 3, **50-1** 1, **78** 1, **102** 1, **109** 2, **217** 3 and 5, **219** 3, (John Cook) **121** 3, (David Montgomery) **166** 2, (Hugh Palmer) **287** 3, (Malcolm Robertson) **174-5** 3, (Dennis Stone) **128-9** 1; Derek Gould **291** 2; Susan Griggs Agency/Michael Boys **168** 1, **211** 4; Kari Haavisto **63** 4, **142** 2, **165** 3; Habitat **28** 1, **29** 2, **36** 1, **42** 2, **45** 2, **53** 2, **57** 2 and 3, **59** 3, **71** 3, **76** 1, **78** 2, **82** 1 and 2, **87** 2, **124-5** 1, **134-5** 3, **136** 1 and 2, **137** 3 and 5, **156** 2, **159** 4 and 5, **166-7** 3, **178** 1, **189** 2, **196** 1, **203** 6, **216** 1 and 2; Robert Harding/Brook **16** 1, **223** 2; Pamela Harper **251** 5; Jerry Harpur **243** 2, **249** 6, **259** 9, **269** 3, **272-3**, **274** 2, **281** 5, **287** 5, **290-291** 1, **291** 3, (designer Mackenzie Bell) **228-229**, (designers Hillier and Hilton – Helen and Desmond Preston's garden) **238** 1, (Don Drake) **239** 2, (Geoff Kaye, Clifton Nurseries) **249** 4, **258** 4, (Hillier and Hilton) **258** 5, (Vic Shanley, Clifton Nurseries) **259** 7, **263** 3, (John Brookes) **259** 2, (Alan Mason, Harewood) **279** 2, (Barnsley House, Cirencester) **286** 1, **287** 2; C P Hart and Sons Ltd **214** 2; Marijke Heuff, Amsterdam **234** 1, (Yak Ritzen, Holland) **250** 2, **258** 6, (Wim Lansonder, Holland) **262-3** 1, (Mr & Mrs van Bennekom, Holland – garden open to public 1st weekend in July) **264** 1, (Mien Ruys & Hans Veldhoen, Holland) **264** 2, **274** 4, (André van Wassenhove, Belgium) **264-5** 3; Neil Holmes **230** 1, **243** 4, **259** 8, **279** 3, **288** 1 and 2; Pat Hunt **258** 3; Jacqui Hurst **248** 1; Impact Photos/Pamela Toler **271** 4; Kingswood Kitchens **105** 4; Läger Kitchens **117** 5; Michele Lamontagne **232** 2, **241** 2 and 3, **242** 1, **257** 2, **260** 1, **261** 2; Ligne Roset **51** 2; Georges Lévêque **252** 1, **253** 5, **257** 3, **271** 6 (architect Michel Renévot) **256** 1; John Lewis of Hungerford **115** 5; Maison Française (Arcadia) **6-7** 1, **57** 4, (Philippe Leroy) **112** 1, (Jacques Primois) **187** 2, (Monsieur Gervais) **212** 1; La Maison de Marie Claire (Hussenot/Charras) **22** 2, **189** 3, **223** 5, (Pataut/Bayle) **24-5**, **70** 1, **80-81**, **140-1** 1, (Rozes/C Hirsch-Marie) **39** 5, **41** 3, **56-7** 1, **144** 1, **213** 3, **217** 4, (Bouchet/AM Conte) **46-7** 1, (Bootz/Olry) Michele and Anne-Marie, **49** 4, (Liddell/Puech) **68-9**, (Pataut/

Puech) **74-5**, **149** 3, (Korniloff/Hirsch-Marie) **87** 3, (Dirand/Chauvel) **90-91** 1, (Pataut/Ardouin) **99** 4, (Pataut/Postic) **106-107**, (Bouchet/Ardouin) **125** 3, (Dirand/Comte) **134** 1, (Pataut/Lautier) **149** 2, (Nicolas/Pelle) **154-5**, (Eriaud/AM Comte) **162-3**, **192-3**, (Korniluff/Billaud) **169** 4, (Nicolas/N Vallery-Radot) **169** 5, (Godeau/Belmont) **176-7**, **218** 1, **227** 2, (Pons/Puech) **197** 4, (Eriaud/Postic) **198-9**, **201** 2, (Dirand) **204-5**, (Kukhan/Hirshnani) **206** 1, **207** 2, (Bouchet/Hourdin) **227** 3, (Viane/Belmont) **248** 3; Peter McHoy **252** 3, **270** 1, **271** 5, **276** 1; Tania Midgley **259** 11, **280-1** 1; Miele Sie **104** 2, **110** 1, **116-117** 1, **117** 2 and 4; Mon Jardin et Ma Maison/Kolko **296-7** 1; Neff (UK) Ltd (photography by David Britain) **104** 3, **108-109** 1, **113** 2 and 3, **123** 3, **129** 2; Octopus (Michael Boys) **282** 2, **285** 3, **288** 4, (Jerry Harpur) **279** 4, **282** 1 and 4, **283** 5 and 6, **285** 2, 4 and 5, (George Wright) **275** 5, **281** 2 and 3; Philippe Perdereau **243** 5, **252** 4, **274** 1, **278** 1, **299**; Photos Horticultural **236-7** 1, **289** 5, 6 and 7; Plastiglide Products **131** 6, 7 and 8; Michael Reed (photographer Etienne Bol) **118-9**; Bent Rej **21** 3, **34** 1, **66** 1, **157** 3, **158** 3, **165** 2, **183** 3, **189** 4, **198** 1 and 2; Ianthe Ruthven **144-5** 1; Arthur Sanderson and Sons Ltd **62** 3; SieMatic UK Ltd **98** 1 and 2, **100** 3, **101** 6, **111** 6 and 8, **117** 3, **126** 1, **130** 2, **142** 3; Terry Sims **195** 4; Handpainted bedrooms by Smallbone **181** 2; Harry Smith Horticultural Collection **288** 3; David Stevens **269** 2 and 4, **270** 2, **281** 4, **282** 3, **298** 1 and 2, **301**; Jessica Strang (designer Gerd Seeber) **53** 3; Syndication International (Homes and Gardens) **2**, (Ideal Home) **44-5** 1; Thorn EMI Major Appliances Ltd **95** 4; John Vaughan **188** 1; Deidi von Schaewen **213** 4; Elizabeth Whiting and Associates **258** 1, (Jon Bouchier) **59** 4, **109** 3, (Michael Crockett) **14** 1, (Michael Dunne) **18** 1, 3 and 4, **30** 2, **35** 5 and 6, **62** 1, **139** 2, **151** 2, **166** 1, **179** 3, **226** 1, **232** 1, (Clive Helm) **67** 4, (Tom Leighton) **19** 5, (Michael Nicholson) **12** 3, **16-7** 3, **87** 4, **91** 3, **210** 3, **230** 2, (Tim Street-Porter) **39** 4, **96** 1, **103** 2, **132-3**, **213** 2, (Spike Powell) **9**, **2** **19** 8, **61** 3, **72** 1, **76** 3, **86-7** 1, **88** 2, **95** 2, **125** 2, **211** 5, **215** 4, (Fridhelm Thomas) **15** 3, **67** 3, (Andrea von Eisiedel) **10** 1, **210** 2, (Home Improvement) **88** 1, **197** 5, (Neil Lorimer) **88-89** 3, **100** 2, **139** 3, **142** 3, **225** 5, (Rodney Hyett) **224** 1 and 3, (Jerry Tubby) **203** 7, **223** 4, **224** 2, **243** 3; Shona Wood (designer Chris Hall) **218** 2; Woodstock **120** 1; Wrighton International **110** 2.


The following photographs were taken especially for Conran Octopus:

Bill Batten (designer Hilary Green) **62** 2, **190** 1; David Brittain (Ken Lumsdale, furniture Mothercare UK Ltd) **195** 2 and 3; Simon Brown **191** 3, **202** 4 (architects de Blacam & Megher) **8-9** 1, **13** 5, **18** 2, **60** 1, **61** 2, **72-3** 3, **77** 4, (architect Shay Cleary) **42-3** 3, **53** 4, **77** 5, **138-9**, **146-7** (paint effect by John Edbon) **52** 1, (architect Richard Gooden) **10-11** 3, **11** 4, **32-33**, **191** 2, (architect Ian Hutchinson) **21** 2, **41** 2, **54-5**, **153**, **223** 3, (architects and designers Simon Design Consultants) **20-21** 1; John Heseltine **36-7**; Ken Kirkwood **13** 4, **76** 2, **134** 2 (architect Roger Mears) **13** 7, **22** 1, **48** 1, **183** 2 (interior designer George Powers) **12** 1, **168** 3; Peter Mackertich **16** 2, **94** 1, (designer Denis Masi) **22-3** 3, (Rugs Helen Yardley, floor Anton Nickson) **48** 3, **71** 2.


Source material for the following illustrations was supplied by Homebase: **14**, **49**, **59**, **70**, **71**, **99**, **105**, **121**, **123**, **136-7**, **175**, **181**, **195**, **199**, **206-207**, **211**, **213**, **215**, **219**, **222-223**, **257**, **283**, **298** above, **299** above and centre, **300** above, **301**.